GOD GUARD THEE

NEWFOUNDLAND

GOD GUARD THEE
NEWFOUNDLAND

SEARCHING *for* MEANING.

An Anthology.

AUTHORS - In order of inclusion:

Paul J. Johnson.

Melvin Baker.

Robert H. Cuff.

Aidan Maloney.

Frank J. Kennedy.

Ronald F. Whelan.

Albert B. Perlin.

Jeff A. Webb.

Peter Neary.

John E. FitzGerald.

Raymond B. Blake.

FLANKER PRESS LTD.
St. John's
2009

Library and Archives Canada Cataloguing in Publication

God guard thee, Newfoundland : searching for meaning / edited by Paul J. Johnson.

Includes bibliographical references and index.
ISBN 978-1-897317-60-0

1. Newfoundland and Labrador--History.
I. Johnson, Paul J., 1929-

FC2161.7.G64 2009 971.8 C2009-906698-X

PRINTED IN CANADA

Mixed Sources
Cert no. SW-COC-001271
© 1996 FSC
FSC

This text of this book is printed on Ancient Forest Friendly paper, FSC certified, that is chlorine-free and 100% post-consumer waste.

FRONT COVER IMAGES: Regiment Cap Badge, The Rooms Corporation, Provincial Museum Division; Cabot Tower, Marc Poirier / Melissa Crocker.

BACK COVER IMAGES: Flags, original artwork by David Webber and Melissa Crocker.

Cover Design: Adam Freake

FLANKER PRESS
PO BOX 2522, STATION C
ST. JOHN'S, NL, CANADA
TOLL-FREE: 1-866-739-4420
WWW.FLANKERPRESS.COM

14 13 12 11 10 09 1 2 3 4 5 6 7 8 9

Canada | Canada Council for the Arts | Conseil des Arts du Canada | Newfoundland Labrador

We acknowledge the financial support of: the Government of Canada through the Book Publishing Industry Development Program (BPIDP); the Canada Council for the Arts which last year invested $20.1 million in writing and publishing throughout Canada; the Government of Newfoundland and Labrador, Department of Tourism, Culture and Recreation.

SEARCHING *for* MEANING.

An Anthology.

CONTENTS.

Preface . . . .*vi*

Acknowledgments . . . .*vii*

About the Editor/Author . . . .*viii*

A Selection of Photographs . . . .*ix*

Opening Hypotheses Chapters - - Introduction 1
Paul J. Johnson

1 Newfoundland: Our People & Our Heritage 2
Paul J. Johnson

2 The Commission, The War, and Governance 14
Paul J. Johnson

The War Years Changed Everything Chapters - - Introduction. .30
Paul J. Johnson

3 St. John's – The Garrison Town: 1939–1945 32
Melvin Baker

4 U-Boat Warfare and Convoy Protection 65
Melvin Baker

5 The Newfoundland Railway At War 73
Robert H. Cuff

6 The "Finest Kind" of Newfoundlanders 105
Herbert Russell, Capt. Jack Whalen,
Gerald S. Doyle, Frank O'Leary, Andy Carnell

7 Banking & Boarding – Spanning the War Years 118
Aidan Maloney

8 Wartime in Newfoundland .129
Frank Kennedy

9 *Evening Telegram*: Wartime Topics 154
Paul J. Johnson & Aidan Maloney

10 World War II and Our Newfoundland Seamen 167
Paul J. Johnson

The Historical Chapters - - Introduction 176
Paul J. Johnson

11 This Was Newfoundland 177
Digest from Albert Perlin

12 The Newfoundland Economy – before, during, and after World War II 195
Melvin Baker

13 The Commission of Government, 1934–1949 203
Jeff Webb

14 Great Britain and the Future of Newfoundland, 1939–1945 211
Peter Neary

15 "The Difficult Little Island" That Must Be Taken In . .250
John E. FitzGerald

16 Mackenzie King's Attitude Towards Newfoundland's Entry into Confederation 275
Raymond Blake

Closing Hypotheses Chapters.

17 We Love Thee Newfoundland 311
Paul J. Johnson

18 A Golden Rule for Newfoundland & Labrador 337
Paul J. Johnson

Index 342

PREFACE.

The title "God Guard Thee Newfoundland" is from the words of our beautiful national anthem, the "Ode to Newfoundland".

The *Anthology* sketches out how life unfolded for Newfoundland and Newfoundlanders, from the earliest days to the present. It opens and closes with chapters that include conjecture and speculation, but the conclusions seem to the author to be reasonable.

For the reader's more reliable consideration we include an excellent background of research by highly qualified historians and journalists. This provides well-documented, objective insight into our earlier public, political, economic, and military situations.

Searching for Meaning concludes that, over hundreds of years, those who lived in Newfoundland were "conditioned" to always accept the direction, decisions, and demands of "others", who purported to have that right and that authority.

The *Anthology* also relates how, thanks largely to World War II, Newfoundland gradually emerged from its sad financial and political collapse of the early 1930s. We have survived, despite never-ending manoeuvring and mismanagement by "*others*" in governing our lives and our economy. "Others" have always been the ones to capitalize on *our* resources.

Newfoundlanders now welcome the intention to develop our resources, while steadfastly seeking "just rewards" for Newfoundland and Labrador. We must initiate industry but retain an equitable "owner's share" - - along with the logical participation of our people in industry's management and workforce.

Hopefully you will find the *Anthology*'s hypotheses and historical background worth your time, consideration, and interest.

Paul J. Johnson, CM, ONL, LLD.

ACKNOWLEDGEMENTS.

The following Writers, professional Historians, and Journalists (or their representatives and copyright-holders) have made invaluable contributions for the overall content of *Searching for Meaning*, as brought together in this *Anthology*.

Dr. Melvin Baker,
Dr. Raymond B. Blake,
Robert Cuff, Esq.,
Dr. John E. FitzGerald,
Frank J. Kennedy, Esq.,
Dr. Aidan Maloney,
Dr. Peter Neary,
Dr. Albert B. Perlin,
Dr. Jeff A. Webb,
Dr. Ronald F. Whelan.

Special thanks to the following Johnson Family Foundation Team, for their great collaboration in the compiling and organizing of this *Anthology*.

Dale Russell FitzPatrick, Editorial Coordinator.
Melissa Crocker, Graphic Design and Layout.
Judy Rudofsky, Executive Secretary.
Sally Johnson, B.A. (Journalism)
Composition Review and Proofreading.
Dr. Melvin Baker, Editorial Review and Sourcing.
Dr. Iona Bulgin, Copy and Proofreading.

Our Foundation also expresses sincere thanks to the following (alphabetical) for their vital input and advice in various aspects of this book: the late Fred Adams, Breakwater Books (Rebecca Rose and Kim Pelley), British Merchant Mariners Association (Derek H. Bristow), Brittain Image Management Services (Bern Brittain), Canadian Merchant Navy Veterans Association (J.J. Strong), Celebrity Photo Studio (Robert Young), City of St. John's Archives (Helen Miller), Crow's Nest Officers' Club / Military Artifacts Association (Gary Green), John and Marjorie Doyle, David Freeman, MUN Archives and Special Collections / Queen Elizabeth II Library (Bert Riggs and Linda White), MUN Botanical Garden (Todd Boland), MUN Geography Department (Charles Conway), MUN Maritime History Archive (Tanya McDonald), Naval Association of Newfoundland (Jim Shields), Newfoundland & Labrador Heritage Web Site (Vince Walsh), Keelin O'Leary, Parks Canada (Marilyn Dawe and Dave Taylor), Capt. Joe Prim, Provincial Resource Library (John Griffin and the Newfoundland Collection Staff), Queen's Printer (Earl G. Tucker), Royal Newfoundland Regiment (the late Lt. Col. Kevin Hutchings), The Rooms Provincial Archives (Melanie Tucker and the Resource Room Staff), and *The Telegram* (Kerry Hann).

Editor / Author - - Paul J. Johnson, CM, ONL, LLD.

Born in 1929 at St. John's, Newfoundland, son of Arthur and Marjorie (Jolliffe) Johnson. Attended Holloway School (Newfoundland), King's Collegiate School (Nova Scotia), Mount Allison Academy, and left before graduating at Mount Allison University (New Brunswick). In 1949, he entered the family business, Johnson Insurance. In 1953, he became Managing Director, and in 1955 Chief Executive Officer and bought ownership of the company.

His Leadership Team pioneered 67 innovations in the insurance field. By 1995, Johnson Insurance operated in every province in Canada. It is the fastest growing general insurance company in Canada. By 2007, it had achieved annual billings and group assets over $ 1 billion each. In 1997, Mr. Johnson retired and sold his shares in Johnson Insurance, but ensured its continued autonomy, with head office to remain in Newfoundland.

In 1987, he had established the Johnson Family Foundation. He has devoted his retirement, and most proceeds from sale of his shares, to preserve and present history and natural heritage of Newfoundland. The Foundation, with excellent collaborators, expert teamwork, and co-sponsor financial contributions, has completed over $ 50 million of work, in over 20 projects.

During his business career, he was Chair of the St. John's Heritage Foundation (7 years); the St. John's Housing Authority (7 years); and the Salvation Army Advisory Board (8 years). He was a Director of the Newfoundland and Labrador Development Corporation (9 years). He served as Co-chair of a Foundation which completed the *Encyclopedia of Newfoundland and Labrador*.

In 1993, Paul Johnson received the Order of Canada; in 1994, Doctor of Laws *honoris causa* from Memorial University; in 1997, Freedom of the City of St. John's; in 2004, one of the first recipients of the Order of Newfoundland and Labrador; also in 2004, the Community Service Award from the Canadian Society of Landscape Architects; the Ernst & Young Award as Atlantic Entrepreneur of the Year; the Environmental Award from the Association of Professional Engineers and Geoscientists; in 2008, he was inducted into the Newfoundland Business Hall of Fame.

He is an Honourary Member of: St. John's Rotary Club (Paul Harris Fellow); Newfoundland Historic Parks Association; Salvation Army Newfoundland Advisory Board; Newfoundland Association of Architects; Newfoundland Association of Professional Engineers and Geoscientists. He has received the Salvation Army Distinguished Order of Service Gold Medal; Canadian Parks Service National Heritage Award; Canadian Commemorative Medal for Canada's 125th Anniversary; Distinguished Service Award from the General Hospital Health Foundation.

A Selection of Photographs of

The Where and The Who of Government,

1933 to 1960.

Colonial Building.

(Opened in 1850.) Courtesy Archives and Special Collections, MUN.

Confederation Building.

(Opened in 1960.) Courtesy City of St. John's Archives, CA 2.07.052

The Last Legislature before Commission Government, 1933.

Courtesy Archives and Special Collections, MUN, 5.05.216.

The Commission of Government (1934-1949).

Courtesy The Smallwood Family Collection.

The National Convention Members, 1946.

Courtesy The Smallwood Family Collection.

First Provincial House of Assembly, 1949.

Courtesy The Smallwood Family Collection.

The Opening and Closing "Hypotheses Chapters".

Introduction by Paul J. Johnson.

A professional historian's definition of an hypothesis might be: "A provisional theory, well documented, but not finally proven". An amateur's hypothesis could be: "An opinion, supported with related information, put forward for consideration". The laywriter of the Hypotheses Chapters follows the amateur's approach.

The Hypotheses Chapters contain some potentially startling opinions and interpretations. They include reasons and realities that explain or expand upon some of Newfoundland's past difficulties, as well as our fortuitous occurrences. The final "Golden Rule" Chapter gives reason for us to "take heart" about how we can and should steadily improve our future fortunes.

The Hypotheses chapters about "what happened" (or didn't), and "why" needed delving beneath the surface and behind usual beliefs. The intention was to do so with appropriate questioning and skepticism concerning the performance, wisdom, and motives of the individuals and entities involved - - regardless of whether they were trusted and honoured in the past.

An enquiring mind will search for "The truth, the whole truth, and nothing but the truth". If this writer has failed on conjecture or conclusions, he apologizes to the reader - - and to our professional historians - - but *not* for having *tried to search for meaning*.

1

Newfoundland : Our People & Our Heritage.

From Settlement to "The Crash".

By: Paul J. Johnson.

Few places on the earth have a society as distinctive as Newfoundland's. Living in our "island-world", and with an economy dependent on the fishery, produced a hardy people proud of being the British Empire's "Oldest Colony". The three positive words in our name "new - found - land" also made us feel different, and hopeful. Our strong and friendly Newfoundland and Labrador dogs gave added pride. For 300 years we almost felt like we were a "nation".

The Term "Our People" Relates to Those Who Settled Here.

It is necessary to understand the different approaches to the cod fishery to realize why some fishers eventually decided to stay here year-round (settle). Cod were incredibly plentiful, both on the Grand Banks and around the coastline. "Catching" was the easier part. "Curing" or preserving the cod to sell it later was more involved. Most European countries would clean the fish, then "put it down" in heavy salt. This could all be done aboard the ship.

The English fishery-approach produced a better product because it was "dried" as well as salted. It could then be shipped or stored more efficiently. But, there was another "catch" to the English fishery. To cure the fish took time, sunshine, and required people to go on shore. The English called the places on shore where the fish could best be landed and processed the "Rooms".

Fish flakes, and "stores" to store dried fish, fishing gear, and to cook food were only required during the fishing season. Then "all hands" would sail home.

The English Fishing Method Moved More On Shore.

The English merchants soon realized that to protect their valuable shore-based "Rooms" against appropriation by other fishers or the native Indians, they needed people to stay over the winter. It did not take long for some merchants and fishers to conclude that if a winter camp could tie directly with next season's fishing, the fish could be sold, to produce better prices and a profit.

The resulting merchant-shore-fishery operation would compete with the English-merchant offshore seasonal fishery. Although it took over 200 years, the on-shore settlers eventually prevailed and the English seasonal fishery was replaced. This (in very simple terms) was why and how "Our People" (Newfoundlanders) became established.

Early on, England and Its Merchants Blocked Settlement.

Having been "discovered" by John Cabot for England in 1497, it was not until 1583 that the island was claimed by Sir Humphrey Gilbert as Britain's first overseas "possession". When it came to concluding arrangements for settlement, for various reasons Britain seldom treated Newfoundlanders with any special concern. And, there were few who spoke on behalf of our settlers.

To protect its Empire, Britain had to keep sailors available for the Royal Navy. So, in the earliest years, building a house to actually "settle" in Newfoundland was prohibited. Even putting a chimney in a summer "lean-to" was forbidden. Fishers had to go back to the "old country" over the winter. That restriction was also to discourage the establishment of Newfoundland-owned fish businesses, to compete against those owned in England.

Gradually settlements began to emerge and become viable. Before the end of the 1600s, in addition to St. John's, over 30 outports had been established.

Why Did Thousands of "Settlers" Come to Newfoundland ?

It was to seek a better life than they could find in their "old country". Sometimes this was for relief from no job, poverty, or even starvation. While some aspects of living in Newfoundland might be forbidding, the climate was moderate, and the coastal scenery quite beautiful. Entering the fishery and catching and curing fish required no special training, nor the complication of finding a job. To engage in the normally abundant fishery of Newfoundland took courage, "getting here", and putting down roots. Tens of thousands came seeking a living where they could be their own "master" and enjoy their own land, home, family, and friends. Because of isolation, hard work, and unexpected "tough times", some of our settlers became disheartened and "moved on" - - mainly to the Maritimes or to what we called the "Boston States".

In the 1600s up to the 1800s, nearly everything about our Newfoundland economy centered on the fishery. Cod was the real "King". Settlers, when they came, had to claim their own fishing ground and nearby land. They needed friends to help build a house, boat, wharf, and fish-flake, and to clear land to grow crops and keep a few animals. The family and friends shared in chores.

Life in Newfoundland in the Early Days.

Like the old nursery rhyme, when the fishery and prices "were good, they were very, very good, but when they were bad, they were horrid". Cod could be scarce, prices down, storms could destroy boats and wharves, crops could fail, and illness and death eventually came to all. It often happened that wars prevented competing European countries from fishing on our Grand Banks. Then, prices for our fish would be a bit higher. The rarity of "no fish, no food" was devastating for any family, and could be for an entire community and even a whole coastal area.

In all fairness, the English West Country Merchants, watching a shore-based Newfoundland fishery develop, were indignant about competition for markets, especially because that competition was also

"English" and producing a product that exactly followed the English method for curing codfish.

Our earliest settlers were breaking English laws, which specially forbade settlement, and a local fishery competing with the English-owned fishery.

Despite Opposition and Obstacles, Settlement Grew.

Today, few people realize that, years ago, inshore fishermen had to row their sturdy boats to their fishing ground, work hard for their "daily catch", and row back home - - sometimes battling, or having to seek shelter from, stormy seas.

As each fishing ground became fully occupied, new fishermen had to find new grounds, and another "outport" was started. Few outports would even have a path to nearby communities. The building of churches and schools was an extra burden. Birth, life, sickness, and death had to be faced, with the only support coming from family, neighbours, or in larger settlements possibly the clergyman, teacher, or merchant. It was a hard, hard way to become "free". In fact, most settlers were never really FREE - - not from "King Cod", not from debt, and never from inevitable stormy weather.

Fishermen had few if any "cash wages". Their livelihood depended on catching, drying, and selling fish. Most fishers were tied to a merchant, who bought their fish and provided credit to "charge up" their food, clothing, and supplies. The "balance" (amount due) was determined at the end of the fishing season. Most merchants were fair and considerate, but a decent living in any year depended on a good fishery, good prices, and good weather.

French Military Attacks Destroy English Settlements.

The settler's life was always hard and often stormy, but in the final years of the 1600s it became a living nightmare. French military attacks descended without warning on all settlers in most Newfoundland outports.

The French, from their capital in Placentia, launched their carefully prepared sequence of attacks that burned St. John's and almost all the small English settlements on the eastern Avalon. This was a brutal, systematic crusade of extermination. It killed those who did not surrender, stole all the livestock and fish, and burned every house and fishing property. Survivors were sent back to England. This cruel business was often carried out in wintertime, so those who fled to escape suffered severely from starvation and exposure.

By their own account the well-armed career French soldiers, with imported Indian support, slaughtered 100 mostly unarmed civilian inhabitants for every French attacker who died. It was a deliberate, scorched-earth campaign, meant to eliminate all English settlements.

Of all the outports on the South Shore, Conception Bay, and eastern Trinity Bay, only Brigus and Carbonear Island escaped destruction. The French did not intend to occupy the territory, but certainly never expected any community to rise again from the ashes. As demanding and discouraging as it must have been, the surviving settlers had the great courage to start again, which says a lot about our forefathers.

As those "first Newfoundlanders" were being pillaged, they must have hoped to see the Royal Navy or garrison troops come to the rescue. The English seasonal fishery, having established Rooms onshore, must have been aware of the slaughter of the settlers. In a way, the French were doing in a brutal manner, what British law was trying to bring about - - getting rid of a competing onshore fishery.

Courtesy Department of Geography, Memorial University.

The "Inshore" Fishery and Settlement Expand.

While it never became a combined harvesting and marketing success, the "merchant class" in the fishery did achieve financial rewards. The fisherfolk achieved more freedom than they had in the old country, but their lives would never become trouble-free.

Developing Character: Centuries in the Forge.

Newfoundland settlers, in hundreds of small outports, over hundreds of years, were used to working and thinking together. That developed general attitudes about what to welcome as "good", or resist as "bad". Common opinions created a natural sense of community. But similar reactions about right or wrong did not preclude differences or disputes. These could arise from opposite personal viewpoints, religious "persuasions", fishing grounds, "townies" versus "baymen", or discontent over the merchant's fish-grading or prices.

For the period from 1700 to 1820, outport living and the fishery did not change much. But the understanding of the manifold disadvantages of living in small settlements became more and more of a depressing torment.

What did change was the hope and expectation that having responsible government would somehow relieve the problems of education, medical attention, and fluctuations in fish prices. The never-ending concern about isolation was eating away at any good feeling about freedom.

A Succession of Promising Political Changes.

Incredibly only in 1811, after 228 years as the "Cornerstone of the British Empire", could we apply to "Crown Lands" to obtain a "grant" of "private land". Eventually in the 1820s, Newfoundland was elevated to become a "Crown Colony". By 1855, seeking the "pipe dream" of improved opportunities, Newfoundlanders sought and were granted "Responsible Government" to elect a "House of

Representatives". In 1931, we gained our "Dominion Status" with a "Sovereign Constitution" under the British "Statute of Westminster". Dominion privileges supposedly led to independence and nationhood, but the Dominions Office in London and our Crown-appointed Governors, continued their "duty" to oversee our trade and justice. The British Parliament dealt with international treaties. Much of our north and west coasts remained occupied as the "French Shore", under French control right up to 1904.

Effective Political Planning Seemed Impossible.

Newfoundland's political performance in managing our "Responsible" Government was not always "responsible". Elected representatives met for only a few weeks a year. Most party leaders and politicians began with good intentions but after being elected realized that government did not have the money to carry out promises. Many politicians eventually lost their credibility and some were found seeking personal advantage.

After Newfoundland obtained Responsible Government, and eventually Dominion Status, Governors did consult with our Political Leaders, but they still reported to London on the economy, budgets, and justice. A Governor's role, and the rare visits by Royalty, were put forward as special advantages to being a part of the British Empire. We were dutifully impressed.

From the early 1800s onward, our Governors lived year-round in the splendid new Government House, located between our Colonial Building and the Garrison Church, on Military Road in St. John's - - all strongly representative of Empire and the obviously subservient position of Newfoundland. Most Governors were considerate and conscientious - - and concerned about the proper administration of justice and faithful reporting on our situation to the British Colonial or Dominions Offices.

Overcoming Isolation - - The Universal Dream.

With few exceptions Newfoundlanders faced real hardships living in very small communities. Medical attention was seldom available; one-room schools were usual; and, if there was a church, it often had only a visiting clergyman. Some fishing communities had to rely on a merchant in a neighbouring outport. In the 1800s, the availability of a connecting public road, railroad, or boat service, was thought to be beyond the realm of possibility.

Nevertheless, in the second half of the 1800s politicians could not resist temptation. They started a trial "coastal boat service" (mail, freight, and passenger) and later began to build a railway. Because construction and operating costs were very high, and revenues extremely low, neither boat nor rail transportation could "break even". But that did not stop political rivals from promising additional rail and coastal boat services. Because of the resulting high Government expenditures, the money for health and education, or public works, was severely limited.

Politicians won elections by making far-fetched promises. A trans-island railway and branch lines, and coastal boat services, were eventually established. They produced ever-higher deficits for the owners and Government. To make up for the lack of tax revenues, Government lands were sold. Over 60 per cent of our forest and mineral rights were sold or leased. For some fisherfolk, the right to cut nearby trees for building or firewood became a problem.

For our outport livyers (and their politicians) the universal dream of overcoming isolation became an obsession. Our railway lines and coastal boats proved well beyond Government's ability to finance. Attempts to close unprofitable branch rail lines or eliminate ports of call provoked strong protests. Low passenger and cargo revenues, even with their perceived great importance, made all operations unprofitable. The year-after-year losses became a major reason for Newfoundland's eventual fiscal collapse.

The First World War - - Our Exorbitant Patriotism.

Despite our poor economy, and partially because of it, Newfoundland's wartime contributions went well beyond the level of affordability. A third of our eventual crushing deficit came from debt we incurred in the Great War. In that war, we lost many of our finest young men, and cost over $ 35 million. This expenditure was a major cause of our loss of self-government. Our loyalty toward Crown and Empire was only rewarded by sharing in the victory.

By 1923, adding to Newfoundland's severe postwar money problems, the Government had to buy out and operate the railway, coastal boats, and dockyard. That cost many more millions. By the end of the 1920s, the Great Depression inflicted additional financial problems, and ever-larger Government deficits. At the start of the 1930s, over half of the Government's annual revenues were paid out as "interest due". Emergency borrowing from the Canadian Banks should not have been sought or provided. It only deepened and delayed our financial predicament and the already inevitable "crash".

The Absolute End to Newfoundland's Independence.

In 1932, the public in St. John's showed their anger and disgust with Prime Minister Richard Squires. His political opponents had instigated a riot of 10,000 people. They assembled outside the Colonial Building where Squires had taken refuge. Squires escaped, and fortunately no fatalities occurred. After the next election, a new Prime Minister, Frederick C. Alderdice, came into office with a huge majority. However, with no way to meet financial obligations, and with no further funds available, Alderdice stated:

> Our people must be rescued from the degrading dole [government allowance of six cents a day] which is sapping their vitality, weakening their self-respect, and undermining their independence.

Hard-working Newfoundlanders were thoroughly disheartened.

In 1933, the British Parliament received the Lord Amulree Royal Commission Report about Newfoundland's financial position, which had been requested by our House of Assembly. It stated:

> In the 12 years from 1920 to 1932, there was no balanced budget. Public debt doubled from the previous 12 years. People were misled, and the country was sunk into waste and extravagance. The elaborate pretensions collapsed. Glowing visions were dispelled by the cold realities of national insolvency.

The "cold realities" included our debt of $ 100 million and these major, unresolved problems:

> Over 70 per cent of our debt was accumulated from our extreme expenditures on the Great War, plus extravagant initiatives in the Railway-Coastal Boat services.
>
> Salaries of government employees were cut by half. Government payments for its supplies were a year overdue.
>
> When Britain went off the gold standard, Newfoundland had to reduce its fish prices by over 20 per cent to compete with other fishing countries.
>
> Over two-thirds of Newfoundland's foreign trading vessels had been lost or worn out in the Great War. Every year $ 600 to $ 700,000 had to be spent to ship our fish to markets.

It became obvious that the Newfoundland economy, even with new paper mills and mines, could NOT AFFORD to fund self-government. The "game" of politicians had been to exploit the almost desperate need and desire of our outport people to bring an end to isolation. Most Newfoundlanders concluded that their politicians, as

Lord Amulree had stated, had scandalously offered: "elaborate pretensions", "glowing visions", and "falsifying of government accounts". Now, any such political games would supposedly end.

Was There Any Remaining Hope for Newfoundlanders ?

Political leaders, newspaper editors, and some prominent individuals had suggested that Britain might find a way to:

Pay back most of Newfoundland's $ 35 million Great War contributions;

Provide decent benefits for disabled war veterans, widows, and children;

Propose attractive funding to establish new primary and secondary industries.

But, Britain was struggling with its own huge war expense and the worldwide depression. There was little possibility of such lenience, especially any repayment of Newfoundland's large contributions to the Great War effort. Britain had already forgiven the war debts of several nations in Europe, but was against having Newfoundland default. That could precipitate a flood of other defaults within the Empire. And default would also worry outside nations about the credit-reliability of Empire Members. Britain did help Newfoundland with debt-reduction, grants-in-aid, and a guarantee on our extended financing of debt. That was all that Britain could afford to do.

Fifteen years after World War I, the Dominion of Newfoundland was finally brought to its knees. After "The Crash", our "independence" (Responsible Government) would *never* be recovered - - which is another sad, long, and complicated story.

Paul J. Johnson.

2

The Commission, The War, and Governance.

Commission of Government is "In" - - Independence is "Out".

An Overview - - from 1934 to 2009.

By: Paul J. Johnson.

On February 16, 1934, under a British Proclamation agreed by Newfoundland, our nearly 80 years of Representative Government was replaced with the appointment of a "Commission of Government" directed by the Dominions Office in London. That Commission consisted of three British and three Newfoundland Commissioners, and our British Governor as Chair. Britain gave us assurances that Newfoundland's self-government was merely "suspended", and "as soon as the difficulties are overcome, and Newfoundland is again self-supporting, on request of the people, responsible government will be restored". During debate in the British House of Lords, Lord Snell had said: "In as short a time as possible, responsible government will again be in operation". These reassurances somewhat relieved the shame and discouragement of all Newfoundlanders. However, it must be realized, those explicit promises by the British Parliament were *never* fulfilled.

At first, the Commission was welcomed as a reprieve from the previous "IR-Responsible Government". But the Commission saw it as their solemn duty to pay off the banks and countries to which Newfoundland owed its public debt. To do so, the Commission spent the least possible money to support health and welfare, public works, or development. They acted more like trustees in a bankruptcy than financial managers. The Commission did provide some Cottage Hospitals, Fishery Regulations, and other administrative improvements, but by the year 1939, widespread unemployment, poverty, disease, malnutrition, and starvation made the Commission decidedly unpopular - - and the second "Great War" was upon us.

Newfoundland Sovereignty & Commission of Government.

- In 1931, the Statute of Westminster had declared Newfoundland's status as a "Dominion". That status guaranteed that Britain could no longer impose direction or regulation upon us. Other "Dominions" included Canada, Australia, and New Zealand.

- Only "at the request and consent" of Newfoundland could Britain appoint a Royal Commission pertaining to Newfoundland, and it would need our agreement to implement its recommendations.

- It is now clear the Commission of Government only considered itself to be administering our finances, taxes, and unavoidable services. The Commission ignored asserting Newfoundland's Constitutional Rights under our Dominion Status (Sovereignty). After outbreak of war, enforcement of our sovereignty was vital, but almost never pursued by the Commission, the Governor, or the watchdog Dominions Office.

- In obvious violation of its Statute of Westminster, Britain began making wartime agreements about Newfoundland with Canada and the United States. Even Canada and the United States made their own combined agreements involving the Dominion of Newfoundland's sovereign territory. While these agreements were part of constructive wartime measures, constitutional experts in all three countries *must* have concluded "We will forget Newfoundland's Dominion Status - - they cannot / never complain".

- What would *Canada* have said if Churchill and Roosevelt declared that the Leased Base Agreement included the Maritime Provinces?

- The Dominions Office in London, which was required to enforce the Statute of Westminster, *repeatedly* decided not to intervene.

Deficiency of Governance by the Commission.

Although Newfoundland's elected Government had been suspended, Newfoundland still had its constitutional status as a Dominion. In failing to assert those rights, the Commission was certainly not dutiful nor businesslike. It was just fortuitous for Newfoundlanders that the actions of Canada and the United States involved spending large amounts of money in Newfoundland.

During the war years, the Commission increased our taxes and "banked" large amounts of government "surplus" money. *But*, they continued their deplorable, ultra-miserable mindset.

In the war years, personal, business, and government incomes went higher. However, the population sustained the huge cost of restricted rates of pay, personal dislocations, interrupted business, and the almost-completely-ignored maintenance of our public roads, railway, boats, wharves, and other properties. Part of the Commission's lame excuse was that all our workers were occupied in the patriotic war effort.

The Commission's derelictions of duty, directly and indirectly cost Newfoundland and Newfoundlanders $ 115 million during the war years (approximated by the writer).

The Commission took several *truly despicable initiatives* directly against the best interests of our people. The Commission tried to fix Newfoundlanders' pay rates at the existing low levels. This was to prevent wage increases for employees of Government, the Railway, businesses, the paper mills, and mines. It is certain that the British Dominions Office was notified by the Governor of the Commission's action. They did not intercede. This was disgraceful, appalling, coldly-calculated interference by those intended to be our "quasi-guardians".

This advertisement shows how miserable and arrogant the Commission of Government were in trying to influence the lives of our people to promote the Commission's objectives.

EVENING TELEGRAM, 3 MAR 1942

IMPORTANT NOTICE

EMPLOYMENT OUTLOOK

The Commission of Government have made enquiries regarding the demand for labor during 1942 by construction companies.

So far as can be foreseen at present, the demand will be maintained at a high level until June, 1942, when a reduction in the number of men employed will take place. This reduction will at first mainly take place in the St. John's area but will steadily and rapidly be extended to other parts of the Island. By the end of November, 1942 it is estimated that approximately 90% of the labour now employed will no longer be required by the construction companies.

Those fishermen who have already left the fishery or who may intend to leave it for other employment should consider their position very carefully in the light of the foregoing information, and they should take all possible steps to ensure that their boats and gear are maintained in good condition so that fishing may be resumed without undue delay and expense when the alternative forms of employment come to an end.

P. H. D. DUNN,
Commissioner for Natural Resources.

Failures to Act, By the Commission of Government.

The following are this writer's opinions on urgent and forceful actions the Commission of Government should have taken to pursue, protect, and preserve the Rights of the Dominion of Newfoundland and its people under the wartime conditions:

1. After Newfoundland found itself at war, the Commission should have issued a "Declaration of Intentions" to our public, the Dominions Office, and the Governments of Britain, Canada, and the United States. The Declaration should have stated, "As Sole Governing Authority for the people and the Sovereign Dominion of Newfoundland, we require prior consultation and agreement to any and all wartime measures proposed to involve the Dominion of Newfoundland, its people, laws, lands, properties, and coastal waters".

2. That Declaration should also state: "Newfoundland will consider becoming the host territory for the armed forces of an Allied Nation for military measures they may propose, based upon Newfoundland's prior acceptance and enactment of specific agreements and conditions".

3. The Declaration should state: "In considering any application from an Allied Nation to occupy Dominion of Newfoundland land or coastal property, it is understood and agreed, it will require:

   (a) Surveyed boundaries and means-of-access,

   (b) Government-approved purchase, lease, or expropriation of lands and rights-of-way,

   (c) Compliance with building codes and other regulations published by Newfoundland".

4. The Commission should have established a "Newfoundland Public Works Assessments Act to apply to any Allied Nation for their use or occupancy of any of our infrastructure of public lands, roads, railway and coastal services, harbours, and wharves. The Public Works Scale of Assessments will pay to Newfoundland a contribution toward construction, modification, extension, operation, maintenance, repair, or replacement of Newfoundland public facilities, as established by appointed professional engineers and adjusted annually".

5. The Commission should also have established a "Newfoundland Workers' Compensation Authority to implement and administer a mandatory schedule of minimum payrates for all persons employed by an Allied Nation, to also require specific employer contributions toward workers' compensation, life, accident, sickness, and disability benefits, pension-contributions, vacation pay, and sick-leave".

Not one of these *five*, highly important, very reasonable steps was taken. During the war years, those egregious failures, directly and indirectly, cost our government, our workforce, and businesses (by the writer's approximation) at least $115 million. This amount would have been quite reasonable as an overhead on top of the over $ 400 million (in 1943 dollars) reported to have been spent by the Allied Nations in Newfoundland.

Why Didn't Newfoundlanders Demand Those Measures ?

Newfoundlanders have *always* been conditioned to accept it as our destiny to be "ruled" by "*others*". "Others" included Royalty, British Parliament, Royal Navy, Fishing Admirals, Governors, the Colonial Office, the Dominions Office, the Commission of Government, World War II Allied Nations Military Occupation, (and some would add Water Street "Merchant Princes"), our elected representatives - - and, since Confederation, the Canadian Federal Government. "Others" have always "called the shots" for Newfoundland. With England and France often at war, Newfoundlanders relied on the Empire and the British Navy to protect us - - which was seldom effectively done. But we always concluded that we owed "the Crown" and "the British Empire" our absolute, unwavering loyalty and patriotic servitude.

In the Second World War, the "invasions" of Newfoundland's Sovereignty, by Britain, Canada, and the United States, permitted by the Commission of Government and British Dominions Office, included: The establishment of Canada-United States "Permanent Joint Board of Defence"; The Churchill-Roosevelt "Atlantic Charter"; The "Anglo-American Leased Bases Agreement"; and the British creation of the Canadian Navy "Newfie John" Base. That is not to say Newfoundland would have disagreed, or expected unreasonable compensation. As usual, Newfoundlanders accepted that "We should just cooperate". Our Board of Trade disagreed by quite a number of very strong resolutions, but these proved to be like "whistling in the wind".

Newfoundlanders' Morale: On the Home Front and Overseas.

When War "broke out", Britain and the Commission of Government decided that Newfoundland's military volunteers would go to England to join the British Armed Forces. It happened that that was fine with "our boys", who had joined up "to fight".

A great many of our volunteers going overseas had left behind "sweethearts". Before departing, there were heartfelt promises of waiting, returning, and love forever. And usually there was a bonding and socializing between the families of the two "sweethearts". What often came later, was a romantic "separation", mostly caused by a new romance at home, or sometimes overseas. Such separations were extremely hurtful and demoralizing for possibly 3,000 Newfoundland boy-and-girl "sweethearts"and maybe another 10,000 involved in their families.

Early in the War, the news from "overseas" was non-stop alarming. With every invasion of another country, Germany seemed invincible - - as seen in the swift conquest of most of Europe. Even the celebrated Evacuation at Dunkirk, that Churchill had portrayed as a "victory", was a serious defeat for the British Expeditionary Force in France, with a heavy loss of armaments. The German air raids on England seemed to be a prelude to a blitzkrieg invasion (as had happened with Norway). Newfoundlanders were greatly concerned about the situation in England, and especially about "our own boys" in England, our Foresters in Scotland, and our Seamen on the seven seas.

Strategy by "Others", About Newfoundland and St. John's.

Back in September of 1939, when War had broken out, Canadian Prime Minister Mackenzie King clearly stated "The integrity [meaning survival] of Newfoundland and Labrador is essential to the security of Canada". In August 1940, Canada and the United States formed a "Permanent Joint Board on Defence" (*not* including our Commission) to turn Newfoundland into "the outpost of North American Defence". These presumptuous plans were *not* about safeguarding Newfoundland, but to create a "remote battleground" on which to defend Canada and America. The Joint Board Plan was about how Newfoundland should be occupied, as the "Atlantic front line", a battlefield "for defence of Canada and America". Newfoundlanders naively believed "the Canucks" and "the Yanks" were coming here to defend our Island and Labrador - - and that innocent misconception was cynically encouraged.

On August 14, 1941, on board the Royal Navy Battleship *Prince of Wales* off of Argentia, Newfoundland, the "Atlantic Charter" was signed by British Prime Minister Winston Churchill and American President Franklin D. Roosevelt. The Anglo-American "Leased Bases Agreement" provided the still-at-peace, industrial powerhouse of America with 99-year land-leases to build rent-free military bases in Newfoundland and elsewhere in Britain's West Atlantic "possessions".

In a relatively short time, Newfoundland was to become a "fortress-isle". The so-called "friendly invasions" did provide financial benefits for Newfoundland, but also altered the lives and lifestyles of tens of thousands of our "grin-and-bear-it" Newfoundlanders. The widespread disruption was simply accepted as part of "our patriotic contribution" to the war effort. To this day, very few people have understood the great turmoil and magnitude of the personal and family dislocations and sacrifices. Over 20,000 Newfoundlanders became involved in base construction - - the large majority having to leave their home and family - - with significant interference in the size of our fishery as well.

Newfoundlanders' Notions about Britain, Canada, & America.

It always seemed strange that Newfoundlanders, having come almost entirely from England, Ireland, and Scotland, seldom maintained any "old country" family connections. Most of us do not even know from which town or city our forebears came. Considering our intense loyalty to the Crown and Empire, that estrangement is certainly a big puzzle. On the other hand, there were very few Newfoundland families that did not maintain connections with relatives or friends who moved from Newfoundland to Canada or the United States. Was the old world "bad" and the new world "good" ? If so, how could one explain Newfoundlanders' extreme patriotism ?

What "notions" did most Newfoundlanders have:

About Britain ? - - Kings and Queens, British Empire, London, Westminster Abbey, Parliament, Parades, Royal Navy, Steamship Lines, Quality Clothing, Transatlantic Cables, Our Paper Companies.

About Canada ? - - Our Neighbour, Similar Origins, a Dominion, Competing Fishery, Our Rail and Shipping Connections, the Maritimes, Niagara Falls, Boarding Schools and Universities, Foodstuffs, Building Supplies, and Contested-Labrador.

About America ? - - Fun Place, Movie Stars, Comic Books, Glossy Magazines, New York City, Skyscrapers, Broadway, World's Fair, Baseball, Hot Dogs, Radio Programs, Snazzy Cars, Big Bands, Hit Parade, Sinatra, Mickey Mouse, and Popeye.

It impressed some Newfoundlanders that America, being a much smaller land-size than Canada, had made itself a far more exciting country. America excelled in popular music, movie stars, spectacles, inventions, and manufacturing. In the war effort, Canada had Newfoundland's kind of patriotism, but America seemed to be more "high-minded", trying to assist England, and building bases (as we thought) to defend Newfoundland.

St. John's & Newfoundland, Wartime Situations, & Outcomes.

- Britain, Canada, and America set strategy for Newfoundland.

- The first bases under construction in St. John's were for the Canadian Navy and Army.

- Military Engineers directed construction, by *mainland* contractors, chiefly with Newfoundland workers.

- After the Leased Bases Agreement, the Americans quickly started planning their military installations.

- Hundreds of private Newfoundland properties were expropriated for land-assembly of military bases - - many owners getting less than their overall relocation costs.

- During the war, employment, wages, and business and government revenues all increased (which, compared to the "pre-war Commission Days" we considered "prosperity").

- For thousands of outport Newfoundlanders, turning Newfoundland into a "military-fortress" opened a first-time opportunity for "cash-wages" (instead of never-ending "debt").

- When an outport head-of-family sought a "base job", it usually meant relocation, bunkhouse-living, mess halls, and never-before-separation from wife, family, and the fishery.

- Some outport workers, when moving to the "big city" of St. John's, were a bit unsure of themselves and homesick.

- The overall population of St. John's increased by 50 per cent.

- Base contractors faced labour shortages and wage-competition. In the employment market, the "Yankee Dollar" was supreme. Highest-to-lowest wages: American, Canadian, Newfoundland.

- The first 900 American soldiers came to St. John's on a large, old, converted cruiseship, the *Edmund B. Alexander*. During the four months on-board, American soldiers started inviting local girls to on-board dinner-dances and movies.

- The American troops paraded to a temporary *"Fort Alexander"* tent city, to stay until permanent *"Fort Pepperrell"* was ready for occupancy.

- The American "guys" had personality, "nice teeth", money, "smooth talk", tailored uniforms, and more stripes.

- Most Americans were very friendly and "easy-going" - - but a few were thought to be "stringing a big line".

- American bases were well-designed, with nicely landscaped, resort-like buildings that far outclassed Canadian and Newfoundland Militia barracks - - as everyone fully realized.

- Compared to the Non-Commissioned Officer and Officer Clubs in the American Bases, the local Service Clubs (e.g., K of C, Caribou Hut, and Crow's Nest) were very plain and "cheap".

- By 1943, we had thousands of lonely, amorous, American and Canadian servicemen in St. John's - - many of them "angling" for dates with attractive local females.

- Americans offered impressionable young ladies never-before-experienced drinks, dancing, steaks, chocolates, silk stockings, exciting "dates", and possibly "romance".

- Hundreds of our delighted, yearning-to-be-admired young girls welcomed their "new-found-life". It involved a "hair-do", lipstick, perfume, fancy dresses, and good times. Many found it possible to earn large, never-before-available wages by working on American and Canadian bases.

- Some "sweethearts" of our boys-overseas or local young men, began the "patriotic-hostess" role at various service clubs.

- Some young ladies, overwhelmed by the overtures of Americans or Canadians, "broke off" as sweethearts of our "boys-overseas" or our young, local or Newfoundland Militia men. Most of the men being "ditched" were pretty disconsolate.

- When a Newfoundland boy-overseas was "jilted", his parents and the parents of his "estranged" sweetheart sometimes tried to save the relationship. Pleading and recriminations usually failed, and it became an all-round "downer" for morale.

- Some St. John's families and young ladies, thinking of the "unfair advantage" of the luxurious American Bases; the many "inducements"; and the "stealing away" of our young ladies; gave Americans "the cold shoulder".

- In the 20 years from 1942 to 1962 (when U.S. bases closed), with many thousands of Americans having served in Newfoundland, an estimated 25,000 Newfoundland girls married Americans. Many such girls often left behind disappointed and disgruntled boyfriends.

- Most Newfoundland-American or Newfoundland-Canadian marriages were happy. And, thankfully, there were hundreds of fine Americans and Canadians who married here, making Newfoundland their "home".

- At the high point, over 20,000 Americans and 12,500 Canadians were based in Newfoundland. Most of our 12,000 Newfoundlanders-in-service were overseas or on the high seas, where they wanted to be - - "engaging the enemy".

- Over 700 Newfoundland Royal Navy and Merchant Navy sailors died at sea in the war.

- Some Newfoundland soldiers were required by the Commission of Government to stay in Newfoundland. The "Home Guard" or "Militia", with 27 officers and 543 other ranks, was later elevated to become the "Newfoundland Regiment", but at home they had to stay - - on routine "garrison duty".

Americans' Not-So-Secret Ways of Winning Sweethearts.

How did the Americans, wherever they had bases in Newfoundland and Labrador, manage to win so many young ladies away from previous boyfriends ? Partially because of their dashing manner, smart uniforms, money, and the appeal of drinks, dining, and dancing. But, the not-so-secret weapons of the Yanks were their made-in-America, popular music and movies. Most such songs and shows focused on the subject and language of love.

Hit parade music and Hollywood movies provided endless expressions of endearment. They were all about romance and the promise of "true love". Whether holding hands, dancing, or whispering words of affection, the desire for a favourable reaction could have no better mood-setting support than provided by very talented American songwriters, singers, and glamorous movie stars. Newfoundlanders and Canadians could only "borrow" some of those American advantages.

The romantic nature of the popular music is evident in these examples of some World War II "love songs":

I Dream of You -- Frank Sinatra.
Prisoner of Love -- Perry Como.
Love Letters -- Dick Haymes.
Yours -- Jimmy Dorsey.
Who Wouldn't Love You -- Ink Spots.
Moonlight Becomes You -- Bing Crosby.
It Had To Be You -- Betty Hutton.
I'll Buy That Dream -- Harry James.
All I Do Is Dream Of You -- Glenn Miller.
Dearly Beloved -- Dinah Shore.
You Belong To My Heart -- Bing Crosby.
All The Things You Are -- Artie Shaw.
You Are Always In My Heart -- Kenny Baker.
You Stepped Out Of A Dream -- Tony Martin.

In the courtship habits of Americans there was another approach that added to the favourable impression they made amongst young Newfoundland ladies. They were not shy in introducing themselves, and they almost always asked for a "date", and offered something to appeal like a movie, dinner, or a dance. The American bases had their own radio stations, movie theatres, and Officer and NCO Clubs. Many Americans also had automobiles. The Canadians and Newfoundlanders usually could not offer similar advantages.

"Newfie-John's" Key Role in the "Battle of the Atlantic".

Hundreds of Allied merchant ships transported vital cargoes from North America to ports in Britain. The ships carried Canadian and American troops, foodstuffs, planes, tanks, trucks, munitions, and fuel, all for the intended Allied invasions of Africa, Italy, and France.

Hitler had over 1,000 submarines built, intending to torpedo the war supplies. To try to protect against such attack, merchant ships began to travel in convoys, and were guarded by small, fast, naval escort vessels such as corvettes, frigates, and destroyers.

Merchant ships, steering a straight course, had enough fuel to cross the Atlantic. The small escort vessels would zigzag, to seek and sink German U-boats. They could only go a quarter the distance from North America to Britain, then return to base to refuel. So, the mid-Atlantic sector originally could not be protected by escorts.

Before becoming the British Prime Minister, Sir Winston Churchill had been "First Lord of the Admiralty". Very few in Newfoundland know that Sir Winston had personally decided that Newfoundland and Iceland would become major naval escort bases to protect vulnerable merchant ships crossing the mid-Atlantic. (He did not consult Newfoundland.) Britain (not Canada) met the cost.

By That Strategy, St. John's Really Helped Win the War.

By 1942, we had built the Canadian Naval Station they called "Newfie-John". It fulfilled Newfoundland's absolutely vital role in the Battle of the Atlantic. That Battle was highly visible in St. John's, with usually over 20 Canadian Navy ships in the harbour refitting and refuelling to replace other ships returning from convoy duty. We also provided the haven for torpedo-damaged merchant ships. Ship repair was a major challenge for the Newfoundland Dockyard and its tremendously dedicated, over-stressed workforce.

The hospital-treatment of navy and merchant-ship wounded in St. John's put enormous pressures on our medical and nursing professionals. Adding to our realization of "being-at-war" were the coastal gun-batteries, searchlights, and anti-aircraft guns installed all around St. John's. Our strict nightly blackout convinced most of the "locals" there must be a significant danger of enemy attack.

In addition to its major contribution in winning the Battle of the Atlantic, the Royal Canadian Navy's "Newfie-John" Base was really the major, "active" military force in Newfoundland or Labrador. It was constantly carrying the battle right to the enemy and continuously suffering casualties. No disrespect intended, but, apart from the Canadian Navy and Air Force Anti-Submarine patrol, other armed forces in Newfoundland were seldom, if ever, in actual combat. Those others were mainly on "standby" garrison service, in event of possible invasion.

Sailors of the Canadian Navy in St. John's were under incredible pressure, as they returned to sea over-and-over, to engage German U-boats and protect convoys of merchant ships. It was strange that most people in the seaport of St. John's did not realize the vast difference between the lives of the navy men and other military personnel, who essentially were non-combatants. The navy boys could be excused if they let off steam when on shore leave, but many people in St. John's expected similar behaviour from all those in uniform.

Paul J. Johnson.

The War Years Changed Everything Chapters.

Introduction by Paul J. Johnson.

It is not simple to determine the important questions and answers for Newfoundland that arose out of World War II. Some general observations were included in the previous chapter and more will be found in the following eight. In this introduction, we identify some key concerns and consequences, of the War:

- Before war broke out, we were still coping with our very serious, ten-year-long depression, with tremendous unemployment and heart-wrenching poverty, hunger, illness, and despair.
- Early in the war, we had a dreadful feeling about Hitler's swift blitzkriegs - - leading to dramatic conquests in Europe.
- Newfoundland's patriotic response to defending of King and Country produced a very high level of enlistment. Over 12,000 Newfoundlanders went overseas, or served in the Royal and Merchant Navies.
- We were puzzled but pleased at the interest of Canada and the "States" in believing it was important to defend our peaceful Newfoundland.
- Was it really possible that Hitler could invade and conquer England - - or attack Newfoundland ?
- Could it happen that 22,000 of our men and women would leave home and family, for well-paying construction jobs, in building all the intended military bases in Newfoundland and Labrador ?
- How could our fishery cope with that major change?

- As soon as employment and business volumes increased we were subjected to tax-rate increases - - and our Commission of Government deficits disappeared.

- With as many as 30,000 single military men stationed in Newfoundland, our single ladies were to receive a lot of attention, and our own single men a lot of overwhelming competition.

- By 1943, we realized that England and Newfoundland were no longer in danger of being invaded.

- Knowing of the victories in the Battle of Britain and the Battle of the Atlantic, we counted our blessings.

- Many Newfoundlanders became casualties, with well over 1,000 lives lost, and many thousands grieving over the deaths and injuries.

- There was little if any profiteering in Newfoundland. The unaccustomed high levels of employment and incomes created a gradual, unprecedented, and unreal feeling of "prosperity".

- Somehow we felt a little bit guilty that Newfoundland had come out of the world's most savage war, in a much better economic condition than when that terrible conflict began.

- What we did not clearly understand was the extent to which all our public works, and railway and coastal services, had been almost worn out, because of the extreme use during the war years.

- But - - could the good economy last - - and what was to be our political future ?

3

St. John's – The Garrison Town: 1939–1945.

By: Melvin Baker.

"I expect St. John's is a very busy and cosmopolitan place these days with the Canadian, American and British in and out of it. Let's hope it will mean some measure of prosperity for the people there."

Cyril Stone, writing to Marion Stone (St. John's), 7 April 1942.[1]

In the Second World War, four separate political entities had to determine and implement an overall military strategy for the forces deployed in Newfoundland and Labrador – Newfoundland, Great Britain, Canada, and America. This is an overview of the creation of military infrastructure in St. John's between 1939 and 1945 – as civilian and military residents lived through the tumult and tribulations of the war on Newfoundland's seas and shores. Tens of thousands of "outside" soldiers, sailors, air force personnel, and merchant seamen were in St. John's. Because of the international and transient nature of the agreements and operations, and wartime secrecy, exact numbers of those involved are not always known.

By 1907, Newfoundland had attained Dominion constitutional status within the British Empire, but since 1934, Newfoundland was governed by an interim British-appointed Commission of Government. On 3 September 1939, when Britain declared war on Nazi Germany, Newfoundland was automatically at war. This followed Hitler's invasion of Poland only two days earlier. Newfoundland's suspended government status made it possible for Britain to dictate the political and military arrangements that Newfoundland must follow, with little consultation. The very substantial rights that Britain gave to Canada and the United States on establishing military bases in Newfoundland had far-reaching implications. The ensuing developments radically altered the constitutional, political, social, and economic situations for Newfoundland and St. John's.

On 3 February 1941, a St. John's newspaper, *The Evening Telegram*, observed that, as a result of the war, the City was becoming a "garrison town, occupied by military units, local, Canadian, and American. It has meant an increase in the male population of more than two thousand not including the varying number of seamen in port, and, a matter which cannot possibly be treated lightly, this occupation presents problems which must seriously be considered."[2]

The Call to Arms – Service Overseas and at Home.

In 1939, as in World War I, Newfoundlanders immediately and enthusiastically answered Britain's call to arms. They eagerly responded to the Commission's recruitment efforts to defend the Empire. However, remembering Newfoundland's dreadful casualties of World War I, this time the Commission of Government decided not to raise a separate Newfoundland army unit. Instead, Newfoundlanders would join the British armed forces overseas. By the end of 1942, about 5,000 Newfoundlanders had volunteered for the Royal Navy, with 2,889 in service and another 2,000 not accepted for various reasons. Similarly, another 3,000 volunteered for the British Army, with 1,608 accepted for service in the Royal Artillery, where they formed two artillery regiments. About 600 men were accepted in the militia (home guard). By the end of 1942, 276 Newfoundlanders had joined the Royal Air Force. And, some Newfoundlanders residing in Canada joined the Canadian armed forces.

By the end of 1942, over 3,600 Newfoundlanders had enlisted in the Newfoundland Forestry Unit, serving mainly in the Scottish Highlands, cutting pit props for the British coal industry to supply heat and ship fuel.[3] Because of the population's very great seafaring interest, thousands of Newfoundlanders were already in the "Merchant Navy", and that number increased significantly during the war.

Newfoundland's Proposed Defence Measures.

Until 1939, Newfoundland's principal reliance for defence had been the invincible British Navy. In World War I, the defence of Newfoundland had been only a small, joint Canadian-Newfoundland naval patrol. In March 1939 (six months before outbreak of the war) in an uncharacteristic initiative, the Commission of Government submitted a defence proposal for its "principal military objectives ... the Newfoundland Airport at Gander, the Bell Island iron ore mines, the cable terminals at Bay Roberts and other communities, and the Capital City of St. John's, which "might be the objective of what may perhaps be called a casual raid for propaganda purposes." St. John's was stated to be "very vulnerable to attack from the sea in the form of bombardment or landing parties." Newfoundland's only "armed forces" consisted of a semi-military Constabulary numbering about 260 men of all ranks, and the Newfoundland Rangers, with about 60 men. Their responsibilities were police duties and they had "modern small arms (though in the case of the Constabulary there is a shortage of revolvers)." A supplementary defence force was clearly needed.[4]

Activating the First Defence Measures.

The Dominions Office in London decided to act on the proposal, and assigned Captain Claude Fanning-Evans of the Durham Light Infantry and Sergeant-Majors Edgar Crump and William Renshaw to go to St. John's to train a home defence Militia of 250 to 300 men. The recruits would receive one month of intensive training and report once a month thereafter for drill and rifle practice. But, Captain Fanning-Evans and the two Sergeant-Majors had not arrived in Newfoundland by 3 September, when war was declared.[5]

So, the Commission acted on its own to protect vital installations by sending 50 policemen to Bell Island to guard the massive iron ore mines and landing piers so important to Canadian industry, until 30 World War I veterans could be recruited to replace them.[6] The Commission also placed a net across "The Narrows" (entrance to St. John's Harbour), which would be raised to block entry, or lowered to admit friendly vessels. The establishment of a Newfoundland Militia was authorized by the Commission on 31 October 1939. The Commission sent Justice Department Secretary Brian Dunfield to Ottawa to ascertain what supplies and equipment Canada could provide.

World War I veteran Walter F. Rendell was appointed Lieutenant Colonel of the Militia and Fanning-Evans from England as its Staff Captain. Canada provided Ross rifles (weapons of World War I vintage) that were issued to Canadian infantrymen in training camps. Newfoundland got the rifles, ammunition, and other equipment needed, some on loan, with some for repayment. In December 1939, further recruitment increased the Militia's numbers.[7]

Gordon Wells, a former Militia soldier, recalled that basic training was learning the army way of using a rifle and bayonet and practicing on a firing range. Indoors, they use the Central Fire Station's basement firing range and a Lee Enfield .22 rifle. Outdoors, they marched from the Police Drill Hall at Fort Townshend to the "Sand Pitts" outside the City. There they practiced firing the regulation Lee Enfield rifle with .303 ammunition, and a World War I Lewis machine gun that was "subject to jamming and overheating."[8]

By July 1940, as their training progressed, the Militia's strength stood at 240 men. This enabled a soldier, along with a policeman, to do guard duty at a number of critical sites. These were the radio station and towers at Mount Pearl, the City water supply at Windsor Lake, the Imperial Oil tanks and premises on the south side Hills, the Commercial Cable Building on Water Street, the cable communications facilities at Cuckhold's Cove, and the Railway-owned dry docks. In April 1940, the Militia assumed complete responsibility for these sites, as well as for the Government's enemy prisoner internment camp by Quidi Vidi Lake. In late 1940, this camp housed 28 Germans and 9 Italians, mostly merchant seamen aboard ships in Newfoundland ports when war was declared. By January 1941, they were transferred to internment camps in Canada.[9]

Initial Canadian Involvement in 1940.

On 10 September 1939, Canada's Parliament declared war on Germany. Prime Minister Mackenzie King stated that Canada's own defence depended upon securing Newfoundland's defences. However, Canada's Army only consisted of a permanent force of 4,261 of all ranks, and a poorly trained and equipped militia of 51,418. The Air Force had only 4,153 officers and airmen, and 53 serviceable aircraft. The permanent Navy was even smaller, with 145 officers and 1,674 men. By adding the Navy's volunteer reserve, there were a total of 336 officers and 3,477 men. The Navy had six modern destroyers, five minesweepers, and two training vessels. At Halifax, the Navy had only two destroyers and two mine sweepers.[10]

Given Canada's small armed forces, and the need to quickly expand them, Canada was slow to provide defensive measures for Newfoundland. In the early weeks of the war, Canada's only action was to secure the Commission's specific permission to do aerial reconnaissance of Newfoundland's coastlines to search for any enemy ships. Canada also obtained permission to fly over Newfoundland and to use local landing facilities if need be.

Initially Canada saw the defence of Newfoundland as the urgent protection of its two airports, and had offered to take over the facilities from Britain. However, Britain was reluctant to give Canada any such advantage because that might lead to the loss of postwar civilian aviation rights, which would otherwise accrue to Britain.[11]

In March 1940, after Newfoundland's Commissioner of Justice, Edward Emerson visited Ottawa, he reported that "on the military side there is not much that Canada can do. They are providing two guns and two searchlights for the defence of Bell Island and will lend us the necessary personnel to train our militia in their use."[12] In June, a Canadian engineer officer came to Bell Island to supervise the construction of a gun battery. Canada also sent the 1st Battalion of the Black Watch (Royal Highland Regiment) to Botwood in north-central Newfoundland to defend the port of

Botwood and the Newfoundland Airport at Gander. Some members of the Black Watch were in St. John's until August, when the 3rd Division Unit of the Queen's Own Rifles of Canada came to relieve them. The Black Watch unit returned to Canada and was later assigned to England.[13]

The Concerns Grow More Intense.

By June 1940, the rapid German military advance through Western Europe, highlighted by the evacuation of the British expeditionary force at Dunkirk, gave greater urgency for Canada to protect the air bases at Botwood and Gander, and to guard the Bell Island iron ore mines. Britain continued to be hesitant to give control of the two air bases to Canada, but did allow Canada operational control, with ground forces in place, for security reasons, but only for the duration of the war.

Canada took over training the Newfoundland Militia in the St. John's area. Two Militia lieutenants and nine other ranks attended a three-month course with the Royal Canadian Artillery in Halifax. In late August, they returned to Newfoundland and formed the 1st Coastal Defence Battery at Bell Island, with 37 men in total. To instruct the men in gunnery, that Battery had Captain D.V. Rainnie and an artillery warrant officer on loan from the Royal Canadian Artillery.

In the first week of August, a second group of twelve Militia men under command of Lieutenant Joseph (Joe) O'Driscoll went to Halifax by the Newfoundland Express train. This group remained until December, undergoing extensive training with Royal Canadian Artillery gun crews at forts around Halifax. Upon return, Lieutenant O'Driscoll's men were posted to Bell Island to strengthen and train the other members of the 1st Coastal Defence Battery. In February 1941, O'Driscoll assumed command of the Battery, with Captain Rainnie returning to Canada.[14]

Canadian–American Board on Defence.

On 18 August 1940, the negotiations between Prime Minister King and President Franklin Roosevelt led to the establishment of a Canadian-American "Permanent Joint Board on Defence" (PJBD). The PJBD provided a forum in which to discuss plans for Newfoundland. Only occasionally did PJBD include any Newfoundland Government representatives in deliberations.[15]

On 20 August 1940, Canada's Minister of National Defence, Charles G. Power, visiting Canadian troops at Gander and Botwood, met with Governor Sir Humphrey Walwyn and other Commissioners to discuss mutual defence needs. The Commission offered its full support to Canada's defence of North America and agreed to enact legislation under the "Visiting Forces (British Commonwealth) Act" whereby both governments would declare their forces "enacting in combination." This Act of the Commission appointed the Canadian Military Commander to overall command of Newfoundland defence, as a sub-command of Canada's Atlantic Command.

Canada thereby agreed to: station an infantry battalion at St. John's; provide anti-aircraft and coastal artillery where necessary; develop an "advanced naval base" at St. John's; and "construct a fighter air base near St. John's". St. John's would become the Staff Headquarters for both the Canadian Army and Navy in Newfoundland, but the Air Force did not require a headquarters in Newfoundland. Canada would be also permitted to recruit Newfoundlanders to serve in the Canadian armed forces.[16]

The United States Extends Its Sphere of Influence.

On 2 September 1940, under the "Bases for Destroyers Agreement", the United States could receive 99-year leases for military bases it could establish in British "possessions", meaning Newfoundland and a number of West Indian Islands and British Guiana. This was in return for some badly needed, older American Navy Destroyers. In Newfoundland and Bermuda, the lease for bases was given "freely and without consideration."[17] Establishing American military bases in Newfoundland sounded alarm bells in Ottawa about the possibility of America's future interest in Newfoundland. Canada and the United States subsequently agreed on "Joint Measures for North American Defence" that included coordination of both nations' plans for Newfoundland.

Canada Expands Its Presence in Newfoundland.

On 4 October 1940, Newfoundland's Commissioners of Justice and Defence, Edward Emerson, and Finance, John H. Penson, attended a meeting of the PJBD in Halifax. The meeting was to "ascertain the Newfoundland point of view" on the proposals affecting Newfoundland, which had already been submitted to the PJBD Board. Up to the date of this meeting, PJBD had not made any report or recommendation to its respective governments. Canadian proposals for St. John's were much more modest than they eventually became. They included an army headquarters with one rifle battalion, the provision of anti-aircraft and coastal defence forces and a small naval base at St. John's. The Canadians would also construct an airport near St. John's for "fighter protection for ships at anchorage." Emerson and Penson accepted this one on PJBD's proposals.[18]

In November 1940, Canada approved the creation of a St. John's Headquarters for Canadian Army Troops in Newfoundland. What was called "W Force" was established for Newfoundland as a sub-command of the Army's Atlantic Command. Career officer Brigadier Philip Earnshaw was appointed Commander of W Force. Earnshaw, a veteran of the Canadian Expeditionary Force during World War I, had a long service with the Royal Canadian Signals depot. Since 1937, he was Director of Signals at National Defence Headquarters in Ottawa. On 11 November 1940, Earnshaw arrived in St. John's. Under the "Visiting Forces (British Commonwealth) Act", he also took command of the Newfoundland Militia. His Headquarters in St. John's was in an elegant residence, "Winterholme", located at the corner of Circular and Rennie's Mill Roads.

In September 1940, among the first Canadian soldiers to arrive in St. John's, were "sappers" (engineers) of the 2nd Fortress Company, Royal Canadian Engineers. They started the construction of barracks before winter. Incredibly, the Commission of Government had given consideration to barracking troops at Memorial University College. This was not done, because the College had just opened for a new academic year. Instead, construction began immediately on the Canadian Army's main base, to be located at Lester's Field in the City's centre, north of LeMarchant Road. Lester's Field was the largest open field in the City and a popular area for sporting events and travelling circuses. Base operations would extend from there, along Blackmarsh Road to the shores of Mundy Pond.

By December 1940, the Canadians completed the initial barracks and started on their warehouses, a small hospital, laundry, theatre, and a recreation centre. (After the war, a Canadian transportation compound on Blackmarsh Road became Newfoundland's still-prospering "Purity" biscuit manufacturing plant.) Canadian sappers assisted in construction of the Shamrock Field barracks for the Newfoundland Militia near Fort Townshend. In March 1942, the 5th Fortress Company was activated for duty in St. John's with the No. 1 Headquarters Detachment and a special Camouflage Section.[19]

Arrival of Canadian Infantry.

On 14 November 1940, the first Canadian infantry battalion to be assigned to St. John's was the Victoria Rifles of Montreal, arriving in Newfoundland by train. They remained in St. John's for six months, when they were transferred to Gander. Their place in St. John's was taken by the Royal Rifles of Winnipeg, which remained until August 1941, when they went to Valcartier, Quebec, for a short stay, before their tragic assignment to Hong Kong.[20] From mid-February to mid-March 1941, the Algonquin Regiment from Northern Ontario also served in St. John's before being transferred to Botwood. While in St. John's, one company from this Regiment was at Torbay Airport, another at Cape Spear, and a third on standby, a 15-minute distance, in case a counterattack was needed.[21]

For reasons of morale and training, Canadian infantry battalions generally rotated on a six-month basis between St. John's and Gander. The infantry battalion in St. John's provided sentry and guard duties in and around St. John's until November 1941, when a Company of the Veterans Guard of Canada arrived to take over. They took on responsibilities which included guarding the Headquarters and the Ordnance Depot.[22] One soldier in St. John's recalled in an article of the *Newfoundland Quarterly* that they were "greeted with kindness and hospitality by the people", spent an "enjoyable year in their midst", and were able to "see the latest movies from a choice of several theatres. We were invited to spend weekends at summer cottages. The girls had organized dance nights when all we had to do was to bring ourselves and they looked after the rest."[23]

The Grand Entrance of the Americans.

On Saturday, 25 January 1941, the American troopship *Edmund B. Alexander* arrived at the entrance to St. John's Harbour. It waited for four days, while wind, snowstorms, and fog kept the 21,000-ton former German cruiseship "at bay". The *Alexander* waited at anchor between Bell Island and Kelly's Island, in Conception Bay. On Wednesday, 29 January, shortly after daylight, the *Alexander*, the largest ship to ever enter St. John's Harbour passed through the Narrows under the guidance of Master Pilot Captain George Anstey.

The *Alexander* carried an estimated 1,000 troops and 200 crew. It docked at the fish premises of William J. Bursey on the south side of the harbour. An unknown writer commented a few months later: "The hour after sunrise proved a perfect time for bringing the transport through the Narrows," for the "sky was clear and there was scarcely any wind. The water inside the harbour was as smooth as oil, and the tide was on the rise. As the big grey ship loomed out of the haze in the Narrows, the shipping in the port blared out its welcome and whistles on shore joined in the celebration. Despite the early hour, crowds lined the waterfront, standing on the docks as they had stood, impatiently for hours on previous days. They were doomed to disappointment, however, for the ship was scarcely through the Narrows when a blanket of dense fog settled over the harbour. Visibility for the rest of the day was reduced to a few yards."[24]

Back to the Canadians Again.

Ottawa remained concerned about the growing numbers of American Military personnel, and their major bases being built at St. John's, Argentia, and Stephenville. Canada was determined to expand and play the pivotal role in the defence of Newfoundland. In 1941, Canada increased the number of its troops stationed here. This involved building up the coastal defence system, on which, in August 1940, the PJBD had given responsibility to Canada.

In the fall of 1940, construction had already begun on three Canadian coastal defence batteries – one at the Outer Battery near Chain Rock on the eastern side of the Narrows; another at Fort Amherst on its western side; and the third at Cape Spear, approximately four miles southeast of the Narrows. The two Harbour batteries housed 4.7-inch guns, while Cape Spear had 10-inch guns, to serve as a counter-bombardment battery. All three battery locations had concrete bunkers to provide stable platforms for the guns. The Fort Amherst Battery included wooden frame barracks, messes, and a storage building. At Cape Spear, concrete bunkers also contained infantry support guns, ammunition storage, gun crew, and infantry "ready rooms".[25]

Until a full organization could be in place, in the spring of 1941 Canada put together a makeshift "Q" Battery of men drawn from existing batteries in Nova Scotia and New Brunswick. With the completion of the Battery at Fort Chain Rock in May 1941, Q Battery was redesignated as the 103rd Coastal Battery RCA and, under the command of Major D.V. Rainnie, given responsibility for Fort Chain Rock, Fort Amherst, and Cape Spear.

Canada also organized a Light Anti-Aircraft (LAA) battery, the 16th LAA drawn from existing mainland batteries. The 16th LAA arrived in St. John's in the spring of 1941, equipped with 50-calibre Colt AA machine guns (supplied by the United States Army). A year later these guns were replaced by Canadian-built 40-millimetre Bofors. The 16th LAA was disbanded to become part of other new batteries from Canada. In August 1941, a Heavy Anti-Aircraft (HAA) battery, the 7th Heavy Battery, was posted to St. John's, remaining and training in St. John's until December when it was transferred to Gander. In June and July 1942, two new batteries, the 14th HAA and the 27th LAA, arrived in St. John's, charged with defending Torbay Airport and various strategic positions around St. John's. Both remained in St. John's until March 1944, when the 49th HAA and 24th LAA Batteries replaced them.[26]

A Basic Change Involving Canadian Troops.

Until 1943, Canadian military units sent to Newfoundland had come from units of the "Active Service Force", whose members had volunteered for general service and could be sent anywhere for "Active Duty". Following the passage in 1940 of Canadian legislation for Compulsory Military Service, because conscription was unpopular in Quebec the Canadian Government decided, "for national unity reasons", to have a plebiscite on the issue. The 1942 national plebiscite returned an affirmative vote in favour of conscription, but the Mackenzie King Government decided to offer military persons the alternate choice of "service in home defence".

In September of 1942, the Canadian government decided Newfoundland would be a location where non-"Active Service" troops could be sent for "home defence". The first regiment posted to St. John's under this arrangement was the Regiment de Ste Hyacinthe, which relieved the Lincoln and Welland Regiment in April 1943. The Regiment de Quebec replaced the Ste Hyacinthe Regiment in September 1944.[27]

Inevitable Confusion at the Command Level.

In 1940, after assuming command Brigadier Earnshaw improved the training of Newfoundland Militia. However, occasional misunderstandings arose between Earnshaw and Newfoundland Police Officials, who sought to use Militia members for police duty without first seeking Canadian approval. In June 1941, Earnshaw resolved this problem by putting the Militia on "Active Duty" and appointing a Canadian, Lieutenant Colonel Alfred T. Howell (a Montrealer, born to Newfoundlanders from Carbonear), as Commander of the Newfoundland Militia. The Militia took on some responsibilities outside St. John's, such as the main hydro dam at Deer Lake and the cable stations at Harbour Grace and Bay Roberts.

In March 1943, the home guard Militia was elevated to regimental status and became the "Newfoundland Regiment". It now consisted of headquarters based at Shamrock Field, two infantry companies, and a coastal defence battery on Bell Island. The Militia also became a pool of trained soldiers that might wish to transfer to one of the two Newfoundland Artillery Regiments in the British Army. Newfoundland women could join the Canadian Army, which began recruiting in Newfoundland after July 1943. Within six months, 250 women enlisted for service.[28]

The British Admiralty Changes the Pivotal Role of Newfoundland and Canada.

In 1940, Canada's plan had been to establish a small naval base at St. John's. Canada supported a small, coastal-patrol defence force of about 12 ships and a maintenance service at St. John's. In December 1940, the HMCS *Mascin* arrived to participate in the work.[29] But, the expansion of the German submarine presence westward in the Atlantic prompted the British Admiralty to create a new, stronger, anti-submarine strategy. This would improve the safe crossing of convoy-vessels from North America to Britain and returning.

The Admiralty proposed three naval escort forces. The first group would operate from Britain to a point in the Atlantic, where a second group of escorts from Iceland would take over. The third group would operate from St. John's. On 21 May 1941, partially in concern over being outmaneuvred by the Americans, Ottawa enthusiastically agreed to become the escort force in St. John's. The British Admiralty wished to have Canada build and maintain a much larger naval base. Because of ever-present British politics, ownership of the land under the bases would remain either with Newfoundland or the British Admiralty – i.e., not Canada.[30]

Canada Builds Naval Forces in St. John's.

For convoy escort service, Canada offered seven corvettes immediately, 15 more by the end of June, and 48 more within six months. By mid-June of 1941, Canada proposed having eight destroyers and 20 corvettes for St. John's. The Admiralty accepted the offer and requested the appointment of Commodore Leonard W. Murray, RCN, as Commander of the "Newfoundland Escort Force" (NEF). Murray arrived on 15 June to assume command. He established his temporary headquarters in the Newfoundland Hotel until a headquarters building could be erected at the rear of the hotel.

Near its headquarters, the RCN also erected a hospital off Quidi Vidi Road, close to Newfoundland's main General Hospital. Because of the large number of injured seamen brought into St. John's from the torpedoed British and Allied vessels in the Atlantic, the need for increased hospital accommodation was great. This placed a tremendous strain on both civilian and military hospital facilities. E.G.M. Cape Co. of Montreal had the contract to build a naval hospital, which went into operation in April 1942.[31]

The Development of St. John's as a Major Naval Port.

St. John's Harbour is small, just over 700 yards at its widest point, and 2,100 yards in length. Commercial wharves and breastworks covered all of the waterfront. These were crucial to Newfoundland's import and fish-export trades. Under the Bases Agreement, the Americans had acquired the right to lease 1,000 feet of the least-used Harbour shoreline. The RCN was left to renovating the wharves on the Harbour's south side and the redevelopment near the northwest corner of the harbour, where the Newfoundland Dockyard was located.[32] This required expropriation of private property to clear the site of structures and construct a naval dockyard and machine shops. It also involved acquiring further land, midway on the south side, where the RCN excavated tunnels into the Southside Hill for the storage of munitions.[33]

By July 1941, the RCN had 150 officers and 750 men in St. John's. By November 1942, there were over 2,000 in total. June 1943 saw a total of 2,700 officers and men. By the end of 1943, this had risen to 3,600. By December 1944, it stood at 5,000. Included in the ratings were some Newfoundland women who had enlisted in the Women's Services of the RCN (WRNS) and returned to be on duty "at home". A total of 568 Wrens did service in Newfoundland, doing mainly administrative work with the North Atlantic Convoy Duty.[34]

Of all the different forces based in or near St. John's, the RCN was present in the greatest number. They served as a strong counterbalance to the large number of American personnel. In that regard, the St. John's Naval Base served Canada's military objectives in prosecuting the war and simultaneously serving Canada's postwar-Newfoundland geopolitical ambitions.[35] After the War, although American bases operated for another 16 years under their 99-year leases, Canadians, despite their political concerns, demobilized and dismantled their bases.

Canada's Extraordinary Effort at Torbay Airport.

In October 1940, Canada, having received approval from the PJBD and Newfoundland, moved quickly to build an airport fighter and surveillance aircraft base at Torbay, near St. John's. In November, the site chosen was 881 acres, about six miles north of the City, the Canadian Government acquiring fee simple title ownership of the land on which the airport would be built. Canadian military rights at the base would be decided after the war. Canada spent a total of $ 11,709,431 on the base by April 1945. It was named by the Royal Canadian Air Force (RCAF) as "Torbay Airport" – after the nearby, small fishing village. During the difficult winter of 1940–41, surveyors laid out all the boundaries, with construction to begin in the spring. The contract was awarded to McNamara Construction of Toronto, with the priority being runway construction. Another base that Canada constructed in Newfoundland was in Goose Bay, Labrador, where Canada, after long discussions with the British and Newfoundland Governments, negotiated a 99-year lease.[36]

Torbay Airport – A Huge Construction Job.

As a 1944 RCAF History of Torbay observed, the "enormity of this task can be appreciated considering the equipment employed. There were eighteen tractors, seven power shovels, eight earth-movers, six bulldozers, two earth rippers, and a fleet of trucks". Time was the big concern. Night and day, men hardened to rough work, forced themselves at a grueling pace. Solid rock ridges were blasted; oozing swamps were drained; and an incredible 1,700,000 cubic yards of earth were moved." Another Canadian company, E.G.M. Cape, had been contracted to erect the buildings and install a water main to the City's water supply at nearby Windsor Lake.

Fortunately, on 18 October 1941, when extreme bad weather forced three American B-17 Flying Fortresses and one Canadian Digby plane to force-land, a single runway was ready. By mid-November the airport had two runways – 5,000 feet by 150 feet, and 5,000 feet by 200 feet.[37]

Integrating Torbay with the Navy in the Battle of the Atlantic.

In 1941, the construction of Torbay Airport was a vital part of Canada's overall plans for the St. John's naval base. By 10 July 1941, the RCAF had established Group I Headquarters at St. John's, with Group Captain C.M. McEwen taking command on 15 August. His first headquarters was at the Newfoundland Hotel, to be close to senior officials of the Canadian Navy, to coordinate their joint efforts. He was responsible for all RCAF units in Newfoundland. Torbay provided air-support for the RCN's Newfoundland Escort Force.

Until 20 January 1942, the St. John's Headquarters reported to Eastern Air Command at Halifax, when Group I took on this responsibility. For much of 1941, Captain McEwen's work was establishing command communications and approving airport construction.[38]

Although first considered a fighter base, with the arrival of the RCAF's 11 Bomber Reconnaissance (BR) Squadron, Torbay became a reconnaissance and anti-submarine/defence base. That Squadron remained until 30 May 1942, when 145 Bomber Reconnaissance came to St. John's, with Hudson and Ventura aircraft, for anti-submarine duty. The RCAF also stationed Liberator and Canso bomber planes at Torbay. In June 1942, the RCAF had Hurricane fighter planes at Torbay, forming the 125 (Nfld) Squadron. In 1943 and 1944, many other aircraft were used at Torbay for anti-submarine work.[39]

Changes Involving Torbay Airport.

From May 1942 to 1945, the Commander of the Torbay Base was Newfoundland-born Group Captain Roy Grandy. Born in Bay L'Argent, Grandy had served in Britain's Royal Flying Corps in 1916 and had joined the Canadian Air Force in 1920. He left in 1922 and rejoined in 1925.[40]

In May 1942, to protect the base Canada posted an Army unit at Torbay Airport. The summer of 1942 also saw 30 members of the RCAF's Women's Division (WD) posted to Torbay in administrative office positions. WD began recruitment in January 1943, and between 27 January and 26 November 1943, the WD had 208 recruits in Newfoundland, with a majority having returned home to serve as clerks, stenographers, and supervising the laundries.[41]

On 1 May 1942, Trans-Canada Air Lines inaugurated its air service to St. John's, on the civilian side of the airport. The RCAF provided emergency transportation of military and civilian patients to hospitals in St. John's. Torbay was also used extensively by the United States Army Air Force, which based some communications and transportation personnel there, in support of Pepperrell Base. No overall figures are available on the number of Canadian and U.S. air force personnel in St. John's between 1940 and 1945.

The American Army Strategy in St. John's, starting 1940.

In September 1940, under the agreement Britain made with the United States on bases for destroyers, the Americans sent an advance party to St. John's aboard the USS *St. Lewis* to survey the sites where bases might be built. American Rear-Admiral John W. Greenslade led the party. He met with the Commission of Government on 16 September and received permission to begin the survey.

Greenslade expressed an interest in an area near Kilbride. It provided easy access to the Railway and was in close proximity of the Harbour. He also agreed to consider a farming area by the Government's internment camp near Quidi Vidi Lake. After consideration, the Americans chose the Quidi Vidi site. On 7 October 1940, Lieutenant Colonel Philip Bruton was appointed District Engineer for the Newfoundland District Office of the U.S. Army Corps of Engineers. On 15 October, Lieutenant Colonel Bruton and a group from the U.S. Corps of Engineers arrived in St. John's aboard the USS *Bowditch* to begin actual surveying. On October 16, Bruton opened the Newfoundland Engineer District Office at St. John's, with his temporary headquarters in the Reid Building on Duckworth Street. This District Office functioned until 1 April 1943, when responsibility for construction passed to the Commanding General of the Newfoundland Base Command.[42]

Americans Negotiate Wharf Rental on the Southside.

There is an interesting story about the business acumen of W.J. Bursey, a Newfoundland merchant. On 16 October, when the *Bowditch* docked at the St. John's fish premises of W.J. Bursey on the south side of the Harbour, the Americans wished to rent his premises. Bursey's site had been chosen because it was the only one with water deep enough for the large American ship that was coming to St. John's. Bursey was asked how soon he could move, because the Americans wanted the premises "by tomorrow noon." Because Bursey was in the midst of preparing fish for export, he convinced the Americans that he needed more time. He worked an arrangement with them to finish his work, and they would pay him on a rental basis for the time the *Edmund B. Alexander* would be docked. Also they "would give Bursey the contract to supply the ship" while it was in port.[43] This was a "shrewd deal" for Mr. Bursey.

The Beginning of Large-Scale American Bases.

On 22 October 1940, over a year before the United States entered the war, the American War Department issued a letter (WD AGO 580 {10-14-40}) stating which army units would comprise the garrison at St. John's. It was to be commanded by Captain Maurice D. Welty. The *Alexander*, when it arrived, carried 977 U.S. Army troops made up of 58 officers and 919 enlisted men. The ship itself had a crew of 200 and carried 2,000 tons of armaments and construction materials. The troops on board were the Minnesota-based, U.S. 3rd Infantry, the 24th Coast Artillery, and the 62nd Anti-Aircraft Artillery. (They came from the Second, Third, and Seventh Army Corps – from New York, New Jersey, Delaware, West Virginia, Pennsylvania, and Maryland.)[44]

With no onshore facilities yet available, the troops remained aboard the docked *Alexander* until May 1941. Fishermen from the Battery (a small fishing village located at the eastern end of the Harbour below Signal Hill) and Fort Amherst (on the opposite side of the Harbour entrance) ran an unofficial water taxi service, carrying soldiers back and forth to Water Street. The fishermen used their taxi-boats as "bumboats", as they were called by locals.

On 15 April 1941, the U.S. Army entered into an agreement with a local company to lease a 15-acre field off Carpasian Road to build a temporary tent-camp for 1,000 troops – until the base near Quidi Vidi Lake was completed. It was named "Camp Alexander" after the troopship and became occupied within one month and five days, on 20 May 1941. The Camp housed nearly 1,000 troops "under canvas", in temporary wood-frame, pyramidal tents. Troops were fed in temporary frame and tarpaper mess halls; with sanitary conditions to be strictly enforced by the medical authorities of the Command.[46]

Construction and Size of Fort Pepperrell.

Between October 1940 and April 1941, Lieutenant Colonel Bruton employed local workmen to erect temporary office buildings at Quidi Vidi, as quarters for handling the administrative work of the District Office and the base contractor. Construction began on 8 February 1941. By 22 February 1941, there were over 600 Newfoundlanders employed at the new base. Twelve large sheds were erected to house supplies off-loaded from the *Alexander*. By 9 July, there were over 2,200 men employed in the Pepperrell base construction, including 400 civilians from the United States.[47] In 1942, the Corps of Engineers also constructed a new power transmission line through the City to supplement the diesel-based generator at Pepperrell. The local United Towns Electric Company reimbursed the Americans for the construction cost.[48]

On 23 April 1941, the American base at Quidi Vidi was officially named "Fort Pepperrell" in honour of Sir William Pepperrell, an American colonial soldier.[49] On 20 May 1941, the Headquarters for the Newfoundland Base Command moved from the cruiseship *Alexander* to a large dwelling at 44 Rennie's Mill Road. Some of the Pepperrell officers and enlisted men had brought their wives and families, who stayed in rental accommodations in the City. Following the 7 December 1941 Japanese attack on Pearl Harbor and the entry of the United States into the war, the families had to return to the United States.

In the spring of 1941, the arrival of the USAT *Chateau Thierry* added another 1,800 American soldiers and 200 sailors.[50] On 1 May 1941, the 805th Military Police Company arrived on the USAT *Leonard Wood* to help the Newfoundland Constabulary patrol

City streets. They replaced the 3rd Infantry that previously did this work. The Military Police previously used a "brig" aboard the *Alexander* as a jail. Later, the Americans set up a jail and first aid station above the York Theatre on Water Street. Eventually similar facilities became available at Pepperrell.

Pepperrell was originally designed to accommodate 3,500 troops, with a warehouse space of 146,315 square feet. Inside there was storage capacity for 310 vehicles. Following the American declaration of war against Japan on 8 December 1941, and Germany on 11 December, plans for Pepperrell changed, with accommodation growing to 5,500 troops and the warehouse capacity increasing to 248,588 square feet. The major structures and facilities of the base were for housing, recreation, administration, supplies, operating equipment, water supply, sewage-disposal, power facilities, and gasoline and oil storage tanks.

On 19 May 1941, a consortium of American construction companies known as "Newfoundland Base Contractors" assumed responsibility for construction work. Using Newfoundland labour, the base was ready for the transfer of troops from Camp Alexander – beginning on 24 November 1941, with the 21st Signal Service Company and all other troops making the move in early December. War, for the United States, began 8 December 1941, in the midst of all the ongoing work the Americans were doing in Newfoundland.

The Stars and Stripes was raised at Pepperrell for the first time on 14 December 1941, within days of America being at war. On 29 September 1942, the 821st Signal Wire Maintenance Company arrived at Pepperrell to help with the installation of telephone line connections across the Island to improve communications. In total, American military records indicate that in 1942 and 1943 there were as many as 7,000 troops stationed at Pepperrell. The 3rd Infantry remained at Pepperrell until November 1943, when it returned to Camp Butner, North Carolina. Troops from the 470th and 471st Infantry Division formed the core of Pepperrell's troops right to the end of the war.[51]

Cooperation & Collaboration Between the U.S. & Canada.

The Canadians were involved with early efforts when the *Alexander* docked in St. John's. Canadians had considered establishing an anti-aircraft battery on Signal Hill. Instead, they now encouraged the Americans to do so. On 4 February the Americans agreed to place their four-gun 155-millimetre mobile coastal artillery battery guns, a four-gun 3-inch anti-aircraft battery, and a 16-gun battery of 50-calibre machine guns on Signal Hill. By the end of February, the 155-millimetre guns were in place, manned by men of the 57th Coast Artillery Regiment, which had been redesignated as a separate battalion.

The first of May 1942 saw the arrival by train in St. John's of two American, 8-inch coast defence guns. On 1 May 1941, 132 American officers and men of Battery D, 52nd Coast Artillery Regiment arrived aboard the USAT *Leonard Wood* from Brooklyn. On 16 February 1942, the Regiment was redesignated Battery D, 24th Coast Artillery Separate Battalion. On 1 April 1941, the Americans began construction of gun positions just north of George's Pond, where they placed 3-inch guns and four machine guns, manned by Battery B, 62nd Coast Artillery Regiment, from Fort Totten, New York. Because the Canadians had not completed their batteries at Cape Spear, Fort Amherst, and Fort Chain Rock, the Americans on Signal Hill were the only defence for St. John's. In December 1941, when the Canadian 10-inch guns went into service, the 155-millimetre American guns were moved from Signal Hill to coastal defence elsewhere in Newfoundland.

The Americans had built extensive barracks opposite George's Pond on Signal Hill to accommodate 478 men. Included were a dispensary, post exchange, machine-and-carpentry shops, two mess halls, and two recreation buildings. A pump-house took water from George's Pond to supply a 10,000-gallon wooden storage tank. There were 5,070 feet of water and sewerage lines.[52] In December 1941, the 58th Engineers constructed and opened a road (known as the "Burma Road") north across Signal Hill to Pepperrell. In January

1942, the Commission of Government agreed to give American personnel on Signal Hill the same rights as if stationed within Pepperrell.[53]

In late 1941, the Corps of Engineers designed and built a U.S. Army Dock at the east end of the Harbour for unloading cargoes of supplies and equipment. It was 605 feet long, 160 feet wide, with a 3,000 square foot transit shed, and stevedoring equipment. It was completed in 1943 at a cost of $1,726,274. Gasoline and oil for the military were off-loaded at the U.S. Dock from military tankers, and stored in adjacent underground tanks. The fuel was shipped by truck daily, from the dock to Pepperrell.[54] Eventually an underground oil line was completed from the Dock to the north end of Fort Pepperrell.

The Different Approaches of Canada and the United States.

The Canadian buildings and facilities were only designed to last for a short time-frame, with presumed early departure of the troops. The Americans built based on their 99-year leases. A public relations officer for Pepperrell wrote in a special year-end 1943 edition of the St. John's newspaper *The Daily News* that in the third year of their occupation the "Americans have built solidly and well", and that the bases had taken on a permanent appearance, being built as "small cities" with all "amenities".[55] The Americans had substantial recreational facilities for off-duty personnel, as well as clubs, theatres, retail facilities, and even a radio station.

In early November 1941, Captain Hiatt of the Army Engineers approached Commissioner for Justice and Defence Emerson for permission to erect a United States Services Organization (USO) Recreational Centre in St. John's. It would house "a Reception Hall, clubrooms for reading and other leisure, quite a fair-sized theatre-dance-hall, and in the basement a bowling alley". The only site found suitable was the garden at the back of the Central Fire Hall on Merrymeeting Road.

On Saturday, 7 January 1942, the USO was opened. Beginning at 8 p.m., the official ceremonies were broadcast over the stations of the Broadcasting Corporation of Newfoundland. The leaders of state and churches and the American and Canadian military were present on stage. This was the first USO building to be built outside of continental United States.[56]

Britain Assesses How Newfoundland Is Doing.

In 1943, an astonishing commentary by the British Dominions Office, sent confidentially to Governor Walwyn, stated that the establishment of Pepperrell had far-reaching effect because:

> almost overnight unemployment was swept away and the many labourers employed on construction work have, for the last two years, been earning wages in excess of what they were previously accustomed to receive. These higher rates of pay, coupled with the physical presence of so many service men, of a nation whose wealth and daily comforts are so much in advance of Newfoundland standards, have led to a realization amongst average Newfoundlanders that they have missed much in the past. Consequently, it may be said that the establishment of United States bases on the island has led to a demand amongst poorer sections of the community not only for the basic domestic requirements, but also for what might be termed luxury articles, such as radio sets, etc. and to a desire for better and more expensive foodstuffs.

They concluded that:

> On the whole the relationship of the United States forces with the general public is satisfactory. This was because the facilities provided for the former are so lavish that they have little need to make calls on Newfoundland hospitality. None-the-less Americans are to be found on duty or on leave in

> all sections of the island and although their primary attraction arises perhaps from their monetary value, their presence is none-the-less cheerfully tolerated. Americans in the mass are often inclined to be overbearing and contemptuous of any country but their own, particularly when they are themselves abroad, but it cannot be said that Newfoundlanders as a whole bear them any ill will.[57]

These condescending remarks tell better than any attempt to describe the superior attitude of the Dominions Office toward the people of Newfoundland or the Americans, just how little regard and respect they had for people they considered beneath them.

A Conclusion of War, But Some "Occupation" Continued.

With the end of war in 1945, the Canadians did not retain their bases. By 1946, they had disposed of most of their assets in St. John's, and the naval base was being dismantled. The Newfoundland Regiment Militia was demobilized in 1946. Following Newfoundland's entry into the Canadian Confederation in 1949, in the fall of that year some Canadian armed forces returned to St. John's.[58] Pepperrell and other American military bases remained until 1961 when the bases were closed and the assets turned over to the Canadian and Provincial Governments.

In December 1942, a public relations officer of the Canadian Army wrote in a St. John's newspaper: "Anchored like a battleship across the mouth of the St. Lawrence," Newfoundland had become the first outpost of the defence of North America.[59] The impacts of the occupation on St. John's were many and varied. The war had forever changed the face and character of the small port city, referred to by happy, returning naval personnel as "Newfie-John".

Melvin Baker.

Biographical Sketch

Melvin Baker is a native of Catalina, Newfoundland, and is the University Archivist-Historian (President's Office) for Memorial University of Newfoundland. He is a graduate of Memorial University and the University of Western Ontario and has written extensively on 20th-century Newfoundland History.

I want to thank James Feehan, Aidan Maloney, Peter Neary, and Paul Johnson for their comments and advice on this essay. Aidan shared with me his personal reminiscences as an employee of the Royal Bank of Canada and as a boarder living in St. John's during the war years.

Endnotes

1. Rooms Provincial Archives, MG358, Box 1, file 4, Cyril Stone to Marion Stone, 7 April 1942.

2. *Evening Telegram* 3 February 1941.

3. Peter Neary, *Newfoundland in the North Atlantic World, 1929–1949* (Kingston & Montreal: McGill-Queen's University Press 1988), pp. 116-18.

4. Rooms Provincial Archives, GN38, Box S4-2-1.1, file 1, Administrator of Newfoundland to Secretary of State for Dominion Affairs (SSDA), March 1939.

5. Gordon C. Wells, *The Newfoundland Regiment (1939–1946): War – "On the Home Front"* (Trinity: Oceanside Press 1997), p. 4; and Neary, *Newfoundland*, pp. 112-14. Fanning-Evans arrived in St. John's on 15 September 1939. See *Evening Telegram* 15 September 1939.

6. Neary, *Newfoundland*, p. 115.

7. Neary, *Newfoundland*, pp. 116-17; and Rooms Provincial Archives, GN38, Box S4-1-2, file 1, Dunfield's report dated 30 September

1939, and Box S4-2-1.1, file 2, Governor of Newfoundland to Commander-in-Chief, America & West Indies, 19 October 1939; G.W.L. Nicholson, *More Fighting Newfoundlanders* (St. John's: Government of Newfoundland and Labrador 1969), pp. 523-24; and C.P. Stacey, *Six Years of War: The Army in Canada, Britain and the Pacific, vol. 1* (Ottawa 1957), p. 178.

8. Wells, *The Newfoundland Regiment*, pp. 5 and 10-11.

9. Wells, *The Newfoundland Regiment*, pp. 6-15; and Gerhard P. Bassler, *Vikings to U-boats: The German Experience in Newfoundland and Labrador* (Montreal & Kingston: McGill-Queen's University Press 2006), pp. 223-43.

10. Robert Kavanagh, "W Force: The Canadian Army and the defence of Newfoundland in the Second World War" (M.A. thesis, Memorial University 1995), pp. 41-44.

11. David MacKenzie, *Inside the Atlantic Triangle: Canada and the Entrance of Newfoundland into Confederation, 1939–1949* (Toronto: University of Toronto Press 1986), pp. 38-46; and Kavanagh, "W Force," pp. 47-49.

12. Rooms Provincial Archives, GN38, Box S4-1-4, file 5, Emerson's memo J.12-1940, dated 23 March 1940.

13. Stacey, *Six Years of War*, p. 179.

14. Nicholson, *More Fighting Newfoundlanders*, pp. 526-27; and Wells, *The Newfoundland Regiment*, pp. 16-18.

15. Stanley W. Dziuban, *Military Relations between the United States and Canada, 1939–1945* (Washington: Department of the Army 1959), p. 30; and MacKenzie, *Inside the Atlantic Triangle*, pp. 44-45.

16. Rooms Provincial Archives, GN38, Box S4-1-7, file 6, memorandum for Commission, J&D 1-1942; MacKenzie, *Inside the*

Atlantic Triangle, pp. 43-44; Kavanagh, "W Force," pp. 75-76; and Paul Bridle, ed., *Documents on Relations between Canada and Newfoundland, Volume 1, 1935–1939* (Ottawa: Department of External Affairs 1974), pp. 160-61.

17. Neary, *Newfoundland*, p. 135.

18. Rooms Provincial Archives, GN38, Box S4-2-1.1, file 8, Report by Newfoundland Representatives of Meeting with Permanent Joint Defence Board at Halifax, 4 October 1940; Dziuban, *Military Relations*, p. 367; and Neary, *Newfoundland*, p. 240.

19. Kavanagh, "W Force," pp. 78-79, 85-86, and 131; Catherine F. Horan, "Buckmaster's Field," in *Encyclopedia of Newfoundland and Labrador, vol. 1* (St. John's: Newfoundland Book Publishers 1981), p. 285; William Clarence Parrott, "On the Perimeter: A Reconstruction of the Military Geography of Newfoundland and Labrador during the Second World War, 1939-1945" (MA thesis, Memorial University 1993), pp. 88-90; and *Daily News*, December 31 1942.

20. Peter A. Henderson, *Guarding the Gates: A History of Canadian Forces Station, St. John's* (St. John's: CFS St. John's 1992), p. 18.

21. http://www.algonquinregiment.com/history.html.

22. Kavanagh, "W Force," p. 94; and Henderson, *Guarding the Gates*, pp. 86-87.

23. Sgt. C.S. McKnight, "A Canadian Soldier Reviews two years Newfoundland Duty," *Newfoundland Quarterly* (Autumn 1944), p. 24.

24. Paul O'Neill, *The Oldest City: The Story of St. John's, Newfoundland* (Portugal Cove-St. Philip's: Boulder Publications 2003), p. 75; John Cardoulis, *A Friendly Invasion: The American Military in Newfoundland, 1940-1990* (St. John's: Breakwater 1990), p. 44; and "U.S. Troops arrive in St. John's," *Newfoundland Quarterly* (Spring 1941), p. 21.

25. Parrott, "On the Perimeter," pp. 90-94.

26. Kavanagh, "W Force," p. 94; Henderson, *Guarding the Gates*, pp. 119-25; and Tony Murphy and Paul Kenney, *The War at our Doorstep: St. John's During World War Two – An Album* (St. John's: Harry Cuff Publications 1989).

27. Kavanagh, "W Force," pp. 165-67 and 173.

28. Kavanagh, "W Force," p. 94; Henderson, *Guarding the Gates*, pp. 81-83; and *Daily News* 31 December 1943.

29. Gilbert Norman Tucker, *The Naval Service of Canada: Its Official History, Vol. II* (Ottawa: King's Printer 1952), pp. 186-88.

30. Tucker, *The Naval Service of Canada*, pp. 190-91.

31. C.P. Stacey, *Arms, Men and Governments* (Ottawa 1970), pp. 310-12; Marc Milner, *North Atlantic Run: The Royal Canadian Navy and the Battle for the Convoys* (Toronto: University of Toronto Press 1985), pp. 40-43; Tucker, *The Naval Service of Canada*, p. 189; Donald E. Graves, *In Peril on the Sea: The Royal Canadian Navy and the Battle of the Atlantic* (Toronto: The Canadian Naval Memorial Trust 2003), pp. 75-90; and Rooms Provincial Archives, GN38, Box S3-5-2, file 8, Governor of Newfoundland to SSDA, 13 June 1941, and Box S3-5-3, file 18, Governor of Newfoundland to SSDA, 15 February 1943.

32. Rooms Provincial Archives, GN38, S4-2-4, file 5, Governor of Newfoundland to SSDA, 19 July 1941, memorandum for Commission of Government, 29 August 1941, and L.W. Murray to Sir Wilfred Woods, 25 August 1941; and Tucker, *The Naval Service of Canada*, p. 192.

33. Details of the expropriation process are in Rooms Provincial Archives, GN4/1/D, Box 35, files G/454/1 and G/454/6; and GN38, Box S4-2-4, file 5, E.A. Seal to Sir Wilfred Woods, 9 July 1941.

34. Tucker, *The Naval Service of Canada*, pp. 193-97; *Daily News* 31 December 1943; and Jeffrey A. Keshen, *Saints, Sinners, and Soldiers: Canada's Second World War* (Vancouver: UBC Press 2004), p. 182.

35. Bernard Ransom, "Canada's 'Newfyjohn' Tenancy: The Royal Canadian Navy in St. John's, 1941-1945," *Acadiensis*, XXIII, 2 (Spring 1994), p. 49.

36. Mackenzie, *Inside the North Atlantic Triangle*, pp. 72-73 and 166-68; Neary, *Newfoundland*, pp. 197-203; *Per Ardua: A Pictorial History of RCAF, Torbay* (1944), pp. 10-12; and Parrott, "On the Perimeter," p. 106.

37. *Per Ardua*, pp. 10-12; and Parrott, "On the Perimeter," p. 106.

38. W.A.B. Douglas, *The Creation of a National Air Force* (Toronto: University of Toronto Press 1986), pp. 387 and 390.

39. http://www.rcaf.com/squadrons/1-100series/145squadron.php; http://home.thezone.net/~ainal/torbay.htm; and Henderson, *Guarding the Gates*, p. 22.

40. http://home.thezone.net/~ainal/torbay.htm;
http://www.stjohnsairport.com/index/index.cfm; and Bert Riggs, "Captain Roy Stanley Grandy," in *Encyclopedia of Newfoundland and Labrador, vol. 2* (1984), pp. 694-95.

41. *Per Ardua*, p. 15; Keshen, *Saints, Sinners and Soldiers*, pp. 176-77; and *Daily News* 31 December 1943.

42. Rooms Provincial Archives, GN38, Box S4-2-1.1, file 13, Notes of a meeting of the United States and Military Experts with the Commission of Government held at Government House, 16 September 1940; John Cardoulis, *A Friendly Invasion*, p. 39; and Corps of Engineers, "Historical Monograph: U.S. Army Bases Newfoundland" (New York, January 1946), pp. iv-1 and iv-3, copy

courtesy of James Candow, Parks Canada, from manuscript on file, Department of the Army, Center of Military History, Washington, D.C.

43. Rooms Provincial Archives, GN38, Box S4-2-3.2, file 1, Telegram from Governor of Newfoundland to Secretary of State for Dominion Affairs, 18 October 1940; W.J. Bursey, *The Undaunted Pioneer: An Autobiography* (1977), pp. 189-90; and Frank J. Kennedy, *A Corner Boy Remembers: Growing up in St. John's* (St. John's: Breakwater 2006), p. 156.

44. Memorial University, Maritime History Archives, John Cardoulis Fonds, file 1.07.010, "History of St. John's Area, Nfld, 1940-1945," p. 1; and Cardoulis, *A Friendly Invasion*, p. 43.

45. Rosalind Power, *Fort Amherst: St. John's Nearest Outport* (St. John's: Jesperson Publishing 1995), pp. 109-12; and Kennedy, *A Corner Boy Remembers*, p. 160.

46. Rooms Provincial Archives, GN38, Box S4-2-4, file 8, Philip G. Bruton to Sir Wilfred Woods, 15 April 1941. An account of army life in Camp Alexander is in John Cardoulis, *A Friendly Invasion II: A Personal Touch* (St. John's: Creative Publishers 1993), pp. 4-6.

47. U.S. Corps of Engineers, "Historical Monograph, U.S. Army Bases Newfoundland," pp. iv-1 to iv-2; Cardoulis, *A Friendly Invasion*, p. 52; and "History of St. John's Area, Nfld, 1940-1945," pp. 2 and 5.

48. Melvin Baker, Robert D. Pitt, and Janet Miller Pitt, *The Illustrated History of Newfoundland Light & Power* (St. John's: Creative Publishers 1990), p. 128.

49. "History of St. John's Area, Nfld, 1940-1945," p. 3.

50. Cardoulis, *A Friendly Invasion II*, pp. 35-38.

51. Cardoulis, *A Friendly Invasion*, p. 52; Ray Owen, "Fort Pepperrell" in *Daily News* 31 December 1945, p. 64; and Dziuban, *Military*

Relations, p. 175; and Cardoulis Fonds, file 1.02.042, Appendix L, "Some of the U.S. Military Units in Newfoundland and Labrador, 1941-1991."

52. James E. Candow, "The Tactical Role of American Armed Forces at Signal Hill, Newfoundland During World War II," *Newfoundland Quarterly* (Summer/Fall 1993), pp. 25-28; and Rooms Provincial Archives, GN4/1/D, Box 35, file 476/2, Welty to Emerson, 7 July 1941.

53. Rooms Provincial Archives, GN38, Box S4-1-7, file 6, Minute of Commission 16-42, J&D 4-42, and Memorandum for Commission, 14 January 1942.

54. Cardoulis, *A Friendly Invasion*, p. 53.

55. *Daily News* 31 December 1943.

56. Rooms Provincial Archives, GN38, Box S4-1-7, J-59-41, Memorandum for Commission, 8 November 1941; "Opening and Dedication of U.S.O. Recreational Centre," *Newfoundland Quarterly* (Spring 1942), pp. 31-33; and Cardoulis, *A Friendly Invasion II*, pp. 117-45. The site chosen on Merrymeeting Road was a vegetable garden at the back of the Central Fire Hall that had been used by members of the Newfoundland Constabulary.

57. Rooms Provincial Archives, GN38, Box S4-2-5, file 8, Machtig to Walwyn, 27 January 1944, with accompanying notes.

58. Henderson, *Guarding the Gates*, pp. 23 and 37.

59. *Daily News* 31 December 1942.

Dates Leading to Arrival of Canadian and American Troops

Canada

10	September	1939	Declaration of War.
	June	1940	First Canadian Engineers Arrive.
18	August	"	U.S.- Canada "Board of Defence".
14	November	"	First Infantry Battalion Arrives.

(Elapsed-time, 14 Months to Troop Arrival and in Camp).

America

18	August	1940	U.S.- Canada "Board of Defence".
2	September	"	Bases-for-Destroyers Agreement.
16	"	"	Admiral Grenslade, Site Survey.
7	October	"	District Engineer, Lt. Col. Bruton.
15	"	"	U.S. Engineers Arrive.
16	"	"	Engineers' Office Opened.
22	"	"	Schedules Jan. Troop Arrivals.
	"	"	Pepperrell Storage Bldgs. Started.
25	January	1941	Troopship *Alexander* Arrives.
8	February	"	Pepperrell Base Construction Begins.

(Elasped–time, 5 months to Troop Arrival, 4 months to Camp).

8	December	1941	America Declares War.

4

U-Boat Warfare and Convoy Protection.

By: Melvin Baker.

In 1953, Gilbert Tucker, the official historian of the Royal Canadian Navy, wrote that the anti-German U-boat campaign in the Atlantic Ocean between 1939 and 1945 had a threefold effect. First, it resulted in a heavy loss of life, shipping, and supplies. Second, it consumed huge resources in manpower, materials, and money. Third, it caused a tremendous interruption of normal trade.

From September 3, 1939 until May 8, 1945, the U-boats sank a total of 14,554,000 gross tons of shipping and damaged another 4,000,000 gross tons. The convoy escort system that was adopted to defend against this U-boat threat was extensive and expensive, and over time reduced the number of sinkings.[1] St. John's and Newfoundland played a pivotal role in that desperate battle, which was eventually called the "Battle of the Atlantic".

Over 370 Newfoundlanders in the Royal and Canadian Navies made the supreme sacrifice. Worldwide, 333 Newfoundlanders in the Merchant Marine were lost in World War II.

U-Boat Activity.

In September 1939, at the outbreak of war, the German navy had only 57 U-boats in service. Over the course of the war, Germany built and commissioned another 1,113 submarines. Only 863 of these were actually used in battle. Of those 863, Germany lost an absolutely dreadful 753. Nearly nine of ten U-boat crews had their submarines sunk. Only a few of the sailors in the sunken U-boats managed to survive.

The most common U-boat series encountered by the Canadian Navy in the North Atlantic was the "Waffe Type VII". This was really a submersible warship, instead of a true submarine. The first of 704 U-boat variants of the VII was designed after a WWI submarine. It carried a crew of 44 men and operated mainly as a surface vessel. Because its electric batteries needed constant recharging, it only dived underwater for limited periods of time. Operating on the surface, the diesel-driven submarine travelled at 18 or 20 knots and manoeuvred quickly to fire torpedoes. Below the surface, with its battery-driven electric engines, it was too slow to pursue an enemy target. This model U-boat was only outfitted with the air-breathing snorkel in 1944, to permit longer, near-surface underwater operation.

In the spring of 1940, after the fall of Western Europe to Germany's blitzkrieg conquests, German submarine warfare in the North Atlantic expanded quickly. The availability of ports on France's Atlantic coast enabled the German Navy to extensively extend its operations, with devastating effectiveness. This largely disrupted Britain's efforts to obtain essential armaments from Canada and the United States.[2]

The Terrifying "Wolf-Pack" Strategy.

In September 1940, U-boats began adopting the wolf-pack tactic, as advocated by Admiral Karl Donitz, Commander of the German U-boat service. Wolf packs saw six or more U-boats stalk a convoy at night, and attack it relentlessly, until all their torpedoes were gone. The wolf-pack strategy was made possible because in 1940 German shipyards were producing an increased number of submarines. Wolf-pack strategy often sank over 20 per cent of a convoy's ships. By the end of 1940, about 2 million tons of Allied shipping had been sunk, or about 14 per cent of the total sunk during the entire war.

Another tactic adopted by Donitz was to send single U-boats as close to the Canadian, American, and Newfoundland shores as possible, not only to destroy shipping but to also force Allied naval and air forces to concentrate on this threat, thus reducing their use in other anti-submarine efforts. The great concern over submarine sightings near shore required that every report be investigated. Manpower, ships, and aircraft assigned for this purpose stretched Allied resources to the limit. Fishing vessels on the water, and people on shore, were always on watch for possible submarine landings.

In the early days of the war, the Allies were ill-prepared to defend convoys against U-boat attacks. At first, Canada only provided escort service as far east as the Grand Banks of Newfoundland. British naval protection extended only as far west as Iceland. Apart from the shortage of Allied naval ships, limitation of fuel on board restricted operational distance for escort vessels. To provide the missing protection for the "Black Pit" (900 kilometres in the mid-Atlantic), on May 27, 1941 Britain had Canada agree to establish the "Newfoundland Escort Force". This was to create a forward base at St. John's, to protect convoys originating from, or returning to, Halifax.[3]

U-Boats Operating Close to North American Shores.

Early 1941 saw an increase in U-boat activity, resulting in the loss of 454,000 tons of shipping in June alone. By September of that year, as Patricia Giesler, one historian of the Canadian Merchant Navy, has described it, North American waters were "under siege". After America entered the war, between January and July in 1942, U-boats roamed the eastern American shoreline, sinking nearly 400 ships, while losing only seven U-boats. The Canadian Navy and Air Force were able to restrict U-boat activity off Nova Scotia and Newfoundland, where the available Canadian defence resources had been concentrated. But, U-boats roamed widely, including in the Gulf of St. Lawrence, where by October 1942 U-boats had sunk 19 merchant ships and two naval escorts. This included the sinking of the Newfoundland Gulf ferry *Caribou*, on its regular run between North Sydney, Nova Scotia, and Port aux Basques, Newfoundland, with the loss of 137 out of 237 people on board.[4]

Beginning in late 1942, Admiral Donitz changed tactics again by concentrating U-boat attacks on convoys in the mid-Atlantic. The German navy now had over 300 submarines in its North Atlantic fleet. Damage inflicted climaxed in March 1943 when the U-boats sank 108 Allied ships, totalling 569,000 tons of shipping.[5]

Turning the Tide Against U-Boat Sneak Attacks.

Beginning in April 1943, the Allies were able to reduce the number of sinkings. They began to minimize and ultimately defeat the U-boat threat. After the outbreak of war, Canada had ramped up its shipyard production capacity so that by 1943, production of both commercial and naval ships exceeded the number of ships sunk by the U-boats. The Allied navies also had better trained, more experienced crews; more escort ships with better armament; and faster, more fuel-efficient escort ships that could better defend the convoys.

Of great importance, British Intelligence had cracked the German secret code of the Enigma machines used by U-boat commanders to communicate with each other and with their naval headquarters. Finally, the long-range Liberator aircraft provided greater aerial surveillance in the mid-Atlantic and also surprised and destroyed U-boats cruising on the surface.[6]

U-Boat Activity Right Inside Newfoundland.

Because of its central location in the northwest Atlantic, "Fortress-Newfoundland" had numerous U-boats around its coastline, but there is only one known example of a submarine crew actually being on shore. That was in October 1943, when *U-537* landed near Cape Chidley, at the northern tip of Labrador. The U-boat crew had set up an unmanned, automatic weather station to broadcast meteorological information for use in the German Atlantic submarine campaign. The weather station only functioned for two weeks. An attempt to re-establish the station in 1944 failed, when the U-boat being sent to do the work was sunk.[7] (This only became known in 1981 through research about German weather reconnaissance in the Arctic.)

There were five tragic attacks upon vessels involving Newfoundland. The first was the previously mentioned sinking of the gulf ferry *Caribou*, en route to Port aux Basques.[8] The others were U-boat sinking of four iron ore carriers off the iron ore mines of Bell Island, Conception Bay, in 1942. The combined number of deaths was 69. *U-513* was cruising the Strait of Belle Isle and, with no available targets, sailed south into Conception Bay on September 4. It entered the waters off Bell Island by following in the wake of the 3,000-ton MV *Evelyn B*, which then anchored off Wabana. The following morning, *U-513* fired torpedoes at the ore carrier *Saganaga*. It sank quickly, with 29 men killed and 14 survivors. A second round of torpedoes sank the *Lord Strathcona*, where, fortunately, there was no loss of life. The submarine escaped the area by again brazenly following in the wake of the *Evelyn B* as it put to sea. (Three weeks later, *U-513* sank the 7,174-ton SS *Ocean Vagabond*, only three and a half miles east of St. John's.)

The second attack near Bell Island was on November 2, 1942, when another submarine, the *U-518*, slipped unnoticed into the ore-ship anchorage off Bell Island. It sank two ore carriers, the *Rose Castle* and the Free French ship *PLM 27*, before safely escaping the area. Casualties for the 43-man crew of the *Rose Castle* were 24 missing, four confirmed dead, and 15 survivors. For the *PLM 27*'s crew of 50, there were three missing, nine dead, and 38 survivors. (Those "missing" went down with their ships.) Of the 69 seamen who lost their lives in the two attacks, five were Newfoundlanders.[9]

The Closing Chapter of the U-Boat War.

On May 8, the date of Germany's surrender, Admiral Donitz had issued orders to all submarine commanders to surface and remain surfaced, and transmit their positions to the nearest Allied wireless station. To indicate their surrender status, each U-boat was to fly a black or blue flag during the day, and to show navigation lights at night. All commanders were forbidden to scuttle their submarines or to damage them in any way.[10]

The only submarine ever captured or surrendered in Newfoundland waters was the *U-190*. On May 11,1945, it surrendered to two Canadian navy corvettes, 500 miles east of Cape Race. (Three weeks earlier, *U-190* had sunk the HMCS *Esquimalt* off Halifax, with a loss of 22 men on the Canadian warship.) The Captain of one of the two corvettes, HMCS *Victoriaville*, was Lieutenant Commander Lester Hickey of St. Jacques, Fortune Bay, who accepted the surrender from U-boat commander Oberleutnant Hans Edwin Reith. Most of the *U-190* crew were taken on board the two corvettes to be brought to Halifax. The remaining crew brought the submarine into port at the Canadian naval facility at Bay Bulls, Newfoundland. It was later put on public display in St. John's Harbour and then taken to Nova Scotia. In 1947, *U-190* was scuttled off Halifax, but its periscope and black flag of surrender became trophies on display at the Naval Military Officers' Club (the Crow's Nest) in St. John's, which had been established in 1942.[11]

Melvin Baker.

Biographical Sketch

Melvin Baker is a native of Catalina, Newfoundland, and is the University Archivist-Historian (President's Office) for Memorial University of Newfoundland. He is a graduate of Memorial University and the University of Western Ontario and has written extensively on 20th-century Newfoundland History.

Endnotes

1. Gilbert Norman Tucker, *The Naval Service of Canada: Its Official History, Vol. II* (Ottawa: King's Printer 1952), pp. 338-339.

2. Patricia Giesler, *Valor at Sea – Canada's Merchant Navy* (Ottawa: Veterans Affairs Canada 2005), p. 5; Gordon Williamson, *Wolf Pack: The Story of the U-Boat in World War II* (Oxford, England: Osprey Publishing 2006), pp. 195-97; Donald E. Graves, *In Peril on the Sea: The Royal Canadian Navy and the Battle of the Atlantic* (Toronto: The Canadian Naval Memorial Trust 2003), p. 38; and Roger Sarty, *The Battle of the Atlantic: The Royal Canadian Navy's Greatest Campaign, 1939-1945* (Ottawa: CEF Books 2001), p. 12.

3. Williamson, *Wolf Pack*, pp. 197-200; Giesler, *Valor at Sea*, p. 17; Michael L. Hadley, *U-Boats against Canada: German Submarines in Canadian Waters* (Kingston and Montreal: McGill-Queen's University Press 1986), pp. 18-19; Marc Milner, *North Atlantic Run: The Royal Canadian Navy and the Battle for the Convoys* (Toronto: University of Toronto Press 1985); Bernard Ransom, "Canada's 'Newfyjohn' Tenancy: The Royal Canadian Navy in St. John's, 1941–1945," *Acadiensis*, XXIII, 2 (Spring 1994), pp. 45-71; and Malcolm Macleod, *Connections: Newfoundland's Pre-confederation Links with Canada and the World* (St. John's: Creative Publishers 2003), pp. 99-134.

4. Giesler, *Valor at Sea*, pp. 19-25; and Williamson, *Wolf Pack*, pp. 214-16.

5. Giesler, *Valor at Sea*, pp. 25-26.

6. Williamson, *Wolf Pack*, pp. 205-06; Giesler, *Valor at Sea*, pp. 2-27; Graves, *In Peril on the Sea*, pp. 164-66; and James A. Boutiler, ed., *RCN in Retrospect, 1910–1968* (Vancouver: University of British Columbia Press 1982), pp. 158-234.

7. Gerhard Bassler, *Vikings to U-boats: The German Experience in Newfoundland and Labrador* (Montreal & Kingston: McGill-Queen's University Press 2006), pp. 290-91.

8. Cassie Brown, *The Caribou Disaster and other Short Stories* (St. John's: Flanker Press 1996); Douglas How, *Night of the Caribou* (Hansport: Lancelot Press 1995); Macleod, *Connections*, pp. 135-51; and Brian Tennyson and Roger Sarty, *Guardian of the Gulf: Sydney, Cape Breton and the Atlantic Wars* (Toronto: University of Toronto Press 2000), pp. 332-34.

9. Joseph Prim and Mike McCarthy, *Those in Peril* (St. John's: Jesperson Press 1995), pp. 101-10; and Steve Neary, *The Enemy on our Doorstep* (St. John's: Jesperson Press 1994).

10. Hadley, *U-Boats against Canada*, pp. 295-300.

11. Bassler, *Vikings to U-boats*, p. 291; and Shannon M. Lewis, ed., *A Safe Haven: Sixty Years at the Crow's Nest* (St. John's: Crow's Nest Officers Club 2002).

5

The Newfoundland Railway at War.

Courage, Commitment, Contribution.

By: Robert H. Cuff.

Introduction by Paul J. Johnson.

Eventually the Obvious Becomes Obvious.

When you spend time with expert collaborators examining research to complete the storyline on the history for a museum (Railway Coastal Museum), you eventually have to ask yourself "Why did all of that happen ?"

From my business person's perspective, it became obvious that the troubles that afflicted both the governing of Newfoundland and the operating of our Railway were *exactly* the same. Neither the Government nor the Railway were ever able to generate enough revenue to "break-even", let alone to develop a surplus. And, if their prevailing leadership was incompetent or self-serving, the deficiency became even worse.

From 1923 onward, when Herbert Russell became the Newfoundland Railway's General Manager, although Newfoundland itself had a steady succession of very serious financial difficulties, management of the Railway and Coastal Services was as efficient as could be expected, allowing for the handicaps imposed by political dictates.

Isolation: A Desperate Problem.

The nature of our inshore fishery caused settlement of 1,400 fishing communities, each of which had to be close by its own fishing grounds. For all of our "outports", shipping dried fish "out" and supplies "in" had to be accomplished "somehow". But, transporting people out and back was a less critical concern. If a livyer was not well, or wanted a different occupation, being "stuck" in a small community could mean a very unhappy lifetime.

Politicians, observing the widespread despair about isolation, began to propose coastal-boat and railway services. As soon as the first examples of those were created, the promises and demands for "more" became loud and insistent. Achieving an "escape from captivity" grew into an obsession.

Successive governments made additional rail and coastal-boat investments. Politicians ignored the reality that the solutions they proposed could *never* earn enough revenue to meet operating costs, let alone a return on the investment. Continued expansion was a sure course for fiscal disaster. It would further impair and eventually undermine our already frail economy.

The Eventual Financial Collapse of Government.

As railway and coastal services grew, so did expenses and losses. That burden consumed more and more government revenue, and curtailed the support of health, education, welfare, and public works. Because of our huge expenditures in the Great War, and an equal amount "sunk" into the Railway, plus other borrowing, in 1933 Newfoundland was forced into receivership, being $100 million in debt.

When Responsible Government could not be sustained, our elected politicians were replaced by a trustee-like Commission of Government. This was proposed by the British Parliament and directed by the British Dominions Office.

The new Commission had to be convinced by Mr. Russell to keep the transportation services in operation. To close them down would have ruined much of Newfoundland's already troubled industry, trade, and public services.

Despite the Commission of Government's tight-fisted handling of expenditures, the Newfoundland Railway proved successful in managing its operations and finances. With strong employee participation, the Railway even initiated employee housing and benefit programs that were unmatched by any Newfoundland business interests.

The Railway Coastal Service, Entering the War.

What difficulties did the Railway face as it responded to the unprecedented demands of turning Newfoundland into a wartime "fortress-isle" ? If you worked for the Railway, long hours and endless personal inconvenience became routine. During the war, thousands of Newfoundlanders had enlisted to go overseas, and another 22,000 earned weekly paycheques in the construction of bases, airports, and naval stations. These major changes in employment caused serious loss of experienced employees for the Railway. The burdens on the Railway to provide even pre-war levels of service were substantially increased.

Another serious problem falling indirectly on the Railway was the reluctance of the Commission of Government to establish adequate maintenance for the island's roads, bridges, wharves, and other public property. As the public facilities became worn down, additional reliance was placed on the Newfoundland Railway, the Coastal Service, and their workforces.

The Railway's own equipment and facilities could have collapsed too, but, because of determined effort, they seldom did. To operate, maintain, and repair rail and coastal systems required a very positive attitude, incredible "makeshift" ingenuity, and non-stop, hard work.

There was a sad sequel to the Railway's wartime story. The postwar commitment to rebuilding the seriously rundown Railway and Coastal Services literally consumed all of General Manager Herb Russell's strength and stamina. In February 1949, at the age of 59, following a heart attack, Mr. Russell was advised to take a mid-winter holiday. Enroute to Florida he died of heart failure in New York City, with his devoted wife Jean at his side. Herb Russell was as great a business manager as Newfoundland has ever produced.

Daily News, 28 February 1949, extract from Obituary for Herbert J. Russell, C.B.E.

"The expansion of transportation activities during the war occurred at a phenomenal rate and the Newfoundland Railway system was required to perform services which few, realizing its pre-war capacities, would have thought possible."

The Newfoundland Railway at War.

Courage, Commitment, Contribution.

By: Robert H. Cuff.

"The increase in traffic has overtaken the Railway like a flood !"
Sir W.W. Woods (Commissioner of Public Utilities 1941a).

Railways and Peacetime, and Wartime Strategies.

Building a railway was often considered "the work of a country" to expand, modernize, and support its economy. In the late 19th century when construction of a railway across Newfoundland was being promoted, some lofty imperial ideals were bandied about, but the railway's appeal was really just domestic. On a limited scale, our railway did accomplish the same goals as elsewhere in North America – extending the reach of government, industry, and people into the interior, and pushing the agricultural and timber frontiers to the north and west. However, as one American observed in 1939, "Newfoundland had not an interior that anyone loved" (Watt 1960:32) and the interior had largely remained the railwaymen's, logger's, and sportsman's preserve. Eventually, Corner Brook, Grand Falls, and Buchans showed "inland" industrial potential.

In wartime, railways are an obvious military asset, providing essential lines of communication within strategically important areas. During World War II, the military importance of the Newfoundland Railway was paramount because we really had no other means of over-ground transportation. The Railway alone enabled deployment of troops and supplies. The efficient movement of materials for constructing fortifications was every bit as important as troop movement. The Railway allowed the American and Canadian military to establish and sustain large forces and supplies, some distant from population centres, and from existing material sources.

Know-how – Like the Palm of Your Hand.

> Service in any capacity within the System should bring to those who accept it, a deep sense of responsibility. The activities of the System, with its far flung operations, produce problems every day that call for concentration and coordinated effort. The responsibilities attaching to these tasks is deepened by the important factor, that the well-being of the country and that of the Railway are so closely related as to be inseparable. (H.J. Russell 1940)

The men who ran the Newfoundland Railway in St. John's were fully experienced, and the Americans recognized that

> These men are all practical operating officers; their organization, while limited in personnel, appears to be thoroughly alive to the problems before it. (Freeman and Dorsey 1941:31)

Railway Management had already seen the effects of the first Great War. The General Manager, Herbert J. Russell, had been with the Railway since 1906 and was the Assistant Superintendent of the line during the Great War. His assistant, James V. Ryan (1894–1974), began as Station Agent / Telegrapher in 1910, and from 1916 was a Dispatcher, where he worked alongside William Chafe, who became Chief Dispatcher during World War II.

The experience of these men during the Great War prepared them to anticipate long hours and extreme working conditions. They had also experienced the severe postwar crisis. Years of neglected maintenance and a postwar economic slump had once before laid the Railway low. The original operators, the Reid Newfoundland Company, were forced to close their Railway, to convince the government to take it over. The Railway Settlement Act of 1923 concluded the issue of ownership and brought about ownership by the Government. At the time of that takeover, "large sums of money would have to be spent on ballasting the roadbed, renewing culverts, replacing wooden bridges with steel and concrete, tie renewals, repair and replacement of rolling stock, as well as extensive repairs to steamers" (Anon 1937:406).

In 1929, the operating departments of the Newfoundland Railway had been divided into two Divisions, separated at the Exploits River. The Western Division was headquartered in Bishop's Falls. The Eastern Division, which included Gander and its supply ports of Argentia, Clarenville, and Lewisporte, was at the Head Office in St. John's.

Newfoundland's Vital Location for Air Traffic.

Railwaymen had also had a taste of things to come because of the building, by British interests, of "aerodromes" at Botwood and Gander in the late 1930s. Although both had originally been conceived as facilitating commercial transatlantic air travel, strategic considerations were never far from the surface. These facilities received far more attention as time went by. So, when the Second World War began in 1939, Botwood and Gander were looked upon as having the most important, strategic military value in Newfoundland.

Back in 1935, the United States, British, and Canadian governments had agreed on Botwood as a landing base for transatlantic flying boats, and built hangars and the facilities for refuelling, communications, weather reports, and service. The first, experimental transatlantic flights landed in July 1937.

Meanwhile, Gander was being built by the British as a commercial / civilian, land-based facility – the "Newfoundland Airport". There were 500 workers at the site in the summer of 1937, when it was first visited by William Chafe:

> My first official visit to Gander left me impressed with the activity at 'Hatties Camp' and 'Cobbs Camp,' which had previously been minor railway sidings… .

> The massive steam-shovels and huge box-type dump trucks were impressive indeed. Less impressive were the labourers quarters. (Chafe 1987:83-84)

By early 1938, one runway was operational. The first official landing was made in January, and, later that year some radio and meteorological personnel were relocated there from Botwood.

Ignoring Reality.

In World War II, when Britain, Canada, and America decided amongst themselves to make Newfoundland into a "fortress isle", they failed to understand that their simplistic notions were both presumptuous and ill-founded. Newfoundland had very few roads, which only connected some of our coastal communities. The Newfoundland Railway was the only, realistic, on-land means of transportation, and it consisted of a slow-speed, small-car rail-line. In 1939, the Newfoundland Railway had only enough rolling stock and employees to look after its own, low-volume, lightweight freight, with limited passenger handling.

In time, the lack of engines and rolling stock could be overcome. And, greater frequency of train movements could be achieved. But, nothing could be done about the disadvantages imposed by the narrow railbed and railcars, or the necessary adherence to safe speeds. To achieve the almost impossible objectives for building-and-supply, Newfoundland Railway men and equipment would be stretched and stressed, right to the breaking point.

Mustering Our Volunteers, 1939–40.

After war was declared in September 1939, the first act of war in North America took place at Botwood, Newfoundland. The German freighter *Christoph von Doornum* had been loading mineral concentrates from Buchans. On 5 September, it was seized by the Newfoundland Constabulary and placed under tow by the Railway steamer *Clyde*. The *Doornum*'s crew were transported to St. John's on a sealed train, and were interred in a hastily built prison camp near Quidi Vidi Lake. The seized ship was temporarily under the management of the Railway. It soon was chartered as a newsprint carrier and renamed *Empire Commerce* (Botwood Historical Society 1992:71-73; Bassler 2006:225-26). From the seizure of the *Doornum* in 1939, to the surrender of *U-190* on 11 May 1945, hostilities in Newfoundland were to last five years and eight months.

The First Railway Duty – Moving Our Volunteers.

In considering the Railway's role in the war, we start with the most immediate concern: troop / personnel movement. From the first, the Railway had an obvious role to play in mustering volunteers for service overseas. The Admiralty issued a call for 625 special-services Newfoundland Naval Volunteers on 14 September. That first contingent was dispatched to Britain from St. John's on the SS *Newfoundland* on 27 December 1939. Although the first Naval draft and the first contingent of the Newfoundland Overseas Forestry Corps departed for overseas directly from St. John's, this was not the case for all volunteers. Many travelled across the island by Railway to Port aux Basques and then across the Gulf, by coastal boat, to ultimately go overseas from a Canadian port.

At this early stage in the war, Canada was unable to provide patrol vessels or reconnaissance aircraft for troop movement directly out of St. John's. Canada was scrambling to provide escort ships for convoys out of Halifax, Sydney, and Saint John. The island of Newfoundland was essentially defenceless. For the 6 January and 1 February 1940 departures of Volunteer Foresters from Port aux Basques, the men had been collected all along the Railway line, at coastal-boat terminals, and in paper towns, by special trains (Curran 1987:10-11).

The departure of the First Contingent of the Royal Artillery on 14 April 1940 gave the citizens of St. John's an opportunity for patriotic demonstration, as Volunteers paraded from the Church Lads Brigade Armoury on Harvey Road to a jubilant send-off at the

Railway Station. Two special trains took "the boys" to Port aux Basques, where the *Kyle* and *Caribou* carried them to Sydney for their train connection to Saint John, New Brunswick, and then on the passenger liner *Duchess of Richmond* to England (Nicholson 1969:13-14).

Co-mingling of "Our Boys" and Canadian Arrivals.

An even more circuitous route was that of our Members of the 8th Naval Draft, who came from all over the northeast coast by coastal boat, then by Railway to St. John's for their initial training. They left by train for Montreal on 11 June 1940. On departing Montreal on the troop-carrier *Antonia*, they called at Quebec City and took on the Canadian Black Watch Regiment. On 21 June the *Antonia* landed at Botwood to disembark the contingent of 900 Canadians for service at Gander and Botwood. The Black Watch were the first "foreign" troops to be stationed in Newfoundland. The *Antonia* also took on another 204 Foresters that the Railway had brought to Botwood for the passage overseas to Britain (Nicholson 1969:456; Cook 1991:37-38).

The Naval Volunteers' "round-trip" from and back to Newfoundland was not a military "SNAFU" but rather a result of change in strategy. The war in Europe was not going well. Beginning with the German invasion of Holland and Belgium on 10 May, it was only a matter of four weeks to the vital and heroic evacuation at Dunkirk. As General Manager Russell described the situation in his monthly bulletin, there was "a devil loose in the world." It was a change of plans that the Black Watch, their tanks, trucks, and supplies were not going to Europe but coming to Newfoundland. After the 900 were disembarked at Botwood (the *Clyde* serving as a tender), 500 of them were dispatched by Railway to Gander, and some of the remainder by truck to Philip's Head. Our Newfoundland Naval Contingent and Foresters, apparently being more expendable, went overseas to where the action was.

After Dunkirk, Our Danger Seemed More Ominous.

In the Fall of 1940, the rethinking of the war effort after Dunkirk resulted in a rapid series of changes and developments. An invasion of Britain appeared imminent. (Hitler's initial target date for "Operation Sea-Lion" was 15 September.) That possibility raised fears that Newfoundland could be used as an Axis base to attack Canada and the United States. On 18 August 1940, the "Canada-U.S. Permanent Joint Defence Board" was established. On 2 September, the American and British governments reached agreement-in-principle on "destroyers-for-bases", whereby the U.S. was permitted to erect military installations in the British possessions in the West Atlantic.

On 13 September, a Canadian request that they be given control of Botwood and Gander for the duration was agreed to by the British. Two days later, Rear-Admiral Greenslade and Brigadier General Devers of the Permanent Joint Defence Board arrived in St. John's for "preliminary discussions" on the establishment of American bases. They made a reconnaissance trip to Placentia Bay, returning on 21 September, at which time the Commission of Government was informed that the base locations recommended were St. John's and Argentia. Stephenville was not selected until the following month. Meanwhile, on 20 September, the Commission of Government had passed their "*Emergency Powers (Defence) Act*" which "in short… provided for government by fiat" by the Commission, in consultation with the British Dominions Office (Neary 1988:128; O'Brien 1994:629).

Gander – The Super, Inland "Newfoundland Airport".

Gander's importance was increased by the arrival of the Royal Canadian Air Force in November of 1940, inaugurating what came to be known as the Atlantic Ferry Command. It made arrangements to send hundreds of warplanes from Gander and Goose Bay to airfields in England and Scotland.

> The first air crew arrived, guided by a Colonel... [who] had been stationed in Botwood and knew the coast, we began picking up little villages and later on Botwood itself, and, of course, the railroad... we started up the track to the airport, cautioning the Skipper not to go following the railroad through any tunnels. (Watt 1960:36)

Initially the biggest problem at Gander was accommodation. Partially, "The Newfoundland Railway came to the rescue with three sleeping coaches and a dining car, which it continued to service" (Neary 1988:133). "Such odd quarters, in howling blizzards, in the middle of the wilderness..." (Watt 1960:33).

In the war service, the Railway's main challenge continued to be conveying the supply of construction workers and servicemen at Gander. The Railway's Eastern Division Headquarters at St. John's had several years of transporting civilian and military people. Troop rotations were a regular feature, but, in Gander, there was also the requirement of "making up" trains to haul daily amounts of stone for the ever-expanding system of runways. This stone was quarried and crushed a few miles east of Gander at Hall's Quarry. During the navigation season there were also Railway coal trains, carrying fuel for the generators, arriving daily from Clarenville. There were also provisions and construction materials, most often shipped through Lewisporte, although Curling and St. John's also saw a good deal of that traffic. The single largest task was the shipping of aviation fuel to Gander, most often through Lewisporte, at the rate of 100-200,000 gallons per day. The bottleneck at Lewisporte, caused by its closure for four months of the year by ice, led the Americans to land most of their fuel at Argentia, where it was further transported by the Railway (Chafe 1987:83; Cook 1991:43; Floyd 1941:42).

Understandably, before the war, the Newfoundland Railway did not have a single tank car.

> All gasoline was at first shipped in barrels. In peacetime, cars carried 60 barrels in one tier; wartime emergencies made it necessary to carry two tiers of barrels, or 120 to a car… Freight cars were jacked up to 20% over their rated capacity and often loaded well above the safety margin specified. But the luck held… (Anon 1945?,10)

The Canadians rushed 14 fuel tank cars to Newfoundland early in 1941, and eventually the Canadians and Americans each supplied 50 tank cars. Despite the potential for disaster, there was only one serious accident during the war involving fuel shipment. A tanker train derailed at Salmon River Bridge near Glenwood, closing the line for several days (Cook 1991:29).

The War Strikes Home.

On 21 November 1940, the first of many later scenes of sorrow was played out at the Railway Station in St. John's with the arrival by train from Halifax of three Newfoundland merchant marine survivors of the sinking of the auxiliary cruiser *Jervis Bay* on 5 November: "Suddenly the war was real" (Neary 1988, 162-63).

The *Jervis Bay* was sunk in mid-Atlantic on 5 November by the German naval ship *Admiral Scheer*, with only 65 surviving of a crew of 255. Four of the seven Newfoundland crewmen were killed. The three survivors were George Squires, Lou Tilley, and Art Taylor, all from St. John's (Wells 1981:74-75).

The Americans Assess the Newfoundland Railway, 1941.

The American "friendly invasion" began on 18 January 1941, when the first engineers and construction workers arrived at Argentia. On 29 January, the *Edmund B. Alexander* arrived at St. John's with 900 infantry to eventually man a military base that was to become "Fort Pepperrell". The logistical problems of conveying personnel between the two bases were enormous. "In the first movements to

Argentia, men were packed like sardines on platforms, in lavatories, even on top of furnaces" (Anon 1945?:9-10).

The Railway's Business Dealings with the Americans.

Late in 1940, because of anticipated Canadian and American military requirements, the U.S. Corps of Engineers began a study to assess what steps should be taken to upgrade the Railway capacity. Initially, consultants for the Engineers recommended a $ 5 million upgrade, noting that "the railway is prepared to supply the necessary labour at their expense to place this program of rehabilitation into effect as outlined in this report" (Freeman and Dorsey 1941:12).

Railway Management had understood that equipment for the recommended upgrade would come as a result of an "outright grant of funds" to begin the huge collaboration. However, a committee of the Commission of Government was informed that what the Americans intended to propose was that the Reconstruction Finance Corporation would make the Railway a *loan* of the required amount, at a "favourable interest rate", to be repaid over 15 years. There was to be no outright grant for locomotives and rolling stock unless the equipment was "earmarked for the sole use of the United States." It was also anticipated that "the United States traffic will be paid for at the same rate as ordinary traffic" and that, supposedly, would be sufficient to pay the cost of the improvements over time.

In the spring of 1941, when the Freeman and Dorsey report was made available to General Manager Russell, he raised an objection to the amount of the suggested loan and the proposed conditions of repayment. Herb Russell, born into a small Newfoundland community and working all his life with the Railway, was an impressive, persuasive, and resolute man. Russell did not agree that the Americans would "have something in the lease and loan agreement upon which they could rely, to secure efficient service" (Commissioner of Public Utilities 1941a).

Russell's Very Logical Position on the Railway Loan.

> It is difficult to distinguish between what is required for military purposes only and what is required for ordinary traffic… but I am convinced that the present emergency calls for this outlay at a minimum… I am strongly of the opinion that some concern should come… towards relieving the Railway of bearing the full burden of the costs of new equipment, etc. The fact that the Railway with its limited facilities has been able to transport all supplies, materials, etc, without delay has meant extra expense to the Railway and in many cases the delaying of maintenance to equipment and roadbed… in order to keep orders moving. The added wear and tear will not be taken care of in increased earnings and later on, when [base] construction work, etc, is completed, the Railway will need to spend large sums not alone on roadbed and equipment, but on terminal and wharf facilities that have been called upon to do a very much greater volume of business than ever planned… costs of all supplies continue to advance and labour costs are very uncertain. (H.J. Russell to Sir W.W. Woods, 8 August 1941 re. his meeting with American representatives Snodgrass and Wright, referenced as Commissioner of Public Utilities 1941a)

The Railway had already, on its own initiative, ordered new locomotives and freight cars (which costs were to be paid from the loan). Sir W.W. Woods, Commissioner of Public Utilities, agreed that some upgrades in equipment would be "absolutely unavoidable in a very few years." The Americans were quickly made to understand that the Newfoundland Railway and Government, having no funds to pay for reconditioning the main line, re-railing the Argentia and Lewisporte Branches, and acquiring new equipment, would have to be funded by the Americans if the work was to be undertaken. Also, no agreements would be acceptable that dictated to Railway Management.

In August, after the matter had been raised at the U.S.-Canada Permanent Joint Defence Board, Americans Frank Wright and Russell Snodgrass travelled to Newfoundland as the representatives of the Quartermaster General's Office for further discussions. On 8 August, General Manager Russell communicated his concern to Commissioner Woods that the Americans' forecast of increased Railway earnings were quite unrealistic, and that, based on his experience, "large sums" would be further required to cope with the very extensive wartime volume of business. Russell's analysis was that a maximum of $150,000 a year in debt expense could be accepted.

Petty Politics Amongst Four Government "Partners".

The 1941 Railway Loan from the United States is still shrouded in mystery. In August 1941, Wright, Snodgrass, Russell, and Woods negotiated an arrangement whereby the United States government agreed, at its own expense, to pay for Railway upgrades and to make the Railway a loan of something over $ 2 million mostly earmarked for new locomotives and rolling stock. The U.S. Army already had four new locomotives on order, and one was supplied from Britain. Most of the remaining freight and passenger cars were made in Canada. Although this equipment upgrade has often been identified as a "Lend-Lease" arrangement, the Dominions Office in London denied that was the case and stated the loan was "a normal loan payable in United States dollars on regular terms" (29 August 1941, Commissioner of Public Utilities 1941a).

The Railway Loan was one of a few war measures on which the Commission expressed opinion or opposition. In its budget speech, the Commission had announced it was borrowing a million dollars to upgrade rail service. The Commissioner of Public Health and Welfare, John Puddester, wrote to Emerson (another of the three Newfoundland Commissioners) decrying the "humiliation" of the "hire-purchase" arrangement and noting that the first locomotive to arrive had "letters of 8-inch dimensions showing that the equipment is property of the United States." Russell had the names repainted as soon as they arrived.

An additional, complicating, and controversial factor was that the Commission's budget had directed that Newfoundland's anticipated surplus for 1941–42 would involve an interest-free loan to the British Government (which amounted to over half the $ 7 million surplus). In the public mind, the Railway Loan was linked with the loan to Britain. The Commission responded that "the country's acceptance" of the interest-free loan as announced was "final and binding on the Government" (Commission). Writing as "The Wayfarer" in the *Daily News*, A.B. Perlin correctly criticized the Commission of Government, saying, "This government does not think with the minds of the people of Newfoundland."

Resolving Some of the Difficult Problems.

At the end of the day, $2,183,000 U.S. was borrowed from the Reconstruction Finance Corporation at 2.5 per cent interest. The bulk of this was spent on five locomotives and 127 other pieces of rolling stock. The Americans assumed that five, 40-passenger, self-propelled day coaches were "reserved for use by the military command, U.S. Army." They absorbed the cost of re-railing the Argentia and Lewisporte Branches, and, in the winter of 1941–42, built an 8 mile road from the nearest rail station to the U.S. air base at Stephenville. The U.S. Signal Corps installed a new, dedicated telegraph cable between the American bases at St. John's, Argentia, and Stephenville. These paralleled the old Railway telegraph – "a single iron wire ground return circuit" (Freeman and Dorsey 1941:12). This telephone / telegraph service, known as the "Newfoundland Long Line System" was begun late in 1941 and completed in early 1942. The new system allowed the Railway two lines for train dispatching (a great practical improvement, given the volume and necessary control of traffic). The Americans did this in return for the Newfoundland Railway's moving of thousands of telephone poles and heavy coils of wire to the nearest sidings. There were seven manned, and 57 unmanned, repeater stations across the island, attended to and supplied by U.S. Signal Corps "speeders" (Cardoulis 1990:102-107).

The Huge Burdens of Operations.

By September 1941, passenger traffic had increased by 120 per cent above the previous year. It was estimated that 20 per cent of all traffic was "military personnel on leave or changing station" and that "this kind of traffic [would] increase importantly" in the coming year (Floyd 1941:19-20). By late 1942, it was suggested that military personnel travelling by train made up the majority of passenger traffic (Cardoulis 1990:107). The Railway delivered both men and materials to the bases under construction, and continued to be the major means of supplying the bases with fuel and provisions. It appears the railwaymen kept up with materials and the increase in traffic, largely by increasing their hours of work.

> Snowbanks and frost, broken axles on badly needed rolling stock, overworked locomotives that really required big overhaul but could not be spared from their insistent work of moving traffic, more passenger space than could be found, difficulties of obtaining materials for repairs, train crews dropping with fatigue and trains held while they snatched a brief period of rest, agents and stationmen doing twenty hours duty in twenty-four… even the rowdy antics of "elated" servicemen which resulted in smashed windows and doors failed to produce more than a shrug of shoulders and an immediate start to clear up the mess. (Anon 1945?:3)

The only respect in which things were allowed to lag behind was the movement of pulpwood, which was constantly piling up, as its shipment by rail was put off to allow for more urgent train movements (Floyd 1941:21). Other movements of forest products (which had always been the largest single component of Railway freight) included the supply of pit props to Britain and, after 1942, supplying the Clarenville Shipyard's program of building a fleet of wooden minesweepers. (These boats were later used in general freighting and known as the "splinter fleet".)

During the war, the "turnaround in the forestry sector of Newfoundland's economy was nothing short of spectacular" (Neary 1988:165). In September 1941, it was noted that, using "every serviceable-locomotive-hour available", there was still a backlog of 7,000 cars of pulpwood over the past six months (Floyd 1941:12).

"The urgency of moving civilian freight was also increased, as Britain was constantly short of goods. Pulpwood movement from the various sidings between Grand Falls and Terra Nova was a real problem in the summer months" (Chafe 1987:83). Meanwhile, military construction of projects in St. John's required eight carloads of sand a day, brought east, as time allowed, from a Shoal Harbour pit near Clarenville. In practical terms, this meant that there never was a "down time" for maintenance of the roadbed, for overhauling rolling stock, or for the great mental strain of running a railroad far above its capacity, day after day. There were always many carloads of pulpwood, sand, and coal awaiting their opportunity for movement.

As Chafe later wrote: "Besides the troop movements and moving materials for base construction, we found that Newfoundlanders were using the Railway more than ever as they traveled all over the island working on construction projects and found themselves with a bit of extra cash to visit their families in their time off" (Chafe 1987:83). The Railway's civilian customers were also clamouring for freight capacity. There was intense competition for space between the trades and the military. "The Railway freight department depot at St. John's had to accept, on many occasions without prior notice, large consignments of construction materials, destined for ports around the island" (Cook 1991:43).

The Commission Inflicts Instead of Relieving Pressure.

The Commission of Government's decision was to establish a "Transportation Control Board" under the chairmanship of General Manager Russell "to coordinate the movement of civilian commercial freight, by land and sea". Thereby "the whole burden of the movement and chartering of ships fell on the Railway, including sole responsibility for the transportation and distribution of all fishery salt" (Anon 1945?:14). The 1941–42 fiscal year saw the peak of wartime traffic and, in that year, the Newfoundland Railway recorded its highest operating surplus at $1,450,000. In 1938–39 the last "normal year" (before the war), there had been a deficit of $ 300,000.

During 1942, the American presence in Newfoundland had increased tenfold, from about 2,000 personnel 6 December 1941 to as many as 20,000 by the end of 1942. It became the view of the Canadians and Americans that, with the course of the war elsewhere, the threat of an invasion of Newfoundland had become remote. However, there remained a concern that sabotage of the vital Railway components could seriously affect the state of preparedness.

On the Domestic Side.

One of the earliest defence regulations (# 39) adopted by the Commission in September 1939 was to make it an offence for anyone to be "upon any railway, pier, wharf, bridge, viaduct or culvert, with intent to do injury thereof." The Quartermaster General's review had identified a number of railway bridges as being "vulnerable to sabotage" (Floyd 1941:8-9). No information is available on the number of sentries posted to protect Railway property.

"Rumours flew that an unusual number of train derailments was the result of sabotage, but there is no indication as yet to have emerged from the historical record that there was any fifth column activity in Newfoundland during the war" (Bassler 2006:233, 288). In considering the number of derailments, there is every indication that wear and tear, coupled with the increased level of traffic, was the root cause.

> Because derailment meant danger to life and property under wartime conditions of extreme overload, the Railway introduced a system by which each train carried a brakeman on the rear platform while in

> motion. By this method markings causing derailments of a wheel or truck are quickly noted and the train can be stopped by the brakeman pulling the emergency cord. (Anon 1945?:11)

While rumours of fifth column activities became rife during 1942, and are mentioned in accounts and memoirs (Kennedy 2000:7-10; Young 2003), this does not seem to have been a serious threat. There are only three known instances of Germans being landed in Canada – two agents put ashore from U-boats in 1942 (one on the Gaspé and one at Saint John, New Brunswick), and the installation in 1943 of an automatic weather transmitting station in northern Labrador. There is no question that the threat of sabotage was taken seriously, particularly at Gander:

> I have one indelible memory of those years, which perhaps qualifies as the most unusual experience of all my years railroading. I was trainman on a non-scheduled westbound freight that stopped in Gander to pick up empty cars for Bishop's Falls. When we arrived at the airport siding, I was sent by the conductor to check spur lines for empty cars. Unknown to me, some of the spur lines ran quite close to an ammunition dump and oil storage which was quite closely guarded by the Canadian military. Just as I approached the ammunition dump a squadron of 30 Hudson bombers was landing, so I did not hear the guards' order to halt – or the first few shots that they fired at me. I was eventually held and interrogated for five hours. This not only held up our train but also several other trainloads of vital supplies that were waiting for meets with our freight on sidings to the west. (Cook 1989:110)

Fifth column activity appears to have been largely myth and rumour.

Meantime, At the Newfoundland Dockyard – Yeoman Service.

The Newfoundland Dockyard was an important part of the Newfoundland Railway. It was a vital component of the war effort, not just repairing ships damaged by torpedoes, but with a much-increased volume of work from shipping, as well as from collisions between unlit ships in Atlantic convoys. Two tasks taken on by the Dockyard early in the war merit special notice:

> At the start of the war, it was decreed that the harbour entrance required a torpedo net, which the Dockyard improvised in the fall of 1939, out of anything which they could beg, borrow or steal from trawlers in port. The 50 aged four stack American destroyers supplied to Britain late in 1940, required refit and servicing before undertaking the transatlantic crossing. (Anon 1945?:20-21)

The Drydock never closed during most of the War. Even though a shortage of skilled artisans prevented three-shift days, the available workers had their normal workweek stretched to 60 hours. And, by 1941, 80-90-hour workweeks were being taken in stride. The number of Dockyard workers increased from a peacetime 200 to 650.

Our *Caribou* Gulf Ferry Tragedy.

There was one enemy action in 1942 that really brought the war home to all Newfoundlanders: the sinking of the Gulf ferry *Caribou* in October 1942.

> On 14 October, the *Caribou*, carrying 238 passengers and crew, sailing from North Sydney to Port aux Basques, was attacked and sunk by a *U-boat*, *U-69*. Of the total number on board, 137 died, and 101 survived. Of the 191 passengers, 118 were service personnel. Although the *Caribou* was listed in Janes' Naval Register as a troop transport, she was primarily

> a passenger ferry. Service personnel on board were mostly either Newfoundlanders in the Canadian forces returning home on leave, or Canadians and Americans returning from leave. (Wells 1981:69-72)

The *U-69* had *no* knowledge what type of vessel the *Caribou* was.

The sinking of the *Caribou* has been described as the war's "Worst Canadian loss in home waters," and "the only attack on the civilian population of North America". It was described as a "hideous attack" and a "useless crime" by both the Canadian and Newfoundland media (Macleod 1996:1-11). The *Caribou* was the pride of the Newfoundland Railway Coastal fleet. Her loss was closely felt by the entire Railway family, as well as the entire population:

> I reported to work the next morning only to learn that the gulf boat had been torpedoed that night. We shortly got word that about 100 passengers had been rescued. Information about who was missing and who had been saved was a long time coming, and at the office we were deluged by visits and telephone calls.... I spent all that evening contacting relatives of those involved in the tragedy, but I had very few bits of good news to convey. I remember well one of our car repairers, 'Florry' McCarthy, who had two sons in the military who were due home on leave on the *Caribou*. The two boys were not picked up among the survivors, but Florry hung around the office for a couple of days, hoping for some word. I eventually took the step of practically ordering him back to work, knowing that this was the only way he might grow to accept the fact that his boys had given up their lives for their country. (Chafe 1987:87-88)

On 16 October, a special train carrying empty caskets was dispatched to Port aux Basques, returning on 18 October "with bodies to be dropped off at stations across the bony geography of a stricken Newfoundland" (How 1988:119).

> This train also carried one of the survivors, J. Charles Moore, a ticket agent at the St. John's Railway Station, who provided the first survivor account of the tragedy. (*Evening Telegram*, 19 October 1942)

Where Did the Term "Newfie Bullet" Come From ?

Nobody really knows who coined the term "Newfie Bullet". It is generally believed that it came from the Americans. One of the Railway's trans-island trains had been called the Newfoundland "Express" because it reduced time by not making as many stops. For a soldier or sailor going home on leave, the slow chug, chug, chug, clickety-clack, clickety-clack, and many wartime loading-and-unloading stops, must have prompted calling the train "The Bullet". Used either in good humour or as a sarcastic reference, "Newfie Bullet" was a name that "stuck". Like the other words "Newf" or "Newfie", people have to make their own choice whether to be amused or annoyed. The "Newfie" train could have made a greater speed, but at an unacceptable risk of "jumping the tracks".

Speed Is a Relative Matter.

During the 1941 "Newfoundland Railway Assessment", it was determined that, due to its curving railbeds and some deficiencies in the way they were ballasted, the speed that could realistically be expected was, on average, 35 miles per hour (55-60 kilometres per hour) (Floyd 1941:7-8). While this might not seem a very energetic pace, it actually was not too bad for rail transportation in the 1940s. A wide-track, Canadian railroad might be capable of average speeds of 40-45 miles per hour, but the usual average speed of the "Newfie Bullet" was all that safety would permit. The Newfoundland Railway's safety record was incredibly good.

In Newfoundland in the 1940s, a major logistical bottleneck was busy, busy Gander. As the headquarters of the North Atlantic Ferry Command, Gander was a vital strategic component and, as such, had to be manned and supplied as a priority.

> Supplying Gander was the most strenuous task for the Railway during the war years. The base there was entirely dependent upon the Railway for all its fuel, construction materials and supplies for what eventually amounted to 10,000 people. We had only 15 flatcars to handle the freight, so there was a constant shuttle between Gander and Lewisporte. (Chafe 1987:83)

Troop movements, and the decision to have regular, six-month rotations of troops between St. John's and Gander, led servicemen to complain long and loudly. In the war years, Gander was a generally unpopular posting. St. John's had restaurants, clubs, and theatres – in short, places to go, and "girls". Even Botwood and Stephenville offered the diversion of a nearby town. Men could wangle a ride by a truck or motor car to Grand Falls or Corner Brook. Gander, on the other hand, was "all mud and bulldozers" (Kavanagh 1995:71, 86).

Over 20,000 Newfoundlanders were employed at the many American and Canadian bases or moving to and from construction or service jobs throughout the island and Labrador. Over 20,000 Canadian and American servicemen were stationed here. This was an economic boom such as the Newfoundland Railway had never seen. The boom increased Newfoundlanders' own use of the Railway, which was greater than at any other time in its history. The demands of constant use and the "ever-present emergencies" were so high that only the most essential maintenance was carried out. Railway lines, as well as the rolling stock, suffered continuously from maintenance deferral. "The motive power was over-extended and in bad repair, [and] this sometimes applied to the manpower as well" (Chafe 1987:58).

Seeing the Light in 1943.

With hindsight, we can see that the war effort started to recede during 1943. The threat to Newfoundland and North America was considered to have almost vanished. In July, the invasion of Sicily began the slow process of retaking Europe. By the end of 1943, the overall Battle of the Atlantic was going very much in our favour. Newfoundland's epicentre position and strategic importance remained high. The St. John's Naval Station and the Newfoundland Dockyard were a safe haven for harbouring, repairing, and supplying the ships that kept supply lines open between North America and Europe. There was also heightened activity in supplying the Air Ferry Service from Gander and Goose Bay Airports, to send crucial aircraft to support the new, long-anticipated ground battles in Europe.

By every measure, the Newfoundland Railway's activity had doubled during World War II. The number of Railway employees had increased from 1,784 in 1940 to 3,635 by 1945. The number of passengers had increased from 162,000 to 346,300. Nine new locomotives, 30 passenger coaches and sleepers, 100 boxcars, 100 tank cars, and 50 flatcars had been added to the service. The Railway had proven equal to the demands of supplying and servicing many large bases and fortifications.

> For most Railwaymen this had been the busiest time of their lives. Railway workers and equipment were pushed to the limits of their endurance and beyond. Like many Railwaymen, I would just as soon forget the hardships and the tragedies of the war years. (Cook 1989:102)

World War II was indeed a *total* war effort. While wide-ranging, and with full and dedicated general support, it cannot be denied that the Newfoundland Railway's management and workforce deserve a very large "heroes' share" of recognition and admiration. William Chafe's experience may be typical:

> I would walk to work every morning through a dim, blacked-out city, work long hours dispatching trainloads of material to military installations and come home late at night through the pitch black streets, while being constantly reminded of the importance of my every work and leisure activity to the war effort. (Chafe 1987:82)

One of the Greatest Casualties of World War II.

The never-ending strain of the war years, and afterward his struggles to rebuild the worn-out Newfoundland Railway while dealing with the tight-fisted Commission of Government, certainly shortened the life of the Railway's greatly admired General Manager, Herbert J. Russell, C.B.E. Following ten exhausting, war-related years (from 1939 to 1949), he suddenly passed away. Hundreds wept openly as his funeral procession passed along the streets of St. John's.

Robert H. Cuff.

Biographical Sketch

Robert Cuff is a historian with Gerald Penney Associates Ltd. of St. John's, archaeological and heritage consultants. He is a former managing editor of the *Encyclopedia of Newfoundland and Labrador*. Bob has written extensively on the history of the Newfoundland Railway for the *Newfoundland Quarterly*, Newfoundland and Labrador Heritage website, *Dictionary of Canadian Biography*, and the Railway Coastal Museum.

References

Anon, "The Newfoundland Railway." *The Book of Newfoundland: Volume Two.* St. John's, Newfoundland Book Publishers, 1937.

Anon, *The Story of Newfoundland Railway in Wartime*, 1945?.

Bassler, Gerhard P., *Vikings to U-Boats: The German Experience in Newfoundland and Labrador.* Montreal and Kingston, McGill-Queen's University Press, 2006.

Botwood Heritage Society, *Botwood: History of a Seaport.* Grand Falls, Robinson-Blackmore, 1992.

Cadigan, Sean, "Unions." *Encyclopedia of Newfoundland and Labrador: Volume V.* St. John's, J.R. Smallwood Heritage Foundation / Harry Cuff Publications, 1994.

Cardoulis, John N., *A Friendly Invasion.* St. John's, Breakwater Books, 1990.

———. *A Friendly Invasion II.* St. John's, Breakwater Books, 1992.

Chafe, W.J., *I've Been Working on the Railroad: Memoirs of a Railwayman (1911–1962).* St. John's, Harry Cuff Publications, 1987.

Colbourne, B. Wade, "Leased Bases Agreement." *Encyclopedia of Newfoundland and Labrador: Volume III.* St. John's, J.R. Smallwood Heritage Foundation / Harry Cuff Publications, 1991.

Cole, D.H. (Capt.), *Imperial Military Geography.* London, Sifton Praed & Co., 1929.

Collins, Paul, "'First line of Defence': The establishment and development of St. John's, Newfoundland as the Royal Canadian Navy's premier escort base in the second world war." *Northern Mariner*, July 2006, Vol. 16(3), 2006.

Commissioner of Public Utilities, "Newfoundland Railway." Provincial Archives of Newfoundland and Labrador, GN 38/S5-9-1/1, 1941a.

———. "Newfoundland Railway, Steamers." Provincial Archives of Newfoundland and Labrador, GN 38/S5-9-1/2, 1941b.

———. "Railway Matters 1943." Provincial Archives of Newfoundland and Labrador, GN 38/S5-9-1/3, 1943a.

———. "Railway and Dockyard." Provincial Archives of Newfoundland and Labrador, GN 38/S5-9-1/5, 1943b.

———. "Railway 1946." Provincial Archives of Newfoundland and Labrador, GN 38/S5-9-1/4, 1946.

Cook, Clayton D., *The End of the Line.* St. John's, Harry Cuff Publications, 1989.

———. *Tales of the Rails.* St. John's, Creative Publishers, 1991.

———. *Tales of the Rails: Volume III.* St. John's, Jeff Blackwood, 1996.

———. *Tales of the Rails: Volume IV*. St. John's, Flanker Press, 2005.

Cuff, Robert H., *Locomotives Since 1880.* St. John's, Railway Coastal Museum, 2003.

Curran, Tom, *They Also Served.* St. John's, Jesperson Press, 1987.

Ferre, Sandine, "Once Upon a Train, a study of the Railway in Newfoundland." L'Universite Catholique de l'Ouest, M. de L. Thesis, 1993.

Floyd, Jesse E., "Report on the Newfoundland Railway and Transportation to, and within, Newfoundland." Centre for Newfoundland Studies, MUN, 1941.

Freeman, L.D. and L.W. Dorsey, "Report on the Rehabilitation of the Newfoundland Railway" [for the U.S. Army Corps of Engineers]. Centre for Newfoundland Studies, MUN, 1941.

High, Steven, "From outport to outport base: The American occupation of Stephenville, 1940–1945." *Newfoundland Studies*,

Spring 2002, Vol. 18(1), pp. 84-113, 2002.

Houlihan, Eilen, *Uprooted!: The Argentia Story.* St. John's, Creative Publishers, 1992.

How, Douglas, *Night of the Caribou.* Hantsport, Lancelot Press, 1988.

Janes, Percy, "The naval career of Peter Jensen." *Newfoundland Quarterly*, Winter, 2001.

Johnson, Paul J. and Harry A. Cuff, *Herbert J. Russell, C.B.E., The Man, His Work, His Words.* St. John's, Johnson Family Foundation, 2004.

Kavanagh, Robert L., "W force: the Canadian Army and the defence of Newfoundland in the Second World War." M.A. Thesis, MUN, 1995.

Kennedy, Frank J., *Flashes From the Past: Forty-Two Years Covering the News.* St. John's, Breakwater Books, 2000.

Kenney, Paul F., "War Measures." *Encyclopedia of Newfoundland and Labrador: Volume V.* St. John's, J.R. Smallwood Heritage Foundation / Harry Cuff Publications, 1994.

Lake, Harold, *Perhaps They Left Us Up There.* St. John's, Harry Cuff Publications, 1995.

Lingard, Mont, *The Newfy Bullet.* Grand Falls-Windsor, M. Lingard Publishing, 2000.

Lodge, Thomas, *Dictatorship in Newfoundland.* London, Cassell, 1939.

Mackay, Robert Alexander (ed.), *Newfoundland: Economic, diplomatic, and strategic studies.* Toronto, Oxford University Press, 1946.

MacKenzie, David, *Inside the Atlantic triangle: Canada and the entrance of Newfoundland into Confederation, 1939–1949.* Toronto, University of Toronto Press, 1986.

MacLeod, Malcolm, *Peace of the Continent.* St. John's, Harry Cuff Publications, 1986.

———. "Death by choice or by chance? U-69 and the first Newfoundland ferry *Caribou.*" *Newfoundland Studies*, Spring-Fall 1996.

Morton, H.V., *Atlantic Meeting.* London, Metheun, 1946.

Murphy, Tony and Paul Kenney, *The War at Our Doorstep.* St. John's, Harry Cuff Publications, 1989.

Neary, Peter, *Newfoundland in the North Atlantic World.* Toronto, University of Toronto Press, 1988.

Nicholson, G.W.L., *More Fighting Newfoundlanders.* St. John's, Government of Newfoundland and Labrador, 1969.

O'Brien, Patricia, "World War II." *Encyclopedia of Newfoundland and Labrador: Volume V.* St. John's, J.R. Smallwood Heritage Foundation / Harry Cuff Publications, 1994.

O'Neill, Paul, *The Oldest City: the Story of St. John's, Newfoundland.* Portugal Cove-St. Philip's, Boulder Publications, 2003.

Osmond, Sherman with Jennifer Hart, Steven Rowe, and Shannon Freake, *Lewisporte: The War Years.* Lewisporte Green Team, 1999.

Penney, A.R. with Fabian Kennedy, *A History of the Newfoundland Railway (1881–1988) –100th Anniversary Edition.* St. John's, Harry Cuff Publications, 2003.

Porter, Helen, *Below the Bridge.* St. John's, Breakwater Books, 1979.
Powell, Griffith, *Per Ardua Ad Astra: A Story of the Atlantic Air Ferry.* Montreal, Herald Press, 1946.

Ransom, Bernard, "Canada's 'Newfyjohn' Tenancy: The Royal Canadian Navy in St. John's, 1941–1945." *Acadiensis*, Spring 1994, Vol. 23(2), 1994.

Snow, Jaqueline Chantal (ed.), *Gander, From Past to Present.* Gander, Gander and Area Laubach Literacy Council, 2000.

Watt, Sholto, *I'll Take the High Road.* Fredericton, Brunswick Press, 1960.

Wells, Herb, *Under the White Ensign.* St. John's, Robinson-Blackmore, 1981.

Young, Ron, "The spy among us." *Downhomer*, October 2003, Vol. 16(5), 2003.

6

The "Finest Kind" of Newfoundlanders.

Introduction by Paul J. Johnson.

Newfoundlanders tend to believe that "as a bunch" we are "a fairly decent lot". We might think some of us are "a cut above". Only a small number would we consider as being the "finest kind".

In this chapter we have singled out five Newfoundlanders who would likely have been on everyone's list of the "finest kind" during World War II. We have described who they were, and what was their special contribution to the tremendous war effort in our beloved homeland.

Each of these individuals would be working diligently, with a clear sense of purpose. The importance of their work was a major part of their strong motivation and yet they were always quite humble and approachable. It must also have been part of their inner feeling of satisfaction to realize that their efforts were widely recognized and greatly appreciated.

Herb Russell.
(1890–1949).

By: Paul J. Johnson.

Herbert John Russell.

Before World War II.

Born in 1890 at Musgrave Harbour, son of Eli and Martha (Day) Russell. The family moved to St. John's in 1904 where Herb enrolled in the Central Training School. On graduation, he obtained a position with the Newfoundland Express Company as a messenger and stenographer. Nine months later (at 16) he was recruited by the Reid Newfoundland Company's Railway Superintendent Ferdinand Rioux, as Chief Clerk. He rose quickly to acting Chief Dispatcher and, by 1913, to Assistant to the Superintendent. In 1917 he had become Superintendent of the Eastern Division.

When the Newfoundland Government assumed control of the Railway in 1923, Herb was appointed General Manager. He began a program of rehabilitating the Railway (neglected during the Great War, and allowed to further deteriorate in the early 1920s). This work involved re-railing the main line, purchasing new rolling stock, rebuilding the dry dock, and constructing the new Gulf ferry *Caribou*, all the while reducing operating losses and improving service. Upgrades to the Railway continued until 1930, with a new locomotive shed and machine shops in St. John's. Under Herb, the Railway also proved equal to the substantial requirements of the two newly opened paper mills and the Buchans Mine.

When the Depression came along in 1929 it reduced rail and coastal traffic. With the Commission of Government cutbacks, the mid-1930s were very trying times. By the late 1930s the realization of an impending war and of Newfoundland's vital strategic importance brought about other challenges. The construction of Gander Airport (then the world's largest) was well underway.

During the 1939 Royal visit Herb was invested by King George VI as a Commander in the Order of the British Empire (C.B.E.).

During World War II.

By 1942 the overall base construction and troop movements would strain the capacity of the Railway to the limit. Throughout World War II Herb's workload as the General Manager of the Railway more than doubled. He also chaired an overall Transportation Control Board to coordinate movement of all commercial freight, by both land and sea. Herb and the Newfoundland Railway proved equal to supplying and servicing all the military bases. These were a major part of overall strategy in the war effort. It also clearly established Herb as the single most important civilian person in the overall Newfoundland war effort.

After World War II.

Herb led the postwar Railway rehabilitation, which meant a second almost total rebuilding or replacement of Railway assets. Early in 1949 Herb suffered a heart attack and had been recuperating at home, but upon the advice of his doctor was travelling to Florida for an extended rest. Sadly, while en route, he died in New York City on February 26, 1949 with his wife Jean at his side.

Captain Jack Whelan.

(1887–1972).

By: Ronald F. Whelan.

John Joseph Whelan.

Before World War II.

Born in 1887, his parents were Thomas and Mary (Dunphy) Whelan from Jerseyside, Placentia. Both his father and grandfather were fishermen and schooner owners and participated in the Labrador fishery. There they had their own "room" (fishing ground), "Whelan's Room", south of Battle Harbour, Labrador. He would eventually become one of the most accomplished seafarers of the twentieth century in Newfoundland.

In 1908, when only 21, Jack Whelan joined the Bowring Brothers coastal boat service, which carried passengers and mail around the Island of Newfoundland and to Labrador.

In 1914, he enlisted in the Newfoundland Regiment (regimental number 169) and saw action in Gallipoli and in France. The Great War nearly ended his life. He was seriously wounded on April 23rd, 1917 but continued to serve, being discharged in October 1918 with the rank of sergeant. On his return to Newfoundland, he studied navigation and then became a foreign-going Captain with John Penny & Sons Limited of Ramea on the South Coast.

In 1923, he married Marcella Burke of St. Jacques, a school teacher in Ramea. The house they subsequently owned in St. John's was 169 Pleasant Street (by coincidence, his old regimental number).

Also in 1923, Captain Whelan joined the Newfoundland Custom Services. In 1928 he became master of the Customs Services vessel *Daisy*, one of three that William Coaker, Minister of Marine and Fisheries, acquired from the British Government. (Those three boats were dubbed "Coaker's Navy" by Coaker's political enemies.)

In addition to its Customs Services, the *Daisy* ferried Magistrates and Supreme Court Judges and their clerks to administer justice in the outports. On November 18th, 1929, when the tidal wave struck the Burin Peninsula, the *Daisy*, carrying court officials, was tied up at Burin. The *Daisy* was not damaged and, when the wave subsided, Captain Whelan put to sea and searched the houses that had floated away for any persons still alive. He towed one of the houses to shore that same night, and later saved two marooned schooners, towing them to safe refuge in Burin. Captain Whelan later sailed from Argentia with officials who were to prepare a report for financial and humanitarian assistance for tidal wave victims.

In the second half of his seafaring life what particularly distinguished Captain Whelan was his consistent involvement in the high-level management of ships and shipping (as compared to being master of a single vessel). In 1934, Captain Whelan was appointed Inspector of Preventive Service for the Customs Department. He was head of personnel and maintenance for all Customs vessels. He acquired two new vessels for the government, the *Shulamite* and the *Marvita*, ex-rum-running boats purchased through Al Capone's lawyer.

In 1937, Captain Whelan's "fleet" expanded to include the vessels of the Justice and Fisheries Departments. Also during the late

1930s, the Captain taught navigation at Memorial University College. He was often called upon as an expert witness in Courts of Inquiry about marine incidents.

During World War II.

In September 1939, at the outbreak of war, Captain Whelan was Director of the Customs Examination Services in St. John's. In May 1941, the Commission of Government agreed that the Royal Canadian Navy should logically take over responsibility for the Customs Examination, using both the *Shulamite* and the *Marvita*. Their crews were transferred to the Canadian Navy Volunteer Reserve and given a navy rank and pay. Captain Whelan, now also coming in charge of all ship's traffic in St. John's, was named Lieutenant Commander (LCdr) in the Royal Canadian Navy.

Harbour management of an active port in peacetime is a large responsibility. Managing St. John's Harbour, a super-busy, blacked-out, naval port during wartime, was an extremely demanding job. LCdr Whelan planned the movement and gave instructions to over 30 naval vessels, munitions ships, tankers, and torpedo-damaged merchant ships as they entered or left port. This was complicated by the submarine nets at the harbour entrance and the severely limited wharf space inside the harbour. The arrival, docking-or-anchoring, and departure of every ship had to be promptly and precisely decided, communicated, and then monitored. Omission or faulty judgment could result in a disaster. The return to port of Canadian Navy vessels with dead and wounded crew required the utmost of care.

"Newfie John" (the spoken name put on the Canadian Naval Base in St. John's) deservedly became famous for its crucial role in the anti-U-boat Battle of the (Mid) Atlantic. LCdr Whelan orchestrated the orderly movement of all shipping. Navigating in the confined space was always difficult. Corvettes sometimes had to be tied up four or five abreast. Trying to move the ones inside took extraordinary skill and supervision. Communicating with ships' officers required firm, clear, no-nonsense instruction, carefully melded with tact and respect.

Some of the LCdr's experiences are recounted in Colonel G.W.L. Nicholson's book *More Fighting Newfoundlanders*, published in 1969. In September 1941, Commander Whelan skillfully brought the British HMS *Candytuft* into St. John's after one of her boilers exploded during convoy duty. The HMCS *Bittersweet* had towed the *Candytuft* to within 5.6 kilometres (3.5 miles) of St. John's Harbour. Colonel Nicholson wrote that "because of the problem of negotiating the submarine nets in the Narrows (all *Candytuft*'s navigating equipment having been knocked out) the tow was handed over to [LCdr Whelan and] the *Marvita* and her accompanying tug *Active*. With the former ahead, and the latter at the stern helping to steer, Captain Whelan docked the HMS *Candytuft* at Harvey's No. 2 Pier, where doctors and nurses were waiting to attend to the injured men."

In another very dangerous assignment, with a courageous crew of volunteers, LCdr Whelan, without incident, successfully towed a burning munitions ship out of the Harbour and scuttled it.

In February 1944, in recognition of LCdr Whelan's overall services, on the recommendation of the Canadian Government he was made a Member of the Order of the British Empire (M.B.E.).

After World War II.

At the end of the war, Captain Whelan returned to a senior position as Maintenance Superintendent with the Newfoundland Government, with responsibility for all government vessels. After finally retiring from public service, he became a Newfoundland Marine Surveyor for Lloyd's of London, serving in that capacity for 15 years. At the grand old age of 85, he died at St. John's on February 17th, 1972, one of a small number of Newfoundlanders to have served in both World Wars.

Note: Dr. Ron Whelan is one of Captain Whelan's children.

Gerald S. Doyle.

(1892–1956).

By: Paul J. Johnson.

Gerald Stanley Doyle.

Before World War II.

Born King's Cove (Bonavista Bay), son of Thomas and Margaret (Devine) Doyle. Educated at King's Cove and St. Patrick's Hall School, St. John's. While working in his first job, travelling for a drugstore in St. John's, he quickly observed great need of the population for many kinds of patent medicine, which were very limited in availability. There were few doctos and even fewer druggists accessible. He started with his very first agency in 1917 for the supply of Dr. Chase's medicines. He incorporated "Gerald S. Doyle Limited" in 1929.

In 1926 he launched *The Family Fireside* newspaper, filled with local news of births and deaths, community activities, as well as advertisements for his medicinal products. He also published folk and traditional songs in magazine form, first released in 1927. He distributed these free of charge. Beginning in 1930 he travelled around the coast of Newfoundland in his own boat, *Miss Newfoundland.* During these excursions he visited many of his 3,000 customers and also collected many traditional songs and stories, which he carefully recorded.

During World War II.

From 1932 to 1965 his firm produced and sponsored a radio news programme on the Voice of Newfoundland (VONF) Radio. Known as the *Gerald S. Doyle News*, it was broadcast in a conversational manner and covered the local news. Primarily it was a source of information for people around the island. At the time there were very few telephones, mail service was slow, and telegraph offices were closed in the evenings. Births, deaths, and marriages; news of hospital stays; movements of schooners, workers, servicemen and women; and fishery news were all reported. When the *Doyle News* aired, people gathered around available radios in every community in Newfoundland and Labrador.

With family members dispersed all over Newfoundland and Labrador in wartime construction, and all over the world in naval, army, and airforce service, the Doyle Bulletin was the most intently followed means of learning personal news. Collecting and compiling that news was an immense and demanding task. The *Doyle News* was of immeasurable value and comfort to Newfoundlanders in wartime.

Mr. Doyle's free songbooks were extremely popular with all servicemen and families for singsongs. In 1944 Mr. Doyle was made an Officer in the Order of the British Empire (O.B.E.).

After World War II.

He was active organizing Air Cadets and Navy Leagues. As treasurer of the provincial fund to assist the European Flood Relief Campaign, he used the *Doyle Bulletin* to "spread the word". Our per capita contributions were the highest in Canada. In 1955 he received a Papal Knighthood in the Order of St. Gregory the Great, and was made Commander of the Order of St. John of Jerusalem. He served on many community service executive committees, including CNIB, Red Cross, St. John Ambulance, and the Newfoundland Tuberculosis Association.

Frank O'Leary.
(1894–1963).

By: Paul J. Johnson.

Francis Martin O'Leary.

Before World War II.

Born St. John's, son of Francis and Margaret (Lambert) O'Leary. Educated at St. Patrick's Hall School, St. John's. Frank served overseas with the Newfoundland Regiment in World War I from 1916 to 1918. On returning home he worked as a commercial traveller, calling upon customers in communities all around the island. During that time in our history, travel was very difficult, and he gained a great appreciation for people living in the coastal communities. In 1922 he established his own business, F. M. O'Leary Ltd., and became the exclusive agent and distributor for many well-known manufacturers of consumer products and building supplies. In 1937 his firm began a radio programme called "The Barrelman", which was dedicated to making "Newfoundland Better Known to Newfoundlanders". The Barrelman was produced and broadcast by Joey Smallwood (later the leader of the Confederation movement), and provided fascinating stories from all over the island and at sea.

During World War II.

Beginning in the early 1940s Frank O'Leary sponsored a free monthly newspaper *The Newfoundlander*, which was widely distributed. After the outbreak of WWII, Mr. O'Leary was instrumental in reactivating the Newfoundland Patriotic Association, and originated campaigns to fund its activities. His "One-Per Cent" and the "Fish-A-Man" appeals were widely publicized on "The Barrelman" programme. Citizens' response to these campaigns accounted for more than 60 per cent of the hundreds of thousands of dollars raised by the NPA. He helped establish, and was the first chair of the Allied Merchant Seaman's Club.

Other projects of Rotary in which he took the lead were the maintenance of the Hostel for Newfoundland Servicemen in London and creation of the Newfoundland Tuberculosis Association. (The deadly TB disease was rampant at that time.) The Christmas Seal fundraising campaign assisted Government by providing mobile X-ray services to coastal communities via the motor vessel *Christmas Seal*. In 1944 he was appointed an Officer of the British Empire (O.B.E.) for his work with the Patriotic Association.

After World War II.

Before the end of the War, he had started the O'Leary Newfoundland Poetry Awards, and in 1947 began to provide monetary prizes for essays on "Great Newfoundlanders". These contests were the forerunners of the annual Arts and Letters contest that the Provincial Government sponsored after Confederation. In 1949 while president of the St. John's Rotary Club, he formed and was made president of the St. John's Memorial Stadium Council, comprised of 120 city organizations, to raise funds to create a stadium to replace the Arena, destroyed by fire in 1941. The Stadium stood as a memorial to those who had served in the World Wars. It was the centre for sports and entertainment in St. John's.

Mr. O'Leary was conferred with a Knighthood in the Papal Order of St. Gregory by Pope Pius XII in 1954. In 2009 he was inducted into the Junior Achievement Newfoundland and Labrador Business Hall of Fame.

Andrew Greene Carnell.

Mayor Andy Carnell.

(1877–1951).

By: Paul J. Johnson.

Before World War II.

Born at St. John's, son of John Thomas and Elizabeth (McCoubrey) Carnell. Educated at Bishop Feild College and Methodist College in St. John's and later at United States School of Embalmery, Chicago. In 1895 he entered the family carriage works and undertaking business, which had been begun in 1835 by his father. In 1902 he became Newfoundland's first certified embalmer. In 1903 he succeeded his father as manager, and expanded the family business to include a mortuary, a forge, a garage, a paint shop, and an upholstering department. In 1904 he married Mabel Payne.

Andy was defeated in two Newfoundland House of Assembly elections in 1908 and 1919. He offered himself in a St. John's municipal election in 1929 and became Deputy Mayor, having polled the highest vote amongst the six councillors elected. Following the death of the Mayor Howlett, Andy became Acting Mayor. In the 1933 election he became Mayor by acclamation.

From 1938, he held office as Mayor until 1949. After 1933, when Newfoundland became governed by a committee of Commissioners,

Andy Carnell was often referred to as "Mayor of Newfoundland". During the years of the appointed Commission of Government, under his leadership St. John's became the "stronghold of democracy". There were no other elected mayors in all of Newfoundland. In 1939 he was awarded the Commander of the Order of the British Empire (C.B.E.) by King George VI for his service to his country.

During World War II.

During World War II, the overall economy of St. John's went from bust to boom. But along with prosperity came a huge variety of City governance, defence, building, and administration issues and problems. His administrations faced huge challenges of housing and the influx of nearly double the pre-war population. Those added people included thousands of military and construction personnel, as well as the many who visited port before convoying across or back across the Atlantic. Housing developments sprang up all around the City. Between Canadian, American, and Newfoundland military personnel, over 30,000 were stationed in St. John's. Handling the civilian side of the war effort fell largely on the shoulders of the Mayor. "Andy was the man" who handled a very demanding job extremely well.

After World War II.

The St. John's Housing Commission was first organized in 1944, leading to the formation of the St. John's Housing Corporation. The Mayor was a key individual in enabling that large-scale plan. In 1948, he was much involved in raising public funds for the Memorial Stadium, to be located near Quidi Vidi Lake.

He initiated and maintained a strong programme of water, sewer, and street expansion. Andy was commonly referred to as the "La Guardia of St. John's". He died in St. John's 26 January 1951.

Banking & Boarding – Spanning the War Years.

By: Aidan Maloney.

I was born in King's Cove, Bonavista Bay, Newfoundland, in 1920 and received my education there. Located on the northeast coast of the island, King's Cove was referred to by many as the "Athens of the North" – renowned for its learned residents. But, in the midst of the great depression, King's Cove offered few job opportunities. That was also the case with most other outport communities. I had decided that a future in a community where fishing was the only industry was not for me, so I had to look for other possibilities.

In 1938 I became aware that the Trinity branch of the Royal Bank had an opening for a "Junior Clerk". I applied for the position and was accepted. So began my six-year banking career, and as well my life as a wartime "boarder" in the Newfoundland towns of Trinity, Placentia, Gander, the capital city of St. John's, and the south coast, island-town of Ramea.

Trinity – 1938 to 1941.

To a beginning employee, Trinity provided an ideal working experience for me. From the spring to the autumn, it was close enough to bicycle home to King's Cove on weekends. In Trinity, the bank "Juniors", as we were generally known, lived together at the only boarding house in that community. The boarding-house owner's wife was in charge and had one helper. They did the meals and laundry for all the guests. That was a seven-day job for both of them, all year round. The home offered good accommodations and was also the lodging place for commercial travellers who visited Trinity. The travellers represented their St. John's principals, calling upon the businesses in and near to Trinity. It was at the dining table, and later in the evening in the living room, that I heard much about the outside world, particularly what was taking place in St. John's. Also, for a spellbound young audience, there were many tall tales and humorous stories. A radio was available to guests. Attentive listening was of the first importance for me, because at King's Cove we only occasionally shared the few available radios.

The Royal Bank at Trinity regularly opened from 10 am to 3 pm, five days a week, allowing me plenty of free time for soccer, trouting, and cycling to nearby communities. Trinity had a men's club, which I joined, where I learned to play billiards and, more importantly, the card game of "Bridge". That captivating pastime stood me in good stead for many, many years as a great social preoccupation. A bank clerk was also expected to play a role in the local autumn and winter concerts staged by the churches. I cheerfully fulfilled that responsibility as well.

Argentia – March, 1941.

My simple and pleasant introduction to employment in Trinity came to an end in March 1941 when the word came to me that I was to be transferred to the Royal Bank at Placentia. Placentia was the branch nearest the massive construction job of the American Navy and Army bases at Argentia. That work was already well underway when I went there to work.

So, I was off on my first job-transfer, my first train-ride, and, incidentally, my first visit to St. John's. In St. John's, I stayed overnight at the very impressive "Newfoundland Hotel" before taking the train the next morning to Placentia. When I arrived in Placentia, the bank had already arranged for me to stay at the only boarding house in the town. My fellow boarders included three other bank staff, and two Americans, who were superintendents of construction at the American bases in Argentia.

My work at this bank branch was a new and busy experience, with very long hours, six days a week and sometimes part of Sunday. One day each fortnight, the manager and three of us juniors went to Argentia to prepare and dispense payrolls and other financial services. These sometimes-complicated services were needed for a workforce of several thousand Newfoundlanders and Americans.

In Argentia, the bank had acquired from the U.S. authorities one of the very few remaining, expropriated homes, to become a temporary bank. Practically all the other homes and buildings had been demolished or moved to the nearby settlement of Freshwater. (Only some years later did I learn that this particular house had been the home of the family whose daughter was to become my wife.)

I was at my job in Argentia on the day of the signing of the historic “Atlantic Charter” by Churchill and Roosevelt. I had heard rumours but no facts on why the huge battleships that obviously brought them here were anchored at nearby Ship Harbour. (That day I also observed my birthday.)

The bank was a major supplier of financial and accounting services to American contractors and their employees in Newfoundland, engaged in Army, Navy, and Air Force base construction. One such unique service provided to American workers on paydays was a telegraphic transfer of their wages back to their homes in the United States. A personal message of 50 words was allowed with each transfer. As tellers, we arranged the transfer and were expected, when asked, to assist in writing the personal messages. In so doing, we occasionally did become aware of some interesting domestic tangles.

My stay at the Placentia Branch of the bank was less than a year. It was memorable as the place where I made first contact with the U.S. Navy and Army personnel and the Americans involved in base construction. My remaining impression of them was that they were a very polite and generous people.

Gander – October, 1941.

In June of that year, word came from the Royal Bank in St. John’s that I was to move to the Royal Bank Branch at Gander. U.S. Forces,

Canadian Army, and the Royal Air Force Ferry Command were based there. The extensive construction of the airport and related facilities was still underway. By October 1941, I was on the train from Trinity to St. John's to connect with the Newfoundland Railway "Overland Express" to Gander. By good luck the bank arranged my boarding. I found myself at the "Eastbound Inn", which, by the standards of the time, offered fairly luxurious accommodations.

My eight month stay at the Eastbound Inn included my private room, all meals in their high-class dining room, and access to the library, games room, and laundry facilities. All of this cost me $ 25 a month, with the balance subsidized by the Royal Bank. (This was not a good setting to prepare me for the eventual challenge of finding a boarding house in overcrowded St. John's. There I was to be completely on my own, without any contribution from my employer.)

During my assignment to Gander, amongst the many British, Canadian, and American servicemen and hundreds of construction workers who appeared at my teller's wicket, a few personalities still stand out in my memory. One morning I was introduced by my manager to Sir Herbert Holt and Lord Beaverbrook, who were in Gander for a few hours en route from Montreal to London. They were prominent in organizing the operation known as "The Ferry Command", the arm of the British Government that was responsible for flying planes across the Atlantic. I also met Vice-Admiral Emile Henri Muselier, the leader of the Free French Navy, who stopped at Gander en route to St. Pierre. Another visitor to my teller's wicket was "Joey" Smallwood, who was planning to open a large pig farm at Gander. The American and Canadian servicemen who used the bank's services were generous in offering an occasional, scarce pack of cigarettes, and tickets to the movies at their base facilities.

The news of the sneak attack on Pearl Harbor by Japan reached us quite early on the morning of December 7th. This, along with the usual, horrible war news, was a dreadful development. It made us realize that many more days lay ahead, before there could be peace.

Once again I received word from the manager of the bank's Head Office in St. John's that I was to be promoted and transferred there. I was expected to report for duty within three days. I managed to be on board the Railway's "Foreign Express" at midnight in Gander and was in St. John's at about 8 a.m. the very next day.

St. John's – 1942 to 1944.

In 1942, the City of St. John's was a madhouse of activity. Non-stop construction of military accommodations for Canadian and American forces and the growth in business activity saw great numbers of workers move from the outports to the City for employment. This placed extreme pressure on available housing. This was a radical change from conditions under the Great Depression of the 1930s.

The housing situation I faced on my first day in St. John's was potentially unsolvable. The bank was not successful in finding accommodation. With the greatest of good luck, my first move was to contact a friend who was working in the City. He was at a boarding house in the City centre, off Carter's Hill and Cabot Street. He offered two suggestions. The first was to stay overnight at his place, where he knew there was a spare bed. The second was to begin, without delay, an intensive search for a permanent place.

His boarding house was a three-storey, semi-detached, flat-roof dwelling, consisting of a kitchen, dining room, bathroom, and five bedrooms. There was a large coal furnace in the main hallway, with its chimney going through all the floors and out through the roof. This furnace provided heat enough for the entire house, along with hot water for the kitchen and bathroom.

I was introduced to the homeowner, who, with minimum negotiation, offered me a bed for the night and longer, until I found a permanent place. The bed was at a monthly rental just below my entire monthly earnings. The fairly large bedroom was on the third floor and had three single beds. The other two beds were occupied by friendly

Canadian Navy shore-based personnel. That third bed was to become my own, fortuitous, little corner of the world.

I should mention that what was thought to be a temporary accommodation turned into a stay of over two years, largely because of the kindness and hospitality of the hosts at my "temporary" lodging. The lasting memory I have is of the thoughtfulness of that family, with whom I kept in touch for years after I eventually left the City.

With accommodation so speedily taken care of, I set out on foot down Carter's Hill to the bank on Water Street. This was to be another, entirely new banking experience. For some clients, the bank assisted in providing a special payroll service to construction contractors, by filling pay envelopes. This required the customer, on the eve of payday, to present the branch with payroll envelopes showing their workers' earnings. Bank staff would return to the branch at night to correctly fill the envelopes. Occasionally, we would find ourselves using newly minted paper currency. These bills had a tendency to stick together, requiring extra-special attention on our part. On a few occasions we ended the evening's work with remaining envelopes and insufficient cash to fill them. All envelopes then had to be emptied, checked, and re-filled. After an extra-long day's work, this was not a happy predicament.

My own pay was at the bank's standard rate for my position. It allowed no room for the negotiation of board expense or any other costs. My boarding rent included some laundry, but my white shirts were done at a nearby Chinese laundry. I am certain the boarding house owner could have gotten a higher rental from others seeking lodging, but he was not interested in profiteering. My monthly rental included a daily box-lunch. I was very thankful for important favours.

My bed was comfortable and allowed me sufficient sleep-time, except on nights when the Navy boys brought home some small tools and pieces of wood, perhaps mahogany ends, out of which they were making jewellery boxes for their "lady friends". Sawing and sanding the wood sometimes went on until after midnight and disrupted my sleep. (A minor discomfort.)

On cold winter nights, the stovepipe from the furnace going through the bedroom provided welcome heat. I never gave much thought to the risk from fire. Now, 60 years later, when I recall that experience, it can keep me awake.

Walking to and from the bank took 40 minutes. With night-work, this doubled to 80 minutes. Because of the workload at the bank, a six-day week was the general rule.

This reduced my boarding-house-time to sleep-time plus an hour each for breakfast and dinner. The exception, of course, was Sunday. Dinner, beginning around noon, was always a good meal. It saw the whole family – father, mother, two teenaged boys, and the boarders – all sitting at the large table, pleasantly recounting their stories of the past week. The owner worked in the Newfoundland Constabulary with specific duties to enforce "wartime blackout" regulations. His stories were often amongst the most interesting of the many to be heard. The Navy personnel had their own tales, many of which had to do with their "off-duty" hours, and were sometimes exaggerated, particularly when they related to their lady friends.

It became evident to me that operating this boarding house was really in the hands of the owner's wife. My negotiation for a monthly rate for board was with her. With the help of a housemaid, the wife purchased food, did most of the preparation of meals, and saw that laundry was properly done and sorted. Her workday I estimate to be 10 to 12 hours, for a six-day week, with a shorter workday on Sunday.

The "man of the house" was a few years past the normal age for Constabulary retirement. His employment was extended to allow for special duty with the blackout regulations. These duties he carried out on foot, always after dark, covering residential streets in the central and west end of St. John's. He did his duty with a routine that ended at midnight.

Occasionally, he invited me to accompany him for an hour or two of his tour of duty. On evenings when I was not working at the bank, I found this to be an interesting diversion. Although I did not accompany him when he had to go to the door of homes and remind the occupants of an infraction of the regulations (e.g., blinds not drawn or light sneaking out), it was my guess that, for the most part, the offender got away with a mild scolding.

At the boarding house, one amenity available to all of us was a good radio in the living room. It was constantly tuned to a local broadcasting station. On a daily basis, the "Gerald S. Doyle News Bulletin" and the war news were compulsory listening. It so happened that, on the evening of the terrible fire at the Knights of Columbus Hut, I was listening to a live broadcast of the entertainment at the Hut, when the emcee declared that a fire had started in the building. Grabbing my coat, I raced to the corner of Long's Hill and Harvey Road, across from the K of C, and for the next few hours watched the worst fire and human tragedy in my life. When I finally left to go home, I still had no idea of the dreadful loss of life in that terrible fire. I only learned the full extent of the calamity the following morning.

Another recollection which remains with me about my stay in St. John's was finding something to do during my spare time on Sunday afternoon. Not having a car, I often took a bus-ride to Bowring Park or on to the Sanitorium on Topsail Road, in the City's west end. Why the Sanitorium ? I knew some young people who were TB patients at the Sanitorium. Apart from visiting them, they were a welcome source of information on what was taking place back home in the King's Cove area.

It was my impression that the boarding-house owner and family, who opened their home for boarders, quite justifiably felt they were performing a valuable patriotic service for the wartime effort. The two Canadian Navy boys would agree.

Leaving St. John's for Ramea – October, 1944.

Because of their training and experience, bank clerks were a good source to which business owners looked to find key staff. And so it was that on a September afternoon in 1944 Gerald S. Doyle, a fellow-citizen from King's Cove, and later a successful St. John's merchant, came to the bank and informed me of an opening in one of Newfoundland's major fishery enterprises, John Penny & Sons Limited. One month later, I said my thanks and farewell to the Royal Bank, and moved away to Ramea, where I became employed with the Pennys.

Once again I boarded the "Foreign Express" at St. John's, going to Port aux Basques, en route to Ramea. A Penny motor-vessel awaited my arrival at Port aux Basques, and I was on my way to the new job and a completely different occupation. But, a boarding house was to remain a main feature of my life.

In Ramea, my boarding accommodation had been pre-arranged and I moved in with a family where the man of the house was a senior employee in the Penny business. I remained there for three years until I became married and built my own first home.

If I had any belief that my bank jobs at St. John's and elsewhere were demanding, it didn't hold a candle to the work ahead of me at Penny's. The firm was discontinuing the traditional saltfish business, where it had been involved since 1856, and changing to frozen fish for the American markets. Penny's wanted to get an early start on new marketing for fish and be ready as soon as the war was over. They wanted to be one of the early pioneers in the Newfoundland fresh fish business. In wartime that was an almost impossible undertaking. Ramea was located on a small island off the south coast. It was a far more peaceful place than that I had experienced in St. John's during the previous two years. Through the nightly radio broadcast, I kept abreast of what was going on in the war overseas. We heard very little about St. John's and the Battle of the Atlantic, but we did know about the tragic sinking of the SS *Caribou* and the four iron ore boats off Bell Island.

Amongst the memories of my time in Ramea was a visit by Sir John Puddester, the Commissioner for Public Health and Welfare. In speaking to the Public Health Nurse for the community, he asked her what she needed most. I remember her reply was "A radio", which I could well understand.

Captain Jack Whelan.

Once, soon after the war was over, I went with Captain Jack Whelan of St. John's to visit Nova Scotia to inspect the construction of a vessel being built for Penny's. We boarded at the home of one of the shipbuilders. How much the war had impacted all of us was told by the unusual fact that the radio in this house had not been turned on since peace had come. The cryptic reason given us by the owner was that "There is no news since the war ended".

My Conclusions.

During my six years with the bank, I had worked at five of its seven branches in Newfoundland and assisted in the examination of the other two. I have sometimes speculated on my employer's reasons for their handling of my career. Was it that I had shown some special skills or abilities to cope with what was needed ? Or was I merely a convenient worker, available on call, to fill an extra need, or perhaps a gap left by another, departing staff member ? The bank did not enlighten me about this – but I have never lost sleep over those questions.

What is important lies in the fact that I look back on my "time-served" with happy memories and the satisfaction I achieved by what I had learned and contributed. The Bank provided me with sound business training that has stood me in good stead for the rest of my life. I left their employ with confidence in the new opportunity open to me in the fishery. Leaving home and adapting to new living conditions was challenging but the experiences of my first boarding house in Trinity and in those that followed have left me with positive, heart-filled recollections of those years. That is particularly true of the kindness and friendship I received, which I sincerely reciprocated. I kept in touch with many of those acquired friends for years – long after I became settled with my own home and family.

Aidan Maloney.

Biographical Sketch

Aidan Maloney is a native of King's Cove and was managing director of John Penny & Sons at Ramea from 1949 to 1957. From 1957 to 1961 he was special advisor in the Newfoundland Department of Fisheries and Assistant Deputy Minister of Fisheries from 1961 to 1966. He represented Ferryland in the House of Assembly from 1966 to 1971, serving in cabinet first as Minister of Public Welfare and then as Minister of Fisheries. He was President of the Canadian Saltfish Corporation from 1971 to 1979. He was the recipient of the Order of Canada in 1992 and received an honorary doctorate of laws from Memorial University in 1993.

8

Wartime in Newfoundland.

By: Frank J. Kennedy.

This chapter consists of excerpts from two books by the author, *A Corner Boy Remembers: Growing Up in St. John's* and *Flashes from the Past: Forty-Two Years Covering the News.*

Prisoners of War Held in City. September, 1939.

Two days after World War II broke out in 1939, the first German prisoners of war were locked up in St. John's. Downtown shoppers were amazed to see the twenty-five men marching along Water Street under heavy guard. Citizens of the Capital City realized the war had indeed begun.

Britain and France declared war on Germany on Sept. 3, after that country invaded Poland. Although Canada did not enter the war until a week later, this was before Confederation. Newfoundland was a British colony, and as such became involved in the conflict immediately. At Botwood a German merchant ship, the SS *Christoph Doornum*, which was loading newsprint, was seized and its crew were made prisoners of war. They were brought to St. John's by train and marched from the railway station to the Y.M.C.A. building on Water Street east. There they were imprisoned during the construction of a proper internment camp at Pleasantville (later to become Fort Pepperrell). When they were transferred to the new camp, they met some of their fellow countrymen who were unlucky enough to be on board a ship loading iron ore at Bell Island on Sept. 3. After some months all these POWs were moved to a larger facility in Western Canada. At the time nothing was published in the media about these foreigners, but the news got around by word of mouth. Citizens often strolled along the Boulevard on a Sunday afternoon to sneak a peep at "the enemy". For the next few weeks life went on pretty much as usual in St. John's.

Call for Volunteers. February, 1940.

On Feb. 6, Governor Walwyn issued a proclamation asking for volunteers to serve in the British Army for the duration of the war. He wanted 400 recruits and within days that number was reached as patriotic young men, the majority from St. John's, came forward to serve their country. In succeeding months hundreds also joined the Royal Navy and the Royal Air Force.

In Europe during the first year of the conflict things went badly for Great Britain. Not only had Germany invaded Holland and Belgium, but the unbelievable happened: France was overcome by the enemy. Scores of German submarines were patrolling the waters off the British Isles and sinking dozens of merchant supply ships every week, cutting off badly needed war materials. In August, 1940, Germany began bombing London. England was being driven to its knees.

Churchill Asks for Help.

British Prime Minister Sir Winston Churchill appealed to his old friend, Franklin D. Roosevelt, President of the United States, for assistance against the German forces. Roosevelt realized that if Britain was invaded, the next conquest for Hitler would be North America. The stepping stone to that continent was obviously the island of Newfoundland, the nearest territory to Europe, and America was determined to defend that island against possible aggression. And so the famous Lend-Lease Agreement was born, and it would have a tremendous effect on the financial and social life of Newfoundland and especially St. John's.

The Lend-Lease Agreement.

The United States agreed to supply fifty warships (destroyers) to Britain in exchange for a 99-year lease on territories in Newfoundland, Bermuda and the West Indies. The areas would be used as military defence bases. U.S. engineers carried out land, sea and air surveys of virtually all the east coast of the island and

Labrador to decide where the bases should be built. A delegation under the command of U.S. Rear-Admiral Greenslade met with the Commission of Government to discuss their plans. Bases would be set up in Goose Bay, Argentia, Stephenville and St. John's. The largest was to be located at Pleasantville in St. John's and take in more than 200 acres that was mostly farm land, with a few summer houses. Pleasantville was the site where 26 years earlier, the famous "First Five Hundred" young Newfoundland soldiers trained before going overseas to serve in World War I. The new base would be called Fort Pepperrell in memory of a famous 18th century U.S. military leader, Sir William Pepperrell. The boundary to the south would be Quidi Vidi Lake and to the north, Bally Haly Golf and Curling Club on Logy Bay Road. All property owners were notified their land was urgently required for the defence of the country, and they were duly compensated by the U.S. Government and asked to move out as quickly as possible.

Fort Pepperrell, Threat to the Annual Regatta.

For security reasons, the plans for the establishment of a military base at Pleasantville were never published. However, when Mayor Andy Carnell, the city councilors, and the Regatta committee discovered the plans included taking over all the north bank of Quidi Vidi Lake, right to the water's edge, they were up in arms. This action would mean the end of the oldest continuing sporting event in North America, the annual St. John's Regatta, which began more than 120 years earlier. Or at least it would have to be postponed for 99 years. The land in question ran the full length of the lake between the Boulevard and the high water mark of the lake. Just recently the city had designated this whole area as "The King George V Memorial Park" and Mayor Carnell expressed the hope that some day they would build a stadium near the head of the lake. Members of the Commission of Government contacted the U.S. authorities and they agreed to change the south boundary to exclude the Boulevard and the north bank. Instead, the Boulevard would be rebuilt, along with King's Bridge Road, which was the principal route from St. John's harbour to the new base.

Paving the Way. October, 1941.

On a rainy day in October, 1941, a small naval boat came in to the wharf at Bursey's Fish Plant on the south side of St. John's harbour. Several naval officers stepped ashore and asked to see the owner. Mr. W.J. Bursey was surprised to see four men, decorated with gold braid, enter his office at the rear of the plant. He was astounded when, after introducing themselves as U.S. Naval officers, he was told they wanted to rent his premises and hoped he could move out the following day. They told Mr. Bursey that in the interest of the defence of Newfoundland it was essential to have his property. There was a troopship in New York ready to sail for St. John's and his dock was the only place in the entire harbour where the water was deep enough for that ship to moor. Before answering the question regarding moving out the next day, Mr. Bursey said "Gentlemen, let me show you around." Bursey took the visitors to a shed where 1000 quintals (12,000 lbs.) of salt fish were stored, as well as another 12,000 lbs. of pickled fish in vats waiting to be put into casks. In the cod oil factory he showed them 10,000 gallons of cod liver oil that were 'curing' in tanks and barrels. Outside on the wharf, men were gutting fish and extracting the livers. The Americans were very impressed with the scope of Bursey's operation and realized moving out quickly would be impossible. They showed Bursey a drawing of the troopship *Edmund B. Alexander* tied up at his premises. In a few days an agreement was signed and Mr. Bursey was very happy with the arrangement. Not only was he paid a generous price for the rental, but he would be allowed to continue with his business and the Americans agreed to have him supply provisions for the ship during the eight months it would be in port.

The *Edmund B. Alexander.* January, 1941.

On January 29, 1941, the largest ship ever to enter St. John's harbour to that date passed through The Narrows with only two feet of water between the keel and the bottom. It was the 22,600 ton U.S. Troopship *Edmund B. Alexander*, nearly 700 feet long. Although it was wartime, America was not yet involved, and although the ship was not mentioned by the media, everyone knew the ship would arrive, as she had been "hanging around" for four days before entering the harbour. The ship was a prize of World War I, having been in Boston when that war broke out; it was then a German passenger ship, the SS *Amerika.* It was renamed to honor a great U.S. Commander who served in the Mexican war 1846–48.

When the troopship left New York on Jan. 15, none of the 977 military men on board or the 200 crew members had any idea where they were headed, except, of course, a few officers. All they knew was "they were going overseas". Five days later, during a snowstorm, the ship dropped anchor one mile off St. John's harbour. The Customs boat *Shulamite* went out to meet her. On board were Captain John [Jack] Whelan and U.S. Capt. Hiatt, as well as harbour pilot Capt. George Anstey, who would later guide the ship through The Narrows. What they saw as they emerged from a snow squall was startling: a huge gray wall with hundreds of portholes towering above them. It was the port side of the ship. After some discussion the ship's Captain William Joensen and the pilot, Capt. Anstey, decided it would be risky to try bringing this large ship through the Narrows in such rough seas and as the forecast showed no immediate improvement in the bad weather, the *Edmund B.* would weigh anchor and steam to Conception Bay to await better conditions.

The ship lay at anchor for three days between Bell Island and Kelly's Island and was admired by thousands all along Conception Bay South, as well as hundreds of St. John's residents who went out to Topsail to see the big visitor. Very early on Wednesday, January 29, the *Edmund B.* sailed out of Conception Bay and was soon at anchor once more outside the Narrows. Again the *Shulamite* went out to meet her. As they approached, Capt. Anstey and the others were impressed with the large ocean liner. Her five decks, four tall masts and two funnels gave an impression of incredible height. As the customs boat came near 'the great gray wall,' two metal doors swung open in the side of the ship and Capt. Anstey climbed in and was escorted to the bridge. There he met the ship's Captain, William Joensen, for the first time. Once again the anchor was winched up and the two men guided the ship safely through the channel as hundreds watched from Signal Hill, the Battery and Fort Amherst.

When the ship was securely moored at Bursey's premises, the same metal doors swung open again and a long gangway was pushed out to the wharf. Hundreds of soldiers who had been at sea for two weeks began streaming ashore and setting foot on this new found land for the first time. As they poured into the city they were delighted to see U.S. flags flying, and on Water Street many of the mercantile firms were decorated with bunting. "The friendly invasion", as it was so aptly called in John Cardoulis' book of that name, had begun. Capitulation was inevitable. Fraternization was rampant. Surrender was bounteous. By the year 1990, 25,000 Newfoundland women would have married American servicemen. Of course, thousands of these servicemen were stationed in other areas of Newfoundland and Labrador but here we are writing only about the effect of the war on St. John's.

Heavy Artillery. 1941.

Bursey's fish plant workers were amazed to see twelve war tanks come off the ship, as well as many anti-aircraft guns and several large cannon. The ship had carried, as well as the troops, 2000 tons of war materials and building supplies. The latter were taken to Pleasantville and the following month construction of Fort Pepperrell commenced. This would be the largest U.S. base outside America. The cannon were immediately put in place on Signal Hill, at Fort Amherst and other points along the coast to guard against any possible attack from the ocean. An anti-aircraft artillery unit was set up just below Cabot Tower in the location now occupied by the Interpretation Center and was manned 24 hours a day.

Floating Barracks. 1941.

For the remainder of the winter the *Edmund B.* was used as a barracks to house the soldiers. During that time many fishermen from the Battery and Fort Amherst ran an unofficial ferry service back and forth, using their fishing boats, from the ship to the north side of the harbour. In May the troops were moved to a temporary camp near Carpasian Road, named Camp Alexander, to await the construction of permanent buildings at the new base. In Camp Alexander the living conditions under canvas were a giant step down from the comforts of the *Edmund B.* which had all the conveniences of a passenger liner including large dining halls, a movie theater, a swimming pool and a hospital.

Economic Boom for St. John's. 1941–42.

The construction of the base was a great boost to the economy of St. John's and indeed the whole island, for workers came from all across the country to work there. In the summer of 1941 more than 5000 civilians were employed, and even after that work was finished, more than 2000 civilians found employment there for several years. Earlier that same year, several residents of the Lower Battery got their marching orders and their homes were torn down to make room for a U.S. Army dock and two huge storage sheds. Hundreds were employed on that job as well and it cost the U.S. government nearly two million dollars.

With construction at Pepperrell almost complete by November 1941, troops began moving in from Camp Alexander. Now they found they were housed in the most modern accommodations ever built for the military outside the U.S. To add to that opulence, all the married officers were allowed to bring in their wives and families from the States. That luxury didn't last long, however, as on December 7, after Pearl Harbour [*sic*] was bombed, the order was sent out to have all the civilians move out, except workers, to make room for additional troops. Troopships kept arriving and by 1942 there were 7000 military personnel at Fort Pepperrell.

Reprinted from *A Corner Boy Remembers: Growing Up in St. John's* by Frank J. Kennedy (Breakwater Books, 2006) by permission of the publisher.

The Grounding of the two Warships and the Dramatic Rescue.

"My God! We've hit a mountain!"
–Anonymous Sailor on the *Wilkes*

The disaster occurred on February 18, 1942, when three U.S. Warships the *Truxton*, *Pollux* and *Wilkes* were traveling from Portland, Maine, to Argentia. It was wartime, and the small convoy was under blackout conditions and radio silence. The *Pollux* was a supply ship, bringing goods to the naval base at Argentia, and on board, besides the regular crew of one hundred and seventy-five men, were fifty-eight young navy recruits going to the Argentia base for training. The *Wilkes* was the flagship, or leader, and was the only ship with radar. Although this was her eighth trip from the States to Argentia, most of the crew this time were inexperienced sailors. The ships had been warned that German U-boats were operating in the area and could attack even in stormy weather, so the three ships maintained full speed ahead, and sailed in a zigzag pattern to avoid possible torpedoes. Normal night time navigation was done by the stars and compass, with the aid of a fathometer, an electronic device that would tell the depth of water under the ship. However, on the night they were nearing the Newfoundland coast, a snow storm was raging, and the skies had been overcast for the past forty-eight hours.

The captain of the *Pollux* wanted the *Wilkes* to change course and had the signal man flash a message to the flagship to that effect. He felt they were too close to shore. In the radar room of the *Wilkes*, the screen was constantly being monitored to keep track of the other two ships. Now a series of blips began appearing at the top of the screen, increasing in number until there were literally dozens of blips there. The radar operator called a senior officer and asked him what he thought of it. The officer said, "Surely there can't be that many ships out there in front of us! There must be something wrong with the radar. Have it checked when we get to Argentia." The fathometer read 200 feet of water underneath. Outside, the snow had turned to sleet, and the lookout, peering into the darkness, saw what he thought was a huge iceberg dead ahead. It was the snow covered cliffs of

Lawn Head. He sounded the alarm, and immediately the engines were reversed and the rudder put hard over. The ship had slowed to five knots when it hit with a resounding crash. The captain ordered the searchlights manned and shone forward. They lit up the white cliffs. "My God!" someone shouted incredulously, "We've hit a mountain!"

The captain ordered the ship's sirens sounded to warn the other ships, but they would not work. They were frozen up. He would have to break radio silence in this emergency and ordered the radio operator to quickly alert the ships of the danger. Although they were in a "radio silence" mode, all the receivers were left on, and could pick up transmissions without having the enemy home in on their positions. The operator found that the transmitter was not working either, as the outside antenna was covered with ice. Two sailors climbed a ladder on the smokestack and knocked the ice off the aerial, but this took another fifteen minutes, and their distress call was answered only by a radio station in Massachusetts. At least the radio was now working, but it was too late. The other two warships had run aground as well. It was just after 4:00 a.m. The *Wilkes* continued sending out the message, "*Wilkes* aground. Don't know which side [of Placentia Bay]." The mouth of that bay is 100 kilometres (60 miles) across and they didn't even know which side they were on! They were truly lost.

One mile east, the fifteen thousand ton *Pollux* had slammed ashore so violently that men in their bunks were thrown out onto the deck. The noise was so loud that some thought a torpedo had hit the ship. Others were sure they had collided with the *Truxton*. Several distress flares were fired into the dark sky, but this was a deserted area and no one on land saw them. Two miles further on, the *Truxton* ran aground in the relatively sheltered Chambers Cove. The back of the ship seemed to be in deep water, so the engines were put full astern. The warship moved back about ten feet and the propellers were torn off on the rocks. The stern swung around broadside to the wind and immediately the fuel tanks were ruptured, sending thousands of gallons of tar-like bunker-C oil out onto the sea between the ship and shore. On board the *Wilkes* it was noticed that only the bow seemed to be aground, so the captain ordered all cargo, munitions, etc. moved to the stern of the ship, and the oil pumped out of a forward fuel tank, with the hope that the stern would go down, and the bow come up. The idea worked, and three hours after grounding, the *Wilkes* slid slowly astern into deep water with only slight damage. The flagship hove to a half mile from the supply ship, but could do nothing to assist as the seas were far too rough to launch a boat. Five men from the *Pollux* had managed, with great difficulty, to get a raft ashore, but not without the loss of some of their shipmates in the vicious seas. Their life boats had been smashed to pieces by the huge waves. The ship's fuel tanks had also been punctured, and the men were covered with the thick, black oil. Some jumped overboard and attempted to swim ashore; others were swept overboard. Only a few made it. Many drowned. Some that did make it to shore froze to death on the spot. There was no beach here, just an outcropping of rocks, from which rose steep, ice covered cliffs three hundred feet high.

Back on the *Truxton*, their boats had also been smashed in the launching attempt, but the sailors had managed to get a line ashore and many were pulled to land in a breeches buoy, a chair-like device attached to a rope. There was a small beach here, but similar ice-covered cliffs all around. One sailor had some water-proof matches so a bonfire was started, using wooden crates that had been thrown overboard earlier and had washed ashore. But it was too late for some. Here too, several froze to death on the beach. When daylight came just after 5:00 a.m., five men scaled the cliff and found an old shed, eight by twelve feet. Inside was a quantity of hay and they lay down and covered themselves with it in an attempt to get warm. One of the sailors figured if that shed was there, then some houses should be close by, and he decided to look around. His name was Edward Bergeron. Unfortunately there were no houses close by, but he pushed on through the snow regardless, and after two miles, was ready to drop from exhaustion when he saw three men working at the top of a mine shaft. This was the fluorspar mine at St. Lawrence, and the men were Sylvie Edwards, Mike Turpin, and Tom Beck. They ran to the man when they saw him staggering through the snow and were horrified to see he was covered with the black oil. "Where did you come from?" they asked. He could barely speak but managed to tell them he was from a warship ashore below the cliffs with over a hundred men on board, who needed help. Indeed, there were one hundred and fifty-five men on that ship when she struck, not to mention the two hundred and thirty-three on the *Pollux*, which he did not yet know about. The sailor was taken to the nearby mess hall, where there was a large hot stove, a welcome sight for him. The news was quickly spread around and, knowing it was too stormy to put out any boats, seven or eight men took off at once with ropes, and headed for the cove. There was no road; they had to beat their way through the snow. Several men came up from the mine to join the rescue party. Theo Etchegary came across the four men in the shed and told them to walk to the mine head; it wasn't far, he told them, and it was warm in the mess hall and there was lots of food and dry clothes there. They didn't want to leave their buddies on the beach, he was told. "If you stay here, you'll freeze to death," he warned, "and men are already on their way to help your buddies." They were led back to the mine building by Etchegary, who then headed back to the top of the cliff, where he met Tom Beck. They looked down at the shipwreck and were appalled at what they saw through the rain and sleet: the huge warship crashing up and down on the rocks, with forty foot waves smashing over the men hanging on to the railings. Some were jumping overboard and trying to reach a raft bobbing up and down in the oily mess. One man climbed onto it and fell off as a wave hit. He got back on. Theo saw his sixteen-year-old brother, Gus, and their father, Louis, down on the beach helping the survivors ashore. Tom Beck lowered Theo down the icy cliff after he had tied a rope around his waste [*sic*].

At noon it was discovered that a second warship was ashore two miles further along the coast. Mine manager Horwood Farrell closed the mines for the day, and now scores of men from St. Lawrence and nearby Lawn, with horses and sleds, made their way to the two distressed ships. More men were lowered down the cliffs to assist getting the sailors ashore. Some Newfoundlanders even went out shoulder-deep in the freezing muck to drag in sailors who were unable to help themselves, but were kept afloat by their life jackets. A concerted effort was made to get the men up over the cliffs and back to civilization. It was a slow process. Each man had to be tied securely with a rope and gradually pulled up the two to three hundred foot cliff, with five or six men pulling on the ropes. It was found that when they were pulled up too fast, they were bruised and bleeding as they struck small outcroppings of rock on the way along. Most were semi-conscious at this stage and felt very little pain. Those who could still walk were led to the mine building, but most had to be taken by horse and sled. As the blackened, oil-soaked sailors began arriving at the mess hall, the women of the two settlements were alerted, and came with wash tubs, scrub-brushes, soap, food and warm clothes, leaving their teenage children to baby-sit the younger kids. District nurse Sadie Ash was called in and had her hands full attending the injured men. The sailors were stripped of the oil soaked clothes and placed on the mess hall tables, where the ladies began the arduous task of thawing out the half frozen bodies, and scrubbing the black oil from their skin. There was lots of hot water in the mess hall. When cleaned up, the men were given hot soup to bring them back to life.

Meanwhile, the coastal boat, SS *Kyle* had stayed in St. Lawrence over night to wait out the storm, and when the master, Captain Connors, heard about the groundings, he took the steamer out to the wrecks, but found he could do nothing there to help. He immediately brought the ship back to St. Lawrence and ordered the crew ashore with blankets and ropes and axes to help with the rescue operation. In the afternoon two U.S. warships, the USS *Brant* and the USS *Georges E. Badger*, arrived in St. Lawrence from Argentia, and naval doctors and medics were brought to the mine building to further treat the injured. They found the people of Lawn and St. Lawrence had brought much food to the hungry survivors, many leaving their own pantries empty. Several of the sailors had already been cleaned up, given warm clothes, hot soup, and then driven in trucks to various homes in St. Lawrence where they were put to bed. In the mess hall, the scrubbing continued. One of the ladies, Violet Pike, was becoming frustrated. "I can't seem to get the oil off this one!" she said aloud. "Ma'am," said the sailor, opening his eyes, "That's as clean as I get. I'm a black man." Violet was shocked. She had never seen a black man in her life. She smiled and put down the brush. She was relieved to know that at least her work on this man was not in vain. One of the young ladies who helped the victims was nineteen year-old Ena Farrell. She was an office worker, but really had a "nose for news." She felt someone should be taking pictures of the historic happenings. Her mother had given her a five-dollar box camera and a few rolls of film two months earlier, for Christmas. She wanted to go to Chambers Cove and take some snaps, but felt she should not go on this day. I spoke with her in February, 1999, and she told me she thought at the time, that it would just not look right for a young lady to be taking photos of the horror that was going on. (She is now Mrs. Ena Farrell Edwards and is a prominent citizen of St. Lawrence.) The day after the disaster, she put on her skis, and with two other young ladies, went to Lawn Head and snapped the two wrecked warships. She also got shots of men in the process of recovering bodies. Later she photographed funerals of victims and burials in the cemetery at St. Lawrence. I have viewed more than twenty of her historic photographs, and it is my humble opinion that she would have been a top-notch news photographer, in the true sense of the word.

A few days after the tragedy, a lieutenant commander from the U.S. Navy appeared at her door and asked her to pass over the films she'd taken. She refused. He tried to persuade her that for the security of the U.S. Navy, she should comply with his request. She refused again, knowing full well that if she gave them up, even on loan, she would never see them again. Next day another visitor came, this time with an order from the base commander at Argentia, demanding the films. The commander wanted to impress on her the fact that if the enemy got their hands on these pictures, it could be detrimental to the U.S. Navy. She told him not to worry, she would make sure that would never happen. She said to tell the commander that she was sorry she could not comply with his order, but she had taken the pictures with her own camera, on her own film, and so they were hers, and that was that. Smart lady! A week after the disaster, the Associated Press representative in St. John's, Mr. Jeffries of *The Evening Telegram*, requested the films. It was agreed she would send him the films and he would have them developed and send them back to her. She told him they could publish whatever they wished. She sent the rolls to St. John's by registered mail. The store where Miss Farrell worked had a newsstand, and the following week, when she opened the weekly paper *The Montreal Standard*, she was surprised and delighted to see a double-page spread of her pictures with by-line. That was the first time she saw her photos. Later the pictures were returned to her, together with a cheque for $100. Again she was quite pleased, as it never occurred to her that she might get paid. She told me she went right out and bought a good folding camera.

The rescue operations at Lawn Head went on all day, and it was after midnight before the last of the one hundred and eighty-five survivors was hauled to the top of the cliff. When the "round-up" began (which took two days) trucks went about the community, picking up the sailors and taking them back to the warships in St. Lawrence Harbour. There were several stretcher cases, and as these were being carried aboard many young ladies, and older ones too, could be seen walking beside them holding hands with the injured men. A strong bond of friendship had developed in St. Lawrence on these two days.

Bodies kept washing ashore for weeks, and some of the two hundred and three victims were never recovered. Ninety U.S. Navy men were buried in a cemetery in St. Lawrence with full military honors, and forty-eight in Argentia. After the war, all bodies were exhumed and returned to the United States. Over the years, many of the survivors have returned to St. Lawrence to express their gratitude, and some St. Lawrence residents have visited survivors in the United States. In 1988 the town of St. Lawrence held a reunion, and forty United States citizens came to take part. Seventeen were actual survivors, and the others were relatives who wanted to meet the valiant Newfoundlanders who had saved their husbands and fathers. In 1992 an even bigger reunion took place. This time one hundred Americans came along. Again many were survivors, but this time several were retired officers and men of the USS *Wilkes*, the first of the three ships to run aground, and which managed to free herself. The mayor of St. Lawrence, Mr. Wayde Rowsell, and his wife went to New York in 1996 and again in 1998, and on both occasions visited relatives of the survivors. The Rowsells even visited the graves of the men who were originally interred at St. Lawrence and later removed to their final resting place in a Field of Honor in the United States.

Reprinted from *Flashes from the Past: Forty-Two Years Covering the News* by Frank J. Kennedy (Breakwater Books, 2000) by permission of the publisher.

The Sinking of the *Caribou*. October, 1941.

Another wartime disaster I well remember is the sinking of the ferry *Caribou* and the shocking loss of innocent lives. It's very disheartening to realize that when the SS *Caribou* was hit by a German torpedo, that ship was actually a legitimate target, according to the universal rules of war. The *Caribou* was carrying military troops. Notwithstanding, it seems a very cruel act considering the 137 men, women and children who were killed in that disaster. The log of the submarine showed the Germans thought they were attacking a freighter being accompanied by a warship, not that that would have made much difference.

The 2200 ton passenger ferry sailed from North Sydney, Nova Scotia, at 8:00 p.m. on Oct. 13 for an overnight crossing to Port-aux-Basques with 45 crew members and 206 passengers, including 99 servicemen. Some were Royal Air Force men who had just completed training and were coming back to the island on leave before going overseas. Others were army and navy personnel on various assignments. The ship was overcrowded and there were not enough berths for all the women and children. Some servicemen gave up their berths to lady passengers and sat up in the lounge for the night, and that act of generosity was responsible for saving many of their lives.

The *Caribou* was equipped with six lifeboats and four life rafts and before leaving port, all passengers were assigned certain lifeboat stations in case of emergency. However, on that particular night, no lifeboat drill was carried out. By midnight most of the passengers had retired in anticipation of an early arrival at Port-aux-Basques after the ninety-six mile trip across Cabot Strait. Some expressed a premonition of danger and lay on their berths without undressing. Others stayed up late playing cards in the saloon. A few safety-minded men made trips to their assigned life-boat stations so as to be familiar with the route. On the bridge Capt. Ben Tavnor talked with the purser, Tom Fleming. The Captain thought it would have been safer if their escort, the minesweeper HMCS *Grandmere*, sailed along in front of them rather than astern, but these were orders from the Navy. He was also told to sail in a zig-zag pattern to avoid possible torpedoes. Looking out over the ocean, Tom Fleming mentioned what a lovely calm night it was. "Calm, alright," said Tavnor, "but not lovely for us. The smoke is going straight up in the sky and can be seen for miles on a night like this." He was right. Five miles away a German sub had just surfaced to charge batteries. It was 3:00 a.m. and they were only 40 miles from their destination.

The log of the U-*69*, made public after the war, read, *"Oct. 14, 0300 hours NDT Sighted freighter followed by warship. We are preparing to attack."*

In the bright moonlight the *Caribou* was an easy target and at 3:30 a.m. a torpedo hit the starboard side with devastating results. Many passengers died instantly. The ship's boilers blew up, killing everyone in the engine room. The lights went out and there was panic below deck as people tried to find their way up in the darkness. Many could not remember their lifeboat station number and those who went to the starboard side found their lifeboats blown to bits by the torpedo. On the port side two lifeboats that were already hanging out over the side were lowered into the water by the crew. As passengers jumped in, the boats began filling with water. There were holes in the bottom to drain rainwater and someone had neglected to put back the plugs. In the first boat the plugs were found and replaced and that boat got away safely but the second one began sinking and overturned, throwing the unfortunate occupants into the cold water.

At the stern of the *Caribou* the remaining two lifeboats were still on deck attached to the davits, but before they could be swung out over the side, they were filled with people. There was no way the crew could handle the boats now and they implored the passengers to get out so they could pull the boats from the deck and lower them into the water. The frightened people refused to move. The ship was sinking fast and when it went under it pulled the two lifeboats with it as they were still attached to the davits. Purser Tom Fleming had helped many passengers aboard the first lifeboats in the five minutes the *Caribou* remained afloat and was trying to free a life raft when he felt the deck go under. Realizing people are often sucked to their deaths when a ship sinks, he took a deep breath and went down with the ship. But not far. Tom was a strong swimmer and was determined not to die now. With lungs almost bursting he came to the surface, helped in no small way by the lifejacket he was wearing. All around people were clinging to life rafts, pieces of wreckage, and the one lifeboat that managed to stay afloat. Some were crying, others were dying. Still others were shouting the names of loved ones, hoping to hear the reply "I'm here!" Some did. Fleming was the only ship's officer to survive. All the others including Capt. Ben Tavnor and his two sons, Harold and Stanley, were lost.

On board the *Grandmere* the crew heard the explosions and sighted the sub on the surface. The bridge ordered "Full speed ahead," and steered straight for the U-boat, hoping to ram it. The sub crash-dived and barely avoided a collision. The minesweeper immediately dropped a pattern of depth charges but saw no evidence of damage to a submarine. *Grandmere*'s Captain, Lieutenant James Culbert, knew there had to be survivors in the water but was required to follow standing orders and these were basically 'Keep chasing the sub and don't worry about survivors.' The reasoning seems to be that if the minesweeper stopped to pick up survivors, then it too would probably be torpedoed.

After a frustrating and fruitless search, the *Grandmere* returned to the scene of the sinking and as the sun rose at 7:30 a.m., one hundred and three survivors were taken from the water. One man who was saved was R.C.M.P. Corporal W.B. Rouse, who was returning to Newfoundland to be married. Strangely enough, although the ill-fated ship was headed for Newfoundland, all the survivors were brought back to Nova Scotia. Two men died before they reached land. Later that day many fishermen from the Port-aux-Basques area went out in their long liners and recovered several bodies.

Dr. Paul O'Neill ... told me that his mother, my aunt Jo, and another lady were the only women on the previous trip of the *Caribou* and as far as she knew, all the other passengers were military men.

Newfoundland Attacked by German U-Boats. March 1942.

On a quiet, cool afternoon in March, 1942, residents of the city were startled at the sound of 500 lbs. of dynamite exploding in the Narrows. "They must be blasting away some rocks to make the entrance to the harbour deeper," suggested one observer in the east end of the city. Looking towards the narrows he saw a cloud of black smoke rising from the sea near Fort Amherst. Two minutes later there was a flash of orange flame and a great plume of water and rocks went skyward near the Outer Battery. Two German torpedoes had exploded in the Narrows. A submarine just outside the harbour had attempted to sink a large merchant ship at anchor awaiting a convoy. Fortunately the commander's aim was not good and the missiles hit both sides of the Narrows with no serious damage. Immediately the alarm was sounded and guns were manned at Fort Amherst and on Signal Hill. Spotters were at their action stations but there was no sign of the enemy and nothing to shoot at. The sub had made a clean getaway.

The Bell Island Attack. September 1942.

Six months later and 14 miles due west of the Narrows, on Sept. 5, 1942, it was a different story when two 'ore boats' were sunk in Conception Bay near Bell Island with the loss of 29 lives. In November two more ships were torpedoed in the same location and 40 men died. In the first incident, two steamships already loaded with iron ore were at anchor off Bell Island's Lance Cove waiting to join a convoy, and their captains were attending a secret meeting in St. John's making arrangements to meet that convoy. The first victim was the SS *Saganaga*, with 8800 tons of ore in her holds. She went to the bottom in less than a minute, taking 29 crew members with her. There had been no sign of trouble until a torpedo exploded amidships and another a few seconds later finished the job. It was just after 11:00 a.m. on a calm, overcast day. The chief engineer of the nearby *Lord Strathcona*, now in charge in the absence of the captain and realizing they were "sitting ducks," gave the order to man the lifeboats and abandon ship, not only to save themselves but to rescue some of the survivors of the *Saganaga* who were swimming around amongst the wreckage.

As they were preparing to launch the lifeboats they heard and felt a bump. Something had hit the bottom of their ship. They thought it might be a torpedo that failed to explode. There was no panic. The men carried out their duties just as they had often done in practice runs, but this time as they were rowing away from the ship there was a tremendous explosion behind them and their ship disappeared in less than two minutes. When a ship is loaded with iron ore, and a hole as big as a house is blown in the side of the ship, the rush of water sends that ship to the bottom very quickly, quicker than a ship with any other cargo. All the crew of the *Lord Strathcona* escaped injury, due certainly in part to a miscalculation on the part of the commander of the sub that did the sinking.

Submarine's Log.

The log of that submarine, the *U-513*, made public after the war, shows that shortly after sinking the first ship, the commander decided to come up and look around. He was not aware that he was now directly underneath the second ship and as the sub began rising it hit the keel of that ship. He knew the bump would be felt on board the ship and expecting depth charges to be dropped, let the sub sink to the bottom of the bay in 150 feet of water. He was relieved to find the bottom in that location was soft, not rocky as his charts indicated. In the state of panic the sub had hit hard. After twenty anxious minutes, expecting the worst, there was a slight leak but no sound of depth charges and the sub quietly moved ahead and came up to periscope level. Then with the *Lord Strathcona* lined up in the crosshairs, two torpedoes were fired and both found their mark. The ship sank in one and a half minutes with not a soul on board.

Periscope Sighted.

The periscope was sighted by other ships in the area and the Mercantile Navy men on board went into action. First off the mark was the SS *Rose Castle*, a coal boat at the Scotia Pier. She came out with guns blazing. Four-inch shells were exploding in the water all around the periscope, which quickly disappeared as the sub beat a hasty retreat. Many shells ricocheted off the calm water and landed in Beachy Cove, St. Phillip's and Broad Cove. People living there thought they were being attacked but fortunately no one was hurt. A rumor circulated that the Home Defence guns on the island were meant to guard against air attacks and could not be aimed down to the sea from their 300 foot high location and their shells were going straight across the bay. This was not so. These guns also fired shells at the last sighted location of the periscope and in fact, several unexploded shells picked up in the above-mentioned settlements were turned over to the authorities and were found not to match the type fired from the island.

Spreading the News.

Word of these attacks spread like wildfire throughout St. John's and it was reported next day that there were German Submarines trapped in Conception Bay and being hunted down by warships. That day being Sunday, hundreds of curious people went to Topsail and Portugal Cove to view the activity. We went to Topsail and there were two small warships cruising up and down the bay and at one point a bomber flew low over the water. Many spectators hoped to see bombs dropping but that did not happen as the sub was long gone. Actually, shortly after the sinking the previous day the captain of the Bell Island ferry reported seeing the swirling of a sub passing along under water on its way out the bay. The log of that U-boat also shows that before the two ships were sunk, two torpedoes were launched but failed to make contact. The Commander wrote they sank to the bottom. That would mean that to this very day there are two torpedoes rusting away somewhere out there, each containing 500 lbs. of dynamite. Monday's newspapers carried only this very vague item regarding the tragedy:

"It was announced by the Naval Authorities yesterday that a submarine attack was made in Newfoundland coastal water. Further details of the accident have not been released."

Second Attack. November, 1942.

Two months later the Germans were back. A different submarine this time, but with the same deadly mission. It was the *U-518* on its maiden voyage from Germany and it picked Newfoundland as the first stop. Late at night on Nov. 2, residents of the Front on Bell Island were awakened by an explosion that shook them in their beds. They knew what it had to be. Another torpedo. This time the Scotia Pier was blown apart by a torpedo intended for the SS *Anna A* [*sic*], tied up there to unload coal. In the darkness, the sub commander, not realizing he had missed his target, lined up an ore carrier, the SS *Rose Castle*. That ship had narrowly escaped being sunk in September during the first attack and had actually fired at the U-boat, but this time her luck ran out and she went to the bottom with a loss of 28 lives, including several Newfoundlanders one of whom was from St. John's, a Mr. H. King. By now the bay was lit up with flares fired from the island by the Home Defence. The U-boat quickly submerged, but before so doing fired one last torpedo at the 6000 ton Free French ship *PLM 26*, which being already loaded with ore, went down in a few seconds with twelve of the fifty crew members. Searchlights on the island kept scanning the waters in the immediate area but that sub was not seen until well after daylight when a patrol bomber sighted it near Cape Race heading out to sea. A bombing attack was immediately initiated but before that could be accomplished, the infamous Newfoundland fog moved in and the sub escaped once more.

That U-boat continued its mission of destruction for more than two years until April 22, 1945, just three weeks before the war ended, when it was sent to the bottom of the Atlantic with all hands near the Azores by a U.S. Destroyer. At that time, however, the commander who was responsible for the tragedies in Conception Bay had already been retired and was replaced by another ill-fated officer.

Other Wartime Memories.

The Commission of Government ordered a complete blackout for St. John's and all points east of Holyrood in April, 1942. Householders were ordered to cover all windows with shutters, dark blinds, or blackout material and remove bulbs from their porch lights. All motor vehicles were required to have shields on their headlights so that no light was visible from above. Drivers could then see the road only a few yards ahead and thus had to drive very slowly at night. As well, cars had to have four-inch wide bands of white paint on all fenders. Sometimes in summer my older brother took us trouting on the Salmonier Line, where we fished till dark. While driving back home he used the full headlights until we reached Holyrood. Then he put the shields in place and literally crawled back to town. This happened only a couple of times and after that he made sure we got back home before dark.

In town, storekeepers not only were required to have their windows covered, they had to have a dark curtain inside the doors so that when opened, no light was visible from the outside. There was some difficulty walking the streets at nighttime when there was no moon. People kept walking into telephone poles. It turned out to be a great explanation when some guys got into a fight downtown and came home with a black eye. "I walked into a telephone pole." It got so bad the government ordered utility companies to paint white stripes around the wooden poles. The blackout was strictly enforced and a volunteer group of air raid wardens monitored the situation. These men, many of them turned down for military service because of age or other reasons, were issued stirrup pumps and buckets of sand to help douse fires in case of an incendiary bomb attack. Air raid sirens were located on towers in various locations in the city, although we had no air raid shelters. Nevertheless every few days or nights the wailing of a practice alert was heard and residents would say "Peter is at it again." Peter Cashin, the renowned politician, was head of the Home Defence organization. The blackout regulations were relaxed somewhat in August 1943, and street lighting, prohibited entirely during the blackout, was permitted at half the brightness of pre-war conditions. The Light and Power Company found that in the previous fourteen months 150 street lights had been destroyed by vandals.

Car drivers had other problems not related to the blackout. Tires were rationed. Taxis and other commercial vehicles owners could buy new tires but owners of private cars were not permitted to buy them and it was a common sight to see a driver stopped along the side of a road fixing a flat tire. Some men even bought old cars just to get the tires. Tea and sugar were rationed with only a limited amount being allowed for each family member, including children. Ration coupons were issued by the government and had to be surrendered to grocery stores upon the purchase of these products. I remember not liking strong tea and trading my coupons with my siblings for their sugar coupons.

All outgoing mail was opened at the post offices and censored. Any reference to military personnel was deleted, even if it was such a seemingly harmless remark such as "It's nice to have my brother John home on leave." The slogan was "Loose lips sink ships." All photofinishers were instructed to destroy any photos showing coastline or shipping of any kind. My photo of the *Edmund B. Alexander*. . .would have been destroyed had I taken the film to a regular photofinisher, but being an amateur photographer at the time, I developed it myself.

St. John's, being the most easterly port in North America, was often the starting point for trans-Atlantic convoys and many merchant ships from the mainland stopped here to await naval escort to Britain. Many warships lay at anchor in the harbour waiting for what was considered a full complement of ships for a convoy. Consequently sometimes there were thousands of sailors roaming the streets. A Canadian government official who visited the city claimed in a report that there were 8,000 Canadian sailors in port and they were responsible for excessive drunkenness and brawling in downtown St. John's. He went on to say the sailors smashed so many store windows that the store owners had the windows boarded up. That man must have been downtown only at night and didn't realize that the windows were boarded up because of the blackout regulations, not because they were being broken. Local police were kept busy regardless and were helped out by the Canadian Naval Shore Patrol who also patrolled the city. The U.S. soldiers from Fort Pepperrell and later U.S. Airmen were not entirely innocent and they had police patrols in place as well.

Security was beefed up considerably after the disastrous fire at the K. of C. Hostel on Dec. 12, 1942, which killed 99 people, many of them servicemen. That tragedy was described in detail in a previous book, *Flashes From the Past*, and I will not go into it here except to say that an inquiry found the fire was definitely arson, possibly by an enemy agent. Evidence was also discovered at the Red Triangle Club that preparations had been made to torch that building as well. The telephone exchange building on Duckworth Street and the Light and Power substation on the South Side were put under 24-hour-guard for fear of sabotage, as was the power station at Petty Harbour.

End of the War. May 1945.

World War II came to a close on May 8, 1942 [*sic*], when Germany surrendered to the Allies, but not before nine hundred Newfoundlanders had paid the supreme sacrifice. These brave men gave their lives so that we who are left behind may see peace in our day. Their names will be forever remembered.

Many Newfoundlanders stationed in England during the war courted and married English ladies and brought them back to Newfoundland when the war ended. Stories are told of how some of the men enticed their brides back to this land of milk and honey. Some blushing brides were in for a letdown. A sailor from the Northern Peninsula had just returned to the island with his bride, and they were standing at a streetcar stop on Water Street near the Red Triangle Club. After waiting nearly ten minutes the lady was overheard remarking ... in a fine British accent "Well, I hope the streetcar service is better than this in Flower's Cove."

Reprinted from *A Corner Boy Remembers: Growing Up in St. John's* by Frank J. Kennedy (Breakwater Books, 2006) by permission of the publisher.

Frank J. Kennedy.

Biographical Sketch

Taking up photography as a hobby while in high school, Frank Kennedy owned his first camera at age 16. He worked as a professional photographer first during WWII, in Gander. Moving back to St. John's, he worked for a dry goods firm and reverted to 'amateur' photographer status. Beginning in March, 1944, he was a reporter for *The Daily News* for 20 years. His front-page April Fool's Day photos were created long before digital editing became the norm and were the cause of great discussions whether they were "real". He took up movie making as a hobby and in 1964 that, too, paid off, as he was hired by the Canadian Broadcasting Corporation as a motion-picture cameraman. He filmed for CBC-TV for the next 22 years and covered a wide array of historical and interesting events in the Province's history.

9

The Evening Telegram, Wartime Topics.

Introduction by Paul J. Johnson.

The Evening Telegram, started in 1879, is "Newfoundland's Oldest Newspaper". For 130 years, it has been a most reliable, highly respected source of news for generations of our people. *The Telegram* has faithfully lived up to its intention to report and editorialize on the most timely and important subjects, in a manner that is accurate, honest, and objective.

This Chapter of "*The Evening Telegram*, Wartime Topics" relates to our military, patriotic, political, economic, and human-interest happenings, during World War II. These were matters of concern to Newfoundlanders, and to the others who experienced what happened here - - before, during, and after the war.

The sixteen articles are abridgements from *The Telegram*, chosen by Aidan Maloney and Paul Johnson for relevance to the overall *Anthology*, and used with the permission of *The Telegram*.

Evening Telegram **– November 21, 1939.**

Newfoundland to Make War Contribution, In New Tax Increase of $ 750,000.

Commissioner for Finance Announces Increased Taxes on Income, Gasoline and Matches.

Hon. J.H. Penson, Commissioner for Finance and Customs, delivered an address on the subject of "Newfoundland Finance in Time of War".

The conditions with which the British Empire is faced today are among the gravest ever known in its history. The British Empire is struggling for its very existence. It is apparent that the common responsibility resting upon all the peoples of the British Commonwealth is deeply and widely recognised. I do not think you would wish me to pass over the special links and special obligations which bind us with the United Kingdom. The sense of loyalty and devotion to the Crown has long been a characteristic of this country. In the present war our very livelihood in Newfoundland is affected by the struggle. The attack on British shipping involves people here. Newfoundland is primarily dependent on sea-borne trade. Financial strength may prove to be a decisive factor in the present conflicts.

Evening Telegram **– June 7, 1940.**

Newfoundland's Strategic Position.

Major George Feilding Elliott, noted United States Military expert, speculates on the future moves of a Germany "flushed with a blitzkrieg victory." Major Elliott remarks, "Hitler might try to move directly against the United States. Newfoundland could be the centre of air domination of the North Atlantic." It has required a war of such startling dimensions to direct expert attention to the importance of the strategical position that Newfoundland occupies.

Evening Telegram – **June 12, 1940.**

Patriotic Parade Biggest St. John's Has Ever Seen.

The Patriotic Parade held last night shows that the comradeship born of the Great War forged a link that can never be broken. Thousands of people lined the route, and there was imparted a deep feeling of loyalty to the Empire's cause. Weather conditions were perfect. The number on parade was estimated at 3,000 and it made a most impressive sight.

Speech of The Governor Sir Humphrey Walwyn.

"The spirit of Newfoundland today is as brave as it was in 1914. The Empire is going through the darkest hour of her history, but we shall win through. I know I can rely on Newfoundland not to lose faith, but to be of good heart and to face the present situation calmly, with courage, and confidence in our ultimate victory".

Speech of His Worship, Mayor A.G. Carnell, C.B.E.

"My heart is filled with pride as I see this splendid gathering tonight and this rally has been designed to make an open demonstration of our loyalty and our affection for the Great Empire of which our own dear country is a part. We are contributing in a very material way to the ultimate victory. Our young men have responded nobly to the call, with loyalty, courage and devotion".

Speech by C. J. Fox, K.C., Vice-President of the Nfld. Patriotic Association.

"We are now bringing to a close a manifestation of deep-seated loyalty and patriotic fervour and devotion on the part of a solidly united people, [to] truly reflect their traditional sentiments of unquestioned and unquestioning devotion to their King and Country. All sections of our people joined in this never-to-be forgotten exhibition of patriotism – this magnificent open profession of national faith and unity. Great Britain and her Empire are today fighting for their very life – against mighty, merciless and unscrupulous foes".

Evening Telegram – **August 9, 1940.**

Ottawa Sees Closer Relationship Between Newfoundland and Canada.

(Canadian Press Copyright).

It is pointed out that the garrisoning of Canadian troops in Newfoundland makes possible personal contacts which will bring about still closer relationships between the countries.

The future political implications of Canada's active participation in the defence of British territories on this side of the Atlantic give rise to speculation in many quarters, particularly in regard to Newfoundland.

Canada has a financial as well as military interest in Newfoundland and the presence of Canadian troops there will tend to make Canadians generally more familiar with the country.

Evening Telegram – **September 4, 1940.**

Britain Receives Fifty Destroyers For Leasing Bases to United States.

Bases in Newfoundland, Freely Leased for 99 Years.

President Roosevelt notified Congress yesterday that Britain and the United States had reached an agreement whereby the U.S. would obtain naval and air bases. The right to bases in Newfoundland was obtained without payment, but compensation will be paid to private individuals whose land will be chosen for the bases.

"The right to bases in Newfoundland and Bermuda are gifts – generously given and gladly received" – the President said in a special message to Congress.

Evening Telegram **– September 4, 1940.**

Certain Areas Will Be Leased to United States.

The following announcement was issued by the Newfoundland [Commission of] Government last night:

The grant by Newfoundland and Bermuda is expressly disassociated from any rental or monetary payment. No question of sovereign rights arises. Considerable negotiations still remain to take place, and the force of the views expressed by the Newfoundland Government interests is fully appreciated by the United Kingdom Government.

The establishment of American naval and air bases in Newfoundland will be of the utmost importance to Newfoundland whose geographical position is such that she would be exposed to the first attack by an aggressor from the East.

Evening Telegram **– January 3, 1941.**

The American Leases.

In the opinion of *The Telegram*, as far as can be learned the bases are a gift, not made by Newfoundland, but by the United Kingdom Government. There is nothing whatever to show that before the agreement was made, the Government of Newfoundland was even consulted.

With Responsible Government functioning, the British Government would not have attempted to assume such authority. Even a proposal to lease to a foreign Power would have raised protests against what would have been regarded as a usurpation of sovereign rights.

As this paper has been officially informed on several occasions, nothing is known regarding the terms. The agreement between the British and American Governments has been finalized.

Evening Telegram – **February 21, 1941.**

600 Men Employed at U.S. Army Base at Quidi Vidi. Employment for 1000 Men Expected.

Wage Rates. The hourly wage rates approved by the U.S. War Department are as follows [examples]:

Brick Layer	60 ¢	Plumbers Helper	30 ¢
Carpenter Foreman	75 ¢	Electrician	60 ¢
Carpenter	40 ¢	Labourer	30 ¢
Dozer Operator	50 ¢	Mason Stone	60 ¢
Painter	50 ¢	Mechanic	40 ¢
Plumber	60 ¢	Structural Steel Worker	40 ¢

Evening Telegram – **June 22, 1942.**

What Further Is Leased ?

According to a Commission of Government communique, "An Act to authorize the execution of a supplementary Lease to the United States of America" had been recommended to His Excellency the Governor for enactment.

The declared policy of the Commission of Government in the past was that no measure in which public interests were concerned would be enacted until the opportunity for comment had been afforded.

The Commission of Government as trustees have no power to pass over to any other country one inch of territory. If any such legislation is enacted at the dictation of the Dominions Office, the latter is acting in complete disregard of those principles.

The Commission of Government displays a deplorable indifference to the view held by Newfoundland. Either that, or the Government have come to regard their judgment as so profound as to be above question. As to that, let their record speak.

Evening Telegram – **August 29, 1942.**

Headlight Masks.

Penalties for breaches of the Blackout Regulations as regards motor vehicles have been stiffened, and may result in suspension of a driver's license for as long as 6 months, up to 12 months imprisonment with hard labour and or a fine up to $ 5000, the Director of Civil Defence has pointed out.

Evening Telegram – **March 4, 1943.**

Taxation By Decree.

The Commission would be wise to take due cognizance of the fact that in no country in the civilized world is it possible for a government effectively and efficiently to carry out the duties entrusted to it, if by its actions it outrages general sentiment. The imposition of increased taxation, which will be retroactive in effect, and that has aroused considerable resentment. The action, in so far as it applies to Excess Profits, is taken at a time when firms have closed the year's accounts. In the case of private individuals, they are most unreasonably informed that the Government intends to exact from their earnings a further amount.

Let it not be thought that, because the people of Newfoundland have no voice whatever in the administration of public affairs, they are without the means of seeking redress of grievances. They still have the right, as old as the Magna Carta – the right of the subject to petition the King.

Evening Telegram **– March 29, 1943.**

The Supreme Blunder.

What crisis had arisen to justify the imposition of additional taxation by the extraordinary device resorted to by the Commissioner for Finance? Notwithstanding, we may add, the approval by the [British] Secretary of State for the Dominions of the Government's action.

The views of a disfranchised people, the Commissioner felt assured, could be as completely ignored in that matter as were their objections to his high-handed device to pad his revenue returns. With an amassed surplus of $ 11,000,000 and high hopes of being able substantially to increase that amount, there is no telling what method may next be applied to wring further taxes from the public.

Appointed with the special purpose of restoring Newfoundland's industrial stability, the Commission of Government has not included since its inception a single member with the knowledge and experience necessary to be capable of dealing with industrial problems.

Evening Telegram **– April 13, 1943.**

Restoration of Self-Government.

In the [British] House of Commons today Right Hon. Clement Attlee, Secretary of State for the Dominions, announced that he was seriously considering the matter of restoring Self-Government to Newfoundland.

This is the first time since Commission of Government was instituted that there has been any inclination displayed by the Government of the United Kingdom to reconsider this important matter. The Commission of Government has itself to blame for the decision announced today which foreshadows its end. The restoration of self-government carries with it grave responsibilities.

***Evening Telegram* – May 6, 1943.**

Goodwill Mission.

The goodwill mission, which the Secretary of State for Dominion Affairs is sending to this country, would seem from the official announcement to be just what its name implies. Mr. Attlee told the House of Commons that the mission will be of "an informal and goodwill character". It is noted that the London *Times* is severely critical of the appointment of the mission which it regards as likely to disappoint the people of this country and because it "would be a mistake to ignore the widespread discontent with the existing system".

***Evening Telegram* – July 15, 1943.**

Newfoundland's Political Future.

"Canada is prepared to consider sympathetically any clear expression on the part of Newfoundland to become a Canadian province, but the Dominion [of Canada] Government feels that this is a move that must be first initiated by the people of Newfoundland." The above statement was made in the Canadian House of Commons by Prime Minister Mackenzie King.

The Prime Minister was of the opinion that the first move should be made by Newfoundland. Mr. Mackenzie King has refrained from saying anything that could be construed as suggesting that Canada had designs on this country; he has at least made it apparent that when and if Newfoundland chose to initiate negotiations to that end, the Dominion [of Canada] would receive such an approach in a friendly spirit.

Evening Telegram – **December 6, 1943.**

Statement in the [British] House of Commons.

By Mr. Emrys-Evans, Under-Secretary of State for the Dominions, on Newfoundland's Status and Restoration of Self-Government.

The Newfoundland Government appealed to the United Kingdom Government for the assistance and a Royal Commission was set up under Lord Amulree. They recommended the temporary suspension of the constitution till such time as the Island might become self-supporting.

The Newfoundland Bill of 1933 was introduced into Parliament. Among the recommendations of the Royal Commission, reproduced in the Newfoundland Act, is the following: "It will be understood that as soon as the Island's difficulties are overcome and the country is again self-supporting, Responsible Government on the request from the people of Newfoundland would be restored".

In the first place H.M. Government had to be satisfied that the Island was self-supporting and in the second place there must be a request from the people of Newfoundland. It can be claimed that the Island has paid its way for the last three years. With regard to the second condition, it cannot be said that there is yet any evidence of a general wish for the restoration of self-Government. There is certainly no desire for any far-reaching change until after the war and until the Newfoundland public have had an opportunity of assessing their prospects in the post-war world. There is a widespread feeling that the return by even one single step to full Responsible Government would be a great mistake. Opinion is much divided as to what form of self-Government or what form of Government would best suit the Island's future.

(continued)

(continued)

Owing to the existing abnormal conditions caused by the war, which make it impossible for the Newfoundland people as a whole to come to a considered conclusion as to the Island's future prospects, there should be no change in the present form of Government while the war lasts. As soon as practicable after the end of the war, machinery must be provided for enabling the Newfoundland people to examine the future of the Island and to express their considered views as to the form of Government they desire. In the meantime the Secretary of State will take soundings in order to ascertain what kind of machinery would be acceptable to the Newfoundland people.

If the general wish should be for the continuance of the present form of Government or for some change of system which would fall short of full Responsible Government, we shall be prepared to examine such proposals. Possible methods might include, for example, the setting up of some national convention, but this is for further consideration.

I cannot close what I have to say without paying a tribute to the work of the Commission of Government. The Commission of Government unsustained by the advice and support of Parliament has successfully brought the Island through the difficult years since the suspension of the constitution.

***Evening Telegram* – May 4, 1944.**

Newfoundland Affairs Debated in House of Lords.

LONDON, May 3 (Reuter's) – Lord Ammon, one of the British parliamentary mission which visited Newfoundland last year, asked the Government in the House of Lords today for progress on the report on the constitutional position of Newfoundland and their arrangements for the post-war economic development of the island. He said social and economic conditions on the island were no advertisement for the British Empire or the American continent. Some of the worst housing conditions anywhere in the world were in Newfoundland.

He therefore suggested a fair sized loan with low interest or free of interest for the development of a road system, housing and agriculture. There ought to be a big market for Newfoundland exports in the United States. The country's mineral resources included probably the biggest iron ore deposit in the world.

Lord Ammon asked the government for the assurance that hope would be held out for some restoration of self-government and the development of a better economic future for Newfoundland. Viscount Bennett, former Prime Minister of Canada, said there was no one not in favour of restoration of her self-government but he thought it would be a mistake if it were granted hurriedly.

Lord Brabazon thought there was general regret that in the gathering of Dominions Prime Ministers there was not one from the oldest Dominion, Newfoundland. As an aviation expert Lord Brabazon said Newfoundland provides a halfway house between London, the United States and Canada. Lord Beaverbrook, he said, had stated the Newfoundland route was the most important route in the world.

(continued)

(continued)

Lord Brabazon hoped that after the war the aerodromes on which a vast amount of British, American, and Canadian money had been spent, would revert to the sovereignty of Newfoundland and no one else.

Lord Cranborne added, "Our main object is that the Newfoundland people after the war in Europe should choose their own course for themselves". Lord Cranborne said he had arranged for two members of the Newfoundland Commission of Government to visit Britain shortly to go with him personally into the whole matter of the most suitable form of machinery which might then be set up for enabling the Newfoundland people to review their position and give expression to their wishes.

World War II and Our Newfoundland Seamen.

Over 700 Brave Men Paid the Supreme Sacrifice.

Introduction by Paul J. Johnson.

The family, friends, and comrades of Newfoundland sailors who died while serving in the Royal or Merchant Navies, usually had an especially sorrowful bereavement. In very few cases was there a final resting place, gravestone, or monument to visit, to feel a sense of closure. A watery grave never enables paying last respects, much less holding a commemorative service.

In the absence of action by Canadian Veterans Affairs, the Newfoundland Merchant Marine and Naval Associations decided it was long since time to create a fitting monument, to bear the names of all their deceased comrades.

Responding to the approach of each Association, the Johnson Family Foundation and the Marine Institute of Memorial University were tremendously proud to enable the noble ambitions of each Association. The Associations completed the arduous work of gathering and recording the complete and accurate list of those who died (333 in the Merchant Marine, and 373 in Naval fatalities).

Johnson Family Foundation took the lead in the design, with funding from the Foundation, the Province, and City of St. John's. Construction was by the Grand Concourse Authority. The two Memorials comprise a unified, circular monument that looks out on the Atlantic Ocean and the Narrows. There is no more fitting place than the Marine Institute for visitation, memorial services, and for constant observation by thousands of young people pursuing training in their own careers for the challenges and enjoyment of the sea.

SUPREME SACRIFICES

Merchant Marine

Abbott, John
Abbott, William
Adams, Alfred
Anderson, Arthur
Anderson, Edward
Anderson, Elias
Anderson, Leonard
Anderson, William
Andrews, Frank
Armstrong, Michael
Aylward, Thomas
Babstock, Charles
Bailey, Malcolm
Baird, Alexander
Barnes, Lester
Barrett, Israel
Barry, James
Barry, John
Bearns, William
Bennett, Anthony
Bennett, Bertram
Bennett, John
Billard, Maxwell
Birmingham, Llewellyn
Bishop, Lloyd
Blackmore, James
Blagdon, Charles
Blake, Francis
Blake, Howard
Blake, John
Bond, Arthur
Bond, Eric
Boone, Victor
Bowdridge, Frederick
Brenton, Thomas
Brinton, William
Brockerville, John
Brushett, Ernest
Bryant, Samuel
Buckingham, Thomas
Bullen, Joseph
Bullen, Joseph Sr.
Burke, Martin
Burt, Frederick
Burton, Brendan
Butler, John
Cake, Edwin
Candow, James
Carberry, Maurice
Carew, Gordon
Carew, Michael
Carroll, John
Carter, Allister
Carter, Arthur
Carter, George
Carter, Lewis
Carter, William
Cave, William
Ceasar, Austin
Chafe, Albert
Chapman, Basil
Chaulk, Ross
Christopher, William
Churchill, John
Clarke, Cecil
Clarke, Gordon
Clarke, Hazekiah
Cleary, Albin
Coffin, Bert
Coffin, Elias
Coffin, James
Coles, George
Collier, Chester
Collier, Samuel
Collier, Thomas
Cooney, Richard
Cooper, William
Critchell, Joseph
Crocker, George
Croucher, Horace
Cullen, Nicholas
Cunning, George
Curtis, Archibald
Curtis, George
Cutler, Howard
Delaney, Patrick
Dempsey, Edward
Dicks, D.
Dicks, Otto
Domalain, Michael
Dominaux, Charles
Dominey, John
Downey, Francis
Doyle, Robert
Dunn, Adam
Dwyer, Vincent
Ebsary, John
Edwards, George
Ellesworth, James
Evans, Thomas
Fagan, Cyril
Feehan, Henry
Feehan, Richard
Feltham, Richard
Fifield, Chesley

Fillier, William
Fitzpatrick, Bridget
Fleet, William
Foley, Patrick
Ford, Cecil
Ford, Charles
Forsey, Aaron
Forsey, Robert
Fortune, Walter
Fowler, Stephen
Fowles, George
Fowlow, Harvey
French, Maxwell
French, Thomas
Fry, Hubert
Gabriel, Albert
Gale, George
Gale, Jerome
Gillett, Arthur
Goodyear, Charles
Goodyear, John
Goodyear, Reginald
Gordon, Paul
Gosse, Charles
Gosse, Daniel
Gosse, David
Gosse, Timothy
Green, Harvey
Green, John
Green, Leo
Guy, Kenneth
Hall, William
Hann, Clarence
Hann, Harry
Hardiman, Cecil
Harding, Ambrose
Harding, Benjamin
Harding, Kenneth
Hardy, Charles
Harris, Alexander
Harte, John
Hartson, Thomas
Hickey, John
Hicks, Otto
Hillier, John
Hofgaard, Neils
Hogan, William
Holden, Maurice
Hollett, William
Hollmans, Alexander
Hopen, George
Horan, Malachy
Howell, Edgebert
Humphries, Charles
Hurley, Edward
Hynes, Arthur
Ingram, Howard
Inkpen, Nelson
Ivimey, T.
Jackman, Joseph
Jensen, William
Kavanagh, James
Kavanagh, Maurice
Kavanagh, Walter
Kean, Russell
Kearley, Horatio
Kearley, William
Keeping, Cecil
Keeping, Otto
Kendell, George
King, Henry
King, Richard
Knight, Arthur
Laing, William
Langmead, William
Leadingham, John
LeDrew, Alexander
Lee, Edward
Loader, Blowers
Lomond, Victor
Lowe, Roy
Luther, Donald
MacAuley, Patrick
MacDougall, Michael
MacSween, John
Mallay, James
Mare, Robert
Marshall, Benjamin
Marshall, George
Martin, Guy
Matthews, Archibald
Mayo, George
Mayo, Stanley
McDonald, Thomas
McEvoy, Ronald
Mills, George
Mills, James
Monster, James
Moore, James
Moores, Charley
Morgan, John
Morgan, Walter
Morgan, William
Moulton, Sefton
Moyst, Thomas
Mullins, Clarence
Munden, Ernest
Murrins, Joseph
Murrins, William
Nelson, Oswald
Nichols, John
Nolan, Robert
O'Brien, David
O'Brien, James

O'Brien, Michael
O'Brien, Ronald
O'Dea, Andrew
O'Driscoll, Albert
O'Driscoll, Andrew
O'Halligan, Richard
O'Hanlon, Charles
O'Neil, Christopher
O'Neil, Gilbert
O'Neil, James
Osmond, William
Owens, Robert
Paul, Gordon
Payton, Joseph
Pearcey, Charles
Pearcey, Samuel
Penney, Charles
Perry, Chesley
Picco, Ralph
Pieroway, Charles
Pike, Donald
Pike, James
Plowman, Israel
Poole, Reuben
Power, Patrick
Power, Pierce
Prosper, James
Purtin, Charles
Quigley, Augustus
Quigley, Edward
Raike, Samuel
Randell, William
Reynolds, Chesley
Richards, Joseph
Roberts, John
Roberts, Lester
Roberts, Owen
Roberts, Thomas
Rodgers, Lester
Rose, Alonzel
Rose, Simeon
Ryan, Patrick
Samms, William
Sansome, Gideon
Savoury, Charles
Savoury, Silas
Scannell, James
Sceans, Leslie
Shaw, Carl
Sheaves, Israel
Sheppard, James
Sheppard, Hubert
Shirley, Roy
Short, Hubert
Skanes, Leslie
Skeard, John
Skeard, Thomas
Slade, Walter
Smith, John
Smith, Michael
Snow, Henry
Snow, Sutherland
Snow, William
Sparrow, Patrick
Spiteri, Joseph
Spracklin, Ralph
Spurrell, Hezikiah
Squires, Bertram
Squires, Joseph
Squires, Richard
Stockman, James
Stone, Phillip
Stone, Roy
Stratton, Hubert
Strickland, Albert
Strickland, Garfield
Sutton, William
Tavener, Benjamin
Tavener, Harold
Tavener, Stanley
Taylor, Eric
Thomas, Arthur
Thomas, Arthur H.
Thomas, George
Thorne, Henry
Thorne, Kenneth
Thornhill, Abram
Thornhill, Andrew
Thornhill, George
Thorton, George
Throwbridge, James
Tibbo, Henry
Tiller, George
Tiller, William
Tobin, James
Tobin, Martin
Vallis, Chesley
Vatcher, Arthur
Vatcher, Victor
Vokey, George
Wade, Thomas
Walters, Patrick
Walton, Jack
West, Walter
White, Herbert
White, John
Whiteway, John
Wicks, James
Williams, Albert
Winslow, Cecil
Woods, Ignatius
Wylie, Harry
Yard, Stephen
Young, Edward

SUPREME SACRIFICES

Royal Navy

Alexander, Joseph M.
Ash, John E.
Ash, William R.
Austin, Allister C.
Avery, Wilson
Baggs, William F.
Baker, Andrew L.
Baker, George
Ballam, Clifford
Barnes, Harry G.
Barry, Francis F.
Bartlett, Fintan E.
Bath, Frederick P.
Beckett, Oscar
Bennett, John G.
Bennett, Stanley
Bennett, Wallace F.
Bishop, Alexander
Bishop, Eli M.
Bishop, Thomas F.
Blagdon, Hubert
Blanchard, Richard W.
Blandford, Darius C.
Boland, Alexander S.
Bond, Albert C.
Bowdridge, Gordon
Bown, Charles
Branton, George N.
Brewer, Arthur W.
Brewer, George
Bright, Walter S.
Brinston, Douglas V.
Brinston, Gordon
Brown, Heber S.
Burke, William C.
Bursey, Graham
Butler, Aubrey B.
Butler, Ernest
Butler, John E.
Butler, William A.
Butt, Elijah C.
Byrne, Gerald A.
Cahill, Patrick
Canning, Weston K.
Carpenter, Clyde
Carpenter, James R.
Chafe, Robert
Chislett, Percy E.
Churchill, Thomas
Clouter, Sydney H.
Coady, Ronald J.
Cole, James
Combden, Edward
Combden, James P.
Connolly, John M.
Connors, Fergus B.
Conway, Philip T.
Coombs, Albert
Corbett, Michael
Cornect, Algernon J.
Costello, William
Costello, William J.
Cox, Frank A.
Crane, Edward C.
Crane, John W.
Critch, Michael J.
Crocker, William C.
Cross, Frank
Cross, Joseph G.
Crummey, Edwin W.
Cull, Andrew J.
Cull, John R.
Cullimore, Elijah
Currie, Thomas W.
Davis, Herbert A.
Davis, Reginald G.
Dawe, William J.
Decker, Chesley
Delaney, Patrick J.
Devereaux, Albert
Devereaux, Nicholas
Diamond, Woodrow W.
Dicks, Thomas M.
Donnelly, Leo J.
Donnelly, Michael J.
Drover, Willis
Druken, Valentine
Durnford, James W.
Dwyer, Milton E.
Earle, Albert B.
Earle, Robert C.
Evans, Clarence
Eveleigh, Malcolm S.
Everard, Henry J.
Ewing, James T.
Farrell, William J.
Fennemore, William G.
Fewer, Edward
Fitzgerald, Alphonsus
Fitzgerald, Anthony
Fitzpatrick, Bernard J.
Fleming, Frederick J.
Fleming, Michael
Flynn, John
Foote, Harold J.

Forbes, Ralph M.
Ford, Harold E.
Forward, Colin W.
Foster, Ralph
Gabriel, Gordon
Gallant, Joseph
Gallant, William
Galliott, Howard W.
Galpin, James A.
Gaudet, Samuel
George, Kenneth G.
Gilbert, Stephen F.
Gill, Ronald K.
Gillett, George P.
Gillis, John R.
Goodridge, Frederick R.
Gosse, Samuel J.
Goulding, Edward G.
Grandy, Frazer E.
Greeley, Walter
Green, Garfield
Green, Wallace S.
Green, William J.
Greene, Harry J.
Grimes, Francis V.
Groves, Frederick J.
Gullage, Frederick W.
Guy, Woodrow H.
Hancock, Charles C.
Harvey, Clayton W.
Hause, Saul H.
Hayter, Alan C.
Head, John
Hennebury, Ronald
Herridge, William W.
Hewlin, Llewellyn
Hibbs, Kenneth F.
Hiscock, Harold
Hobbs, Thomas
Holden, Gerald
Hollett, Malcolm P.
Holloway, William K.
House, Gordon H.
Howlett, Patrick
Howlett, Robert E.
Hulen, James E.
Hunt, William T.
Hussey, James D.
Hutchings, Samuel
Jack, James A.
Janes, William
Jennings, Daniel
Jesseau, Frederick
Jesso, Henry J.
Johnson, Arthur J.
Joyce, Patrick
Keating, Bernard
Keefe, Abel
Keeping, Chesley
Kelloway, Pearce B.
Kelly, Peter
Kelly, Ronald D.
Kelly, Samuel
Kennedy, Mervil C.
Kennedy, Richard A.
Kent, Peter K.
Kerrivan, Bernard J.
King, David
King, Herbert
Kitchen, Frank W.
Lahey, Robert J.
Lambert, Levi G.
Lane, Herbert K.
Lasaga, Michael B
Lavis, Joseph
Lawrence, Everett A.
Lawrence, George
LeDrew, Rexford S.
Lewis, Joseph
Lewis, Walter P.
Lidstone, Albert E.
Lilley, James H.
Linfield, William S.
Loader, Francis C.
Locke, Raymond
Luff, Ralph H.
Lush, James M.
MacDonald, William J.
Mahon, James T.
Mahoney, Stanley G.
Maidment, Ernest W.
Martin, Guy K.
Masters, Edmund
May, Esrom
McDonald, Peter
McFatridge, Arthur R.
McGrath, Austin
McGrath, Milton A.
McKinnon, Allan
McLennon, William G.
McLeod, Roy B.
Mercer, John H.
Mercer, Philip A.
Mercer, William E.
Messervey, George H.
Mifflin, Reginald S.
Miles, James T.
Miller, Albert L.
Mills, Loyal W.
Mitchell, Hayward S.
Moore, Leslie B.
Morrissey, James P.
Morrissey, Thomas J.
Mouland, Ivan C.

Munden, Frederick
Murphy, James J.
Murphy, John J.
Murphy, John J.
Murphy, William J.
Nash, Aloysius M.
Neil, Edward F.
Nelson, James L.
Neville, Arthur
Neville, William J.
Newell, Richard W.
Newell, William
Noble, Wilfred J.
Nolan, Edward
Nolan, Frederick
Noseworthy, Gordon W.
Noseworthy, Warwick L.
Noseworthy, William L.
O'Brien, Maurice J.
O'Connell, Arthur
Oldford, Augustus A.
O'Neil, Henry
Osmond, Isaac G.
O'Toole, Thomas V.
Packwood, Harold
Parrott, Edgar T.
Parsons, Wilfred
Payne, Eric R.
Pearcey, Raymond F.
Peckford, Francis C.
Pennell, Bernard
Pennell, Roland C.
Penney, Alphaeus
Penney, Cyril H.
Penney, George M.
Penney, Robert K.
Penney, Samuel C.
Penney, Vincent
Percey, Maxwell C.
Perry, Arthur
Piercey, Frederick
Pike, George D.
Pike, William J.
Pitts, Jobey O.
Poole, Philip O.
Poole, Wilfred G.
Porter, George
Porter, Philip H.
Power, Charles J.
Power, Dermot M.
Power, Michael
Power, Osbourne J.
Quigley, John J.
Quinlan, Edmund R.
Reddy, Patrick R.
Reid, Aaron H.
Rendell, Augustus W.
Richards, Arthur J.
Richardson, Francis C.
Rideout, Sidney
Roberts, George H.
Roche, Francis J.
Rose, George S.
Ross, Malcolm P.
Rowe, Hedley J.
Ryall, Patrick J.
Ryan, Henry
Ryan, Michael
Ryan, Richard
Samson, Thomas G.
Sellars, Harold W.
Sexton, Harold J.
Sharpe, William
Shea, William
Sheppard, Fred M.
Sheppard, Gordon K.
Sheppard, Reginald E.
Simms, Robert A.
Skanes, Lemuel
Smith, Edward N.
Smith, Roland H.
Smith, Ronald
Snooks, William H.
Snow, Donald D.
Spencer, Matthew J.
Squires, Henry G.
Stacey, Leslie J.
Stamp, James J.
Stansbury, Cecil
Stares, Meshack E.
Stone, Hubert C.
Stone, James A.
Stringer, Isaiah
Stuckey, Herbert
Sweeney, James J.
Sweeney, John P.
Symmonds, Garfield C.
Taylor, James
Thistle, Cyril R.
Thomas, Walter P.
Tobin, Peter W.
Traverse, Anthony J.
Traverse, Jabez W.
Tucker, George S.
Vatcher, Kenneth N.
Vey, William J.
Vicars, Ronald J.
Walsh, Patrick J.
Walsh, Patrick J.
Wareham, Douglas
Warren, Francis
Warren, Lawrence
Webb, Paul
Wells, Roy G.

SUPREME SACRIFICES

West, Joseph B.
Whalen, John
Whalen, Wallace
Wheeler, Reginald
Wheeler, Sidney M.
White, Charles L.
White, Cyril J.
White, Llewellyn O.
White, Raymond G.
Whiteway, William J.
Williams, Harold
Windsor, William
Winsor, Betram P.
Wiseman, Norman L.
Yetman, James M.
Young, Cecil A.
Young, Leo J.

Royal Canadian Navy

Brenton, George W.
Dicks, George R.
Edmonds, John C.
English, Dermot T.
Fulton, Henry
Grandy, Charles R.
Hillier, George A.
Hooper, Howard F.
Keeping, Robert
Lundrigan, John
McCarthy, John M.
Morrison, Francis A.
Penney, Selby J.
Poulain, Augustine J.
Shave, Chesley N.
Skinner Richard J.
Strickland, Stanley G.
Tapper, John
Wakeley, Stanley G.
Walters, Gordon W.
Young, James L.

United States Navy

Horan, Malachy P.
Morgan, Walter E.

A Requiem.

As you read the names of those who made the supreme sacrifice, you realize you have known many people with the same names. If you are over 70 you likely knew some who died. Very few sailors expected to die until their last moments, with no time for final words. Had they lived, they and their family and friends would have shared a lifetime of dreams. Their passing would be an absolute tragedy, except that, collectively, their sacrifices ultimately gave us the opportunity for our freedom.

PJJ

The Merchant Marine & Royal / Canadian Navy Memorials, St. John's.

The Marine Institute of Memorial University.

The Historical Chapters.

Introduction by Paul J. Johnson.

In assembling this *Anthology* we were extremely pleased and privileged to receive agreement from highly acclaimed historians to include material we requested, that they had published previously. Their chapters follow the original publications and have not been altered except to conform with the print arrangement of the *Anthology*.

We were also most grateful to have permission to include a shortened summary we derived from journalist A.B. Perlin's excellent 1959 book *The Story of Newfoundland*. A.B. Perlin was arguably our most capable and scrupulous "Observer" of Newfoundland issues and events.

The historical and journalistic chapters provide impressive insight and thoroughness. There may be some variations in points of view, but there are more likely to be differences between the Historical Chapters and the first and last Hypotheses Chapters of the lay writer.

In *Searching for Meaning,* the *Anthology*'s Hypotheses Chapters reflect on past events and circumstances. They suggest how we might improve our future, and *possibly* remedy previous unfortunate results. To achieve that will require a determined change in Newfoundland's longstanding submissive behaviour.

The Historical Chapters provide extensive, well-researched background that will assist a reader to arrive at their own conclusions.

11

This Was Newfoundland, from 1497 to 1832.

Introduction by Paul J. Johnson.

We are pleased to have the agreement of Mr. Albert Perlin's son John to let us let us do a summary from Albert Perlin's outstanding 1959 book *The Story of Newfoundland*. We have focused on the period 1497 to 1832, relating to "the way we were". This outlines the woeful obstacles and hardships that ultimately created the resourceful people of Newfoundland.

Albert Perlin, as a journalist and observer of current and historical events, had a remarkable ability to identify and outline important issues, their meanings, and potential outcomes. Cynicism was not his style. Being realistic about recognizing change, he always offered constructive commentary, pertinent to the prevailing circumstances.

He was a remarkable storyteller. There were never hidden motives behind his observations. He was intent on being scrupulously fair and forthright, and clearly succeeded in that intention.

In the late 1940s, Mr. Perlin was considered an advocate of Responsible Government (as opposed to Confederation). His reasoning was that Newfoundland should be independently free (instead of pre-committed to Confederation) to investigate and negotiate our best political, financial, and economic possibilities. Once Newfoundland did commit to Confederation, Mr. Perlin continued offering his insightful views about our most beneficial approaches within Canada.

Biographical Sketch

Albert Benjamin Perlin (1901–1978). Journalist. Born St. John's, son of Israel Perlin and Adele (Adams). Married E. Vera Crosbie. Many would consider A.B. Perlin was Newfoundland's most respected and influential journalist, from the 1930s through to the 1970s. In 1973 Memorial University awarded him an Honorary Doctorate of Letters. The next year he was appointed an Officer of the Order of Canada, and was given an Award of Merit by the American Association for State and Local History.

This Was Newfoundland, from 1497 to 1832.

Abridged from *The Story of Newfoundland*, by Albert B. Perlin.

Newfoundland's story is unique in British annals. In 1620, Newfoundland was the only British possession in North America, yet it was the last to be officially acknowledged to have the status of a colony. Many of our problems had their origin in what the New Zealand historian A.H. McLintock had described as "Britain's greatest experiment in retarded colonization".

Nearly three centuries after the Island's discovery, the British Secretary of State, William Grenville, declared that "Newfoundland is in no respect a British colony and is never so considered in our laws". Instead, Newfoundland was regarded as a great ship moored near the Grand Banks, a source of wealth for the West Country merchants, and a training ground for seamen for the Royal Navy.

Newfoundland consists of the Island of that name and the major part of the Labrador peninsula. Newfoundland itself has an area in excess of 42,000 square miles. The Island has a maximum height and width of about 315 miles. Labrador was confirmed as part of Newfoundland by a Privy Council decision in 1927, and has an area of 110,000 square miles.

In one very special respect, Newfoundland is unique. The population was chiefly settled along the coastline. This fact stems from historical causes, and is at the root of many of the Island's transportation, communication, and financial problems.

The island has been described as a plateau of low, gently rolling relief, with bare rocks rising above the level of vast reaches of timberlands, bogs, and muskeg, surrounding innumerable lakes. Most of the largest rivers empty into the northern bays. Three great watersheds, the Exploits, the Gander, and the Terra Nova, are divided by parallel ridges. The Exploits River has a length of 200 miles. It was the source of the first large hydro-electric development in the Island. The major exception to the northeastward flow is the Humber River, which follows a course of 80 miles, to empty into the Bay of Islands on the West Coast.

The capital city of St. John's lies in the same latitude as Paris, but the shores of Newfoundland are washed by the cold waters of the Labrador current and the climate is less pleasant than that of the European countries in the same latitude.

The climate of Newfoundland is not severe. Temperatures below zero degrees Fahrenheit are rare in winter. In summer the weather is pleasant. Temperatures may rise to 80 degrees, but are rarely excessive. The cool ocean breezes always constitute a moderating influence. The rainfall is ample and snow is variable.

The People of Newfoundland.

In the first census after Confederation, it was disclosed that more than 90 per cent of the population of that time had its origin in England, Ireland, and Scotland. Of the remainder, persons of French origin, numbering 9,841, were in the majority. Of Indians and Eskimos (the former including a small colony of Micmacs on the Island of Newfoundland), there were only 1,127, of whom the largest number was to be found on the northeast coast of Labrador.

There are many Newfoundland people who can trace their ancestry back to the very early days of the eighteenth century. The prevailing isolation of persons living in Newfoundland has preserved the origins in speech and tradition to a degree rarely found elsewhere. We have a vocabulary made quaint and enriched by inherited and preserved words and phrases. These have been part of the development of a very special and unique Newfoundland character and culture, which visitors find is of particular charm.

John Cabot's Discovery of Newfoundland.

North America was discovered by John Cabot on June 24th, 1497. There is excellent reason to believe that Newfoundland had been visited by Spanish and Portuguese fishermen well before Cabot's voyage. But history can accept only that of which there is proof. John Cabot's first voyage in 1497 marked the emergence of Northeastern America into the known western world.

Cabot was a shadowy figure and left no personal records. Born in Genoa in about 1450, he was taken to Venice as a boy, later becoming a merchant captain, trading in the eastern Mediterranean. He was obsessed with seeking a sea route from western Europe to Asia. Moving to England in 1484, he persuaded the merchants of Bristol to send ships in search of a "western passage".

In 1496, he procured from Henry VII letters patent granting him the right to discover new lands (provided the operation was conducted at Cabot's cost and that 20 per cent of the net profits would go to the King). On May 2nd, 1497, Cabot set out from Bristol in the *Matthew*, and 53 days out of Bristol, came within sight of land. But no western passage was to be found.

After Cabot's return from "the new-founde-land", there was entered in the royal accounts: *"To hym that found the new isle £10"*. A pension of £20 a year was also awarded the discoverer. The careful King was induced by Cabot's first account to aid in founding a fleet for a second journey. Among others said to have accompanied him was João Fernandes, a "lavrador" (farmer) of the Azores. That expedition sailed to Greenland and on to Labrador which is believed to have become known as "the land of the lavrador", from which its present name Labrador derives. The fleet moved southward but save for the highly coloured account given by Cabot's eldest son Sebastian, nothing is really known about the second voyage.

The Newfoundland Way of Life.

For the first three centuries after settlement began, the way of life in Newfoundland showed little change. The one industry was the fishery. This was the source of earning and the reason for existence of the population. The repressive laws against settlement and the extraordinary nature of the inshore fishery were the irresistible causes for dispersal of the population around the perimeter of the island.

The people made the very best possible use of what nature enabled. They grew basic root crops. They caught and cured fish and sold or traded it, including to the masters of visiting ships, for sugar, molasses, flour, tea, woollens, iron-mongery and a variety of other useful articles. They supplemented their food supply with ptarmigan, edible seabirds, and the wild fruits that grew plentifully on the neighbouring barrens. They burned wood for heating and cooking. With some improvements from time to time, this was the basic way of life in hundreds of small, separated settlements.

In time, commerce developed in an organized manner. In the outharbours, "planters" (or middlemen) acted as the agents of merchants for the purpose of distributing supplies on credit, and collecting the produce of the people. But, because the risks were enormous, planters' markups were high and often exorbitant. As well, rarely did the fishermen obtain the full value of their fish and oil. This kept almost all settlers in a state of servitude, which was only alleviated in those outports where a benevolent merchant was to be found. This practice meant that a fisherman was almost always in debt. It usually kept the fishermen from the extremities of want, but sometimes ruined the merchants who had uncollectible book debts.

The great majority of settlers experienced a hard and lonely life, depending on the fortunes of the fishery and their crops. Doctors were virtually unknown, schools were few, isolation was extreme, and bitter toil and hardship were the lot of all. But Newfoundlanders were always a deeply religious people. Few were the communities of any size that did not have their churches.

The English Approach to the Fishery.

The English introduced into Newfoundland the methods of catching and curing fish which they had long employed in Iceland. The French and Portuguese did not dry their catch but put the fish down in heavy salt. The English used little salt and dried their cod to a hard consistency. This produced a stock of fish of good keeping quality which was in particular demand not only in the tropical countries but for ships' supplies.

This method of curing required premises on shore. Therefore, there was eager competition for the best shore sites. First-come was first served, but serious disputes often occurred over the most desirable location to establish the best "fishing room". Out of these conflicts may have come the first crude attempts at some means to produce order, by making the first captain to arrive in port the lord of the harbour – or "fishing admiral".

The English seasonal fishermen were not colonists, only summer fishermen. But, out of their methods of fishing, settlement was to grow. No one can say when the practice began of leaving men to winter in the Newfoundland harbours. They were keepers of the "bye-boats" and watchmen to protect property from the Indians and from the early arrivals of other English the following spring.

The West Countrymen brought system to their fishery. Of a crew of 40, there would be 24 to man eight small boats and 16 to work on the room as the shore gang. Seven men removed the heads and split and cleaned the fish; two boys stood by to spread the fish on salting tables; three women salted; and three men spread the cod on the drying flakes. There was one other woman in the shore gang who did the cooking.

Sir Humphrey Gilbert Takes Possession of Newfoundland.

Gilbert was a Devonshire man and half-brother of Sir Walter Raleigh. He turned to soldiering, and was an English Captain in the Irish Wars. His knighthood, conferred when he was 31 years of age, was a reward for his army services to the Queen. He was one of the first advocates of a northwest passage to Asia. But, after writing a pamphlet on colonization, he turned his thoughts to that subject.

Gilbert had a fleet of five ships with 260 men, who sailed from Causet Bay, near Plymouth, on June 11th, 1583. It had been agreed the course should be set for Cape Race from which point the ships would sail north to Fermeuse and St. John's. At the end of the second day, the expedition was deserted by the largest of the ships, the *Raleigh*.

On entering St. John's, Gilbert found 36 ships in the harbour, 20 were Spanish or Portuguese, a few were French and the rest English. It is a remarkable testimony to the influence of the English that they were acknowledged as lords of the harbour. Gilbert was conducted around the harbour by the English merchants. On August 5th, Gilbert had his tent set up on shore, called together all the persons in the port, and read his Commission to take possession for Queen Elizabeth.

Life went on in Newfoundland as if Gilbert had never been here. But, for the purposes of history, the first British possession overseas had been established. From that seed, a mighty empire grew.

The Newfoundland Fishery Grows.

The value of the Newfoundland fishery to England was the reason for the establishment of convoys of the Royal Navy to protect the fishing fleets. It was because of the convoy captains that the most desperate efforts of the West Country merchants to abolish the settlements in Newfoundland were frustrated. The restoration of Charles II to his throne was a bitter time for the settlers in Newfoundland. Charles, at the persuasion of the West Countrymen, added a provision designed to put an end to settlement. All owners of ships trading to Newfoundland were forbidden to carry any persons not of the ship's company. However, worse was to yet follow.

Up to this time, the French had been content to consider Newfoundland as just a convenient base for fishing operations. In 1662, they landed at Placentia on the south coast a military force of 150 men to occupy and fortify the place.

Some well-known Newfoundland ports, chiefly St. John's, were centres of a remarkable and thriving international trade, which offended the English Navigation Acts. These Acts required that all the products of the colonies must be sent directly to England. The biggest illicit trade or barter was of European products for New England and West Indian goods.

The Royal Navy was used to protect the English fishing fleet coming to Newfoundland and also to keep a watchful eye on smuggling. Its Captains were also charged with supervising the laws against settlement, but it is ironic that it was largely on the Navy Captains' advice that the harshness of these restrictions on settlement was ultimately modified.

In 1662, the year that the French moved into Placentia, each of the settled English harbours had its planters, many of them men of substance, having both domestic and fishery servants.

In 1680, Thomas Oxford had said that he and his predecessors had occupied houses and fishing premises in St. John's for about 70 years (est. 1610). But their security was threatened on two sides - - by the efforts of the West Country merchants to uproot the planters and the later armed attempts by the French for total conquest of Newfoundland.

Repression of the Settlers.

In 1662, the English "livyers" were, at best, tolerated. New French colonists, on the other hand, were supported by the French government in the settlement of Placentia. English King Charles II had very likely sold to King Louis XIV the right to occupy and fortify Placentia.

The year 1665 was notable for two events. The first was the descent on St. John's by the famous Dutch Admiral, de Ruyter. His landing parties destroyed flakes and stores, and burned most of the town. The other event was the publication of Sir Josiah Child's *Discourse on Trade* which crystallized the West Countrymen's theory that the settlements in Newfoundland were prejudicial to both the English-based fishery and to national interests.

Child was a man of immense influence, and the chief mouthpiece of the Western Adventurers. He commanded great prestige in policy matters, which was supported by the distribution of rich and well-placed bribes.

In 1675 new rules were added that forbade any livyer to cut down trees or to set up residence within six miles of the shore. The rules also put every master of a fishing vessel under heavy bond to bring back all his crew to England. The rules also continued the vicious rule of the Fishing Admirals.

The English seasonal fishermen, returning now in greater numbers to Newfoundland, took swift action to enforce the reconfirmed rules. They seized and destroyed what settlements they could, threatening the inhabitants with fines and imprisonment.

However, Navy convoy captains saw a need for settlement to check against the French and others who pirated the on-shore, over-winter properties. The Captains' reports supported petitions from the planters and caused an order to be issued in 1677 that "the Planters in Newfoundland be continued in possession of their houses and stages". Our settlers proposed plans for the fortification of the principal harbours and asked again, without avail, for a governor. In 1680, planters and settlers were permitted to build. And then came England's war with France, which was to last for twenty-five years and cause our unfortunate colonists to be subjected to tragic new attacks and harassments.

The French Invasions.

Our settlers were allowed to remain as guardians against French ambitions, but nothing was done to prepare or protect them from French assaults. A strong British fleet appeared one day before Placentia, bombarded the port for six hours to little effect, and went away. The English settlements were defenceless against the French attacks that followed. An attempt on St. John's failed, but the French ships took Bay Bulls and Ferryland, and plundered and burned all the houses. They shipped 150 persons back to England, rather than detain them as prisoners.

On November 1, 1696, Pierre Le Moine d'Iberville, a young French-Canadian officer with a thorough knowledge of Indian warfare, set out overland from Placentia and arrived in nine days at Ferryland. In his military party was a strong force of Indians and Canadian *coureurs de bois*. They prepared for a northward drive toward St. John's. A mile from the main settlement, about 90 ordinary settlers, hidden on the Southside Hills, tried to put up resistance. They were forced to retire after half their number were killed. The St. John's inhabitants left their homes to gather in Fort William.

An English prisoner, having been scalped by the Indians, was sent by the French to the Fort with the message that the same fate would overtake all if they refused to submit. The settlers were horrified and did surrender. The surrender terms provided for the repatriation of all who wished to return to England. Then the town was burned with the exception of a few houses left to house the sick and wounded.

That winter, d'Iberville, having equipped his forces with snowshoes, began a methodical destruction of most English settlements along the shores of Conception and Trinity Bays. Only Carbonear Island, which over 200 settlers defended, and Brigus survived this attack. After ravaging, plundering, burning, and seizing all livestock and fish, the French might well have thought the English colonies had been destroyed. But some inhabitants escaped inland from their villages.

Later, the British King William dispatched a fleet with 1,500 troops to St. John's. No sign of life was found. The town was a place of blackened ruins and the port had been completely abandoned.

Local settlers had suffered horribly, but their miseries aroused no sympathy in London. In December 1698, legislation was passed to establish the ownership by England of the whole of Newfoundland. But again, the existence of settlers was ignored. The role of the notorious Fishing Admirals for each port was again confirmed. The island continued to be regarded as the special preserve of the Western Adventurer merchants. The settlers were once more denied the right to have: a governor, civil law, citizenship, or adequate defence.

The war continued. A powerful English fleet, capable of taking Placentia, looked the port over and withdrew without making an attack. Emboldened by the English Admiral's failure to act, the French renewed their attacks by land on the Trinity Bay settlements. A more aggressive assault on the English settlements was launched in early 1705. The Governor of Placentia, with Indians and Canadians, moved to make a surprise attack on St. John's. They attacked the settlers in their homes, inflicting on them many brutalities. But the French made no headway against Fort William or the batteries on Signal Hill.

The garrison at St. John's made some successful retaliatory attacks on the French and brought some relief to the harassed settlers. One British reprisal took the form of naval action against French fishing ships in their main ports on the eastern side of the Northern Peninsula.

But, on January 1, 1709, another French force took the then badly guarded Fort William by surprise. This was the last French attack of any consequence during the war. War ended in 1713 with French surrender and signing of the Treaty of Utrecht. In the next two hundred years, that Treaty, instead of being of benefit, was a constant source of trouble for Newfoundlanders. In St. John's, John Collins was made Governor of the inhabitants. But the Fishing Admirals still ruled over the fishing harbours.

The French Shore Established.

Under the Treaty of Utrecht, the French supposedly resigned any designs on Newfoundland, but they were allowed to keep, but not fortify, Cape Breton Island. The English asked for concurrent fishing rights but these were refused by the French on the grounds that they might become the source of continuous strife. Yet, when the French requested similar rights in Newfoundland, they were granted. The Treaty provided that it should be lawful for the subjects of France to catch fish and to dry them on land in that part of northern Newfoundland from Cape Bonavista to the northernmost point of the island, and then all the way south along the west coast.

Placentia remained a source of irritation to Newfoundlanders who had no governor, but an English Governor was appointed in Nova Scotia. The surrendered French colony at Placentia was put under his jurisdiction. It had been provided that Frenchmen who wished to remain in Placentia, if willing to become British subjects, were to be continued in the possession of their land. Frenchmen in Placentia were assured the right of property under the protection of the English Governor of Nova Scotia, but Newfoundlanders could still not own land.

Absurdity, injustice, and stupidity could hardly have soared to greater heights. Our people who had actually bought land in Placentia from departing Frenchmen were later dispossessed and their protests were without avail.

The First Naval Governor.

In 1729, Captain Henry Osborne, R.N., was appointed Governor and Commander-in-Chief over all the Island of Newfoundland (including Placentia), with authority to appoint justices of the peace, and to erect court houses and prisons. The authority of the Naval Governor was constantly challenged by the ongoing authority of the Fishing Admirals. These rival jurisdictions only existed between spring and fall. In the period between the first appointment of a Naval Governor and the outbreak of a new war with France in 1756, the laws against settlement of Newfoundland were largely ignored. The fishing ships resumed bringing out passengers who intended to make their homes in Newfoundland.

Life continued to be troublesome for the settlers, but trade flourished. The taking of seals was becoming a winter industry of growing importance. And by 1750, the output of salt codfish had reached 430,000 quintals (48,160,000 pounds of dried fish).

A Settled Society Emerges.

Between the French wars, the emergence of a settled society occurred. In St. John's the few rich merchants were the aristocracy. Below them was the planter class comprised of men who gave credit to the fishermen, encouraged them to patronize their retail stores and taverns, and required them to pay in fish and oil, priced at arbitrary levels – prices just as arbitrary as those charged for the goods provided to fishermen on credit. The end result was to make the third class, the settlers, virtual lifelong serfs.

New Attacks and Counter-Attacks.

In the spring of 1762, four large ships slipped out of Brest, France, setting course for Newfoundland. The fleet, carrying 32 officers and 700 soldiers, captured Bay Bulls on June 24 and three days later easily entered and captured poorly defended St. John's.

Ten weeks later a British fleet carrying troops under Colonel William Amherst arrived off St. John's. Signal Hill was stormed, the British troops defeated the French, and surrender was accepted on September 20th. But the four French ships escaped from the harbour under cover of a thick fog. The war ended with the Treaty of Paris by which all of Canada became part of the British Empire.

Civil Rights Established.

Under the Treaty of Paris, our first Naval Governor was Hugh Palliser, a man supremely dedicated to the proposition that the summer fishery was of vital consequence to British interests and must not be jeopardized by any interference from the inhabitants. In 1775, his representations led to legislation known as Palliser's Act. Its express purpose was to ensure the return to England of all seamen and fishermen who had made the summer voyage to Newfoundland. Once again, Newfoundland was being considered a great English ship, moored near the Grand Banks during the fishing season, for the convenience of English fishermen.

Captain James Cook, the celebrated cartographer, had taken part in the recapture of St. John's in 1762. Two years later, Governor Palliser brought him to the island to be "marine surveyor of the coast of Newfoundland and Labrador". Cook's famous map, published in 1775, was the first to show an accurate and extremely useful representation of the coastline of Newfoundland.

In 1789, the Governor had to improvise a civil court. But out of this came a new appraisal of the situation by the British Government. An official Civil Court was arranged in 1791. The following year a Supreme Court of Civil and Criminal Justice was established. At long last the rule of the Fishing Admirals, and ad hoc quarterdeck courts of Naval Governors were abolished.

In 1811, the British parliament approved a measure to allow much of the waterfront in St. John's which had been reserved for the summer fishermen to be granted, let, and possessed as private property. Thereby the admission of Newfoundland to colonial status and the settlers to perpetual residence were confirmed. By that time, the population of settlers had grown to nearly 50,000 persons.

If, after 200 years of struggle, the settlers finally gained the right to exist and own property in Newfoundland, they were to long–remember the earlier, horrible, unjust suffering and hardship. In that long period, "better times" had only been experienced during the American war of 1812–14, because of the inflation of fishery prices. But at the conclusion of that war, a grave depression occurred. Many merchants went bankrupt. In a single year, a great influx of 11,000 new immigrants from Ireland augmented everyone's distressed situation.

The New Turning Point, Leading to 1832.

The framework of an organized society was developing in St. John's and some of the larger outports. In 1805, Simon Solomon became the operator of a primitive post office and John Ryan was permitted, (under severe restrictions) to publish the newspaper *Royal Gazette*. A Merchants' Society had been formed for collective dealings with the Governor. The best of the numerous taverns, particularly the London Tavern, were clubs which the best people of the town patronized. Appointed to the Governor's office were enlightened naval officers whose efforts speeded the ultimate recognition and civilizing of Newfoundland as a Colony.

But perhaps no event was to have more far-reaching importance than the arrival in St. John's in 1808 of a young and dour Scottish doctor, William Carson, who argued with cold, forceful logic for the establishment of local government. He was subsequently supported in this cause by the more fiery, impassioned eloquence of a dynamic Irish merchant, Patrick Morris. But in the last analysis, it was the past cruelty of the surrogate courts and persuasion of Governor Sir Thomas Cochrane that in 1832, had brought about Representative (Responsible) Government for Newfoundland.

Cochrane has been called the best Governor that Newfoundland ever had. He threw himself with tremendous energy into the tasks of reform. One of his first duties was to be present for the inauguration of a new Supreme Court comprising a Chief Justice and two Assistant Judges. He caused the work that had begun on the island's first roads (to Topsail, Portugal Cove, Torbay and Bay Bulls) to be expedited.

But more than anything else, he dedicated himself to the promotion of a local legislative assembly. In 1832, that long deferred boon was granted, though only over the vehement protests of the West Country merchants. The new constitution called for an elected House of Assembly and an appointed Legislative Council. The first general election was held in the autumn of 1832.

Newfoundland was not short of able and patriotic men but her people were new to the responsibilities of self-government. It was to be expected that the legislature would encounter many difficulties. Many problems came from inexperience, but most arose from the woeful inadequacy of public revenues.

The acquisition of Representative Government did nothing to improve the economy. A population of upwards of 60,000 people was spread over hundreds of harbours along a lengthy coastline. The sea was their only means of contact and communication with one another. There was no organized system of education. The heavy reliance on winter credit kept most fishing familes in virtual serfdom. Few were well-nourished or properly clothed. And even in St. John's itself, winter conditions after a bad fishery saw an immense need for relief.

Such was the state of Newfoundland and the people in 1832 that they began a new experience with Responsible Government and an understandable great hope for an improved life for their families.

Eventually, a Rapid Growth of Population.

In 1638, at the beginning of the repression of settlement in Newfoundland, the desire of most resident settlers was to evade any attempt to estimate their whereabouts or numbers. But in 1644, the number of visiting, English seasonal fishermen was established at 10,800. They came out in 270 vessels, and employed more than 2,000 smaller boats in their fishery.

But, despite the apparent increases in settlement, the crews of visiting summer vessels from England still outnumbered those residents. Life seemed endurable for the livyers, and more wished to come.

The Royal Navy was active and many prizes were taken and brought to St. John's. The British Government was spending vast sums fortifying and developing Nova Scotia but the residents and the defences of Newfoundland remained neglected.

In 1752 (120 years after 1638), English ships in the seasonal fishery numbered about the same, at 284. Commerce was lucrative and great fortunes enriched the virtual monopoly of the English western and southwestern port cities. But now, additional settlers, many of them Irish, were allowed to come on English summer-fishing ships. Almost all vessels touched at Irish ports on the way to and from Newfoundland. The outward passage was much cheaper than the return. Few could earn the cost of the homeward journey even if they did wish to leave. By 1750, about one-half of the resident population were Irish settlers.

The year-round settlers began to encroach more and more on land used by seasonal fishermen. By 1774, there were thought to be at least 12,000 people permanently living on shore. Large local mercantile interests had been established, whose owners made substantial earnings from the Newfoundland fishery.

The numbers for population were not by actual census. The estimate for 1804 was 20,380, or nearly double that of 1774 (30 years before). In 1832 (a further 28 years), when we were granted Responsible Government, the inhabitants had tripled to 60,000.

Although outside the period of this summary, 1497 to 1832, it is interesting to see the further total growth of our settlements. In 1857 (another 25 years) the population had more than doubled again, to total 124,000. In 1891, an actual census revealed a remarkable 202,000, for an additional 78,000 residents in only 34 years. In 177 years, the population had grown from 12,000 to an amazing 202,000 people.

It is remarkable that, despite the difficulties, frustrations, and efforts to prevent settlement, the population that did come to settle and stay were very courageous and determined people – a "good breeding stock", that has produced the fine, homogeneous character of our present population.

Also of interest, the 1891 denominational breakdown was 72,696 Roman Catholics, 69,824 Anglicans, 53,276 Methodists, 1,449 Presbyterians, 782 Congregationalists, 2,092 members of the Salvation Army, and 1,397 Moravians on Labrador. The analysis of occupations (not including tens of thousands of young people) showed 53,502 persons in the fisheries, 180 clergymen, 62 doctors, 43 lawyers, 601 school teachers, 608 civil servants, and 2,681 tradesmen and 1,058 employed in factories. Merchants and traders numbered 767 and employed 1,948 shop assistants. Obviously we still had fewer merchants and fewer teachers then outports, so many outports were doing without. The proportion of the aged was high, with more than 7,000 person of 65 years and over.

Note: The foregoing is abridged from Mr. A.B. Perlin's 1959 book *The Story of Newfoundland*, with the permission of copyright holder Mr. John C. Perlin, CM, CVO, ONL, LLD.

12

The Newfoundland Economy – before, during, and after World War II.

The Great Depression Ends Democratic Government.

By: Melvin Baker.

In 1934, Newfoundland was in desperate economic straits. When the Commission of Government replaced parliamentary democracy, government was financially "on the rocks". Conditions for the general population were bleak and made even bleaker by the worldwide depression. It was predominantly a society of small fishing outports. There were 1,292 settlements along the coast, only 100 with a population of more than 500. In 1935, St. John's, the capital, had 39,886 inhabitants. The largest employer, the fishery, offered a meagre living. Some fishermen could supplement their incomes through part-time work as loggers for the island's two pulp and paper mills and as sealers in the spring. Some outport residents also worked as sailors on the vessels that carried fish to our markets in southern Europe and the Caribbean.

Cash wages were only found in the papermaking towns of Grand Falls and Corner Brook, and in the mining centres such as Bell Island, Buchans, and St. Lawrence. In St. John's, there was a small civil service, some secondary manufacturing, and a sizeable labour force involved in marine-related activities. A high birthrate was offset by a high mortality rate. In 1934, the death rate was 12.1 per thousand of population, compared with 9.5 in Canada. The island had only 450 hospital beds, according to a health survey conducted in 1934 by the St. John's Rotary Club. This represented one bed for every 644 persons, whereas in the U.S. there was one bed for every 130 people. The economy was dependent on the export of fish, minerals, and forest products.

Beginning in 1929, the depression was extremely vicious. Total exports were cut in half and fell in value from $ 40 million in 1930 to $ 23 million by 1933. The value of fishery exports alone fell from $ 16 million in 1928 to $ 6.5 million in 1932. The number of people receiving able-bodied relief of six cents a day rose sharply. During the winter of 1932–33, one-quarter of the population depended on the government to pay for the necessities of tea, flour, pork, and molasses.

Decreased revenues and increased expenditure for relief created a financial calamity for the government. In 1933, about 65 per cent of government revenues went to pay the annual interest charge on government debt. Since 1920, the debt had grown rapidly. From $ 43 million in 1920, it had risen to $ 101 million in 1933. The new prime minister, Frederick Alderdice, and his United Newfoundland Party in 1932 obtained a joint loan from the British and Canadian governments. In return, Alderdice consented to the establishment of a British Royal Commission, to suggest ways for the island to meet its debt obligations and to plan an economic reorganization. The findings of this Inquiry, as reported to the British House of Commons on October 4th, 1933, were that Newfoundland politics was corrupt and that the island needed a respite from parliamentary politics until it was again self-supporting.

Facing the alternative of default, on November 28 the Dominion of Newfoundland asked the British government to replace the existing elected government by an appointed "Commission". The charge that Newfoundland politics was corrupt was relatively unfair. They were no more so than in Canadian politics. But, by focusing on corruption, the Inquiry found justification for the suspension of Newfoundland's democracy. Had the Inquiry focused more closely on the real cause of Newfoundland's economic problems (the international depression), the case for the abolition of representative government would have been harder for the British Parliament to pass.

Government by Committee Begins in Early 1934.

The Commission of Government, consisting of three Newfoundland and three British appointees plus the Governor, assumed office on February 16, 1934. The Commissioners saw their main tasks as the provision of efficient government and paying off the debt. They dropped the political and religious criteria for the hiring and promotion of civil servants. With the help of imported British officials, the Commission made merit the basis for promotion. Young Newfoundlanders with professional training were encouraged to join the civil service. The Commission made its earliest strides in the educational and public health fields. It established a summer-school program for teachers at Memorial College and increased their salaries. It left the denominational school system unchanged, fearing that any tampering would provoke widespread protest. It made textbooks and school supplies available on loan to pupils, and tried to improve their health by providing free, nutritional "cocomalt", a cocoa-milk powder.

Medical services were improved after 1935 through the creation of a network of Cottage Hospitals in the larger outports. By 1938, the government operated 10 cottage hospitals, with a total of 130 beds. This was the first instance in North America of a Government establishing a subsidized medical-care plan on a pre-payment basis. To help combat widespread tuberculosis, a new wing was added to the St. John's Sanatorium in 1938, and a mobile Health Unit was formed to visit communities and check for the disease.

Socialist Ambitions Fail.

In its first few years, the Commission tried to implement an ambitious, land-settlement initiative, emphasizing agricultural development as an alternative to the island's reliance on the fishery. This scheme was the creation of Thomas Lodge, a strong-willed English Commissioner, who imposed his idea of "social reorganization" on a reluctant Commission. By 1938, there were 11 farm settlements established, involving 340 families, but harsh agricultural conditions, with inexperienced farmers, meant that success was rarely achieved. The Commission was forced to drop this expensive program, and concentrate efforts on the fishery.

The Commission encouraged some fishermen to form cooperatives, and gave them financial assistance to enable them to purchase boats, and especially engines and other supplies. In 1936, the Commission set up the Newfoundland Fisheries Board, which was given control over the licensing, marketing, and exporting of fish. The Board was also responsible for quality control.

Despite these improvements, during the 1930s the fishing industry continued to perform poorly. This was largely because of economic and political problems within some of the main export markets. In 1938, the value of salt cod exports was lower than at any other time since 1900. Consequently, there was an increase in the number of people requiring government assistance. Between 1934 and 1940, people receiving relief rose from 31,899 to 39,802.

World War II Construction Builds the Economy.

By 1939, public disillusion with the Commission was strong. Administration was more efficient, but hopes for economic development and substantially higher standard of living completely failed. The outbreak of war changed all that. Strategically, Newfoundland became an important defence base in the Allied war effort. Canada established various large base installations in Newfoundland at a total cost of over $ 65 million. These included air bases at Gander, Torbay, and Goose Bay, and a very large naval base in St. John's (for which the British Admiralty actually paid).

The number of Canadian garrison troops peaked at nearly 6,000 army personnel in 1943. This figure does not include the thousands of naval seamen serving on convoy protection from St. John's. Nor the sizable number of airmen who were stationed at Gander and Goose Bay, in Ferry Command or Anti-submarine Patrol.

Under agreements reached in 1940–41, the Americans were permitted to establish military bases in Newfoundland for a tenure of 99 years. The major facilities they built included an army base at St. John's, a naval base at Argentia, and an air force base at Stephenville. They also shared the use of the Gander and Goose Bay Bases with the Canadians. At its height, in September 1942 the American and Canadian construction boom employed 19,752 Newfoundlanders. They earned an average annual income of $ 1,500, considerably more than the $ 333 earned in the fishery in 1941. There were now jobs for all who wished to work. But the Newfoundland construction workers did not receive wage-parity with their American or Canadian civilian counterparts, because the Commission of Government did not wish to have wages for employees in government, industry, or mercantile firms increase.

Britain and Canada – New Attitudes about Newfoundland.

Increased exports and foreign military expenditures during the early 1940s ended the Commission's budget deficits. They had peaked at $ 4.8 million in the 1939–40 fiscal year. Thereafter, budget surpluses enabled the government to make $ 12.3 million in interest-free loans to Britain, while adding to improvements in health, education, housing, and local government. In view of the large American presence in Newfoundland, the Canadian government took an increased watch on our economic and military interests, appointing a High Commissioner to Newfoundland in 1941.

In considering the postwar restoration of democracy to Newfoundland, Britain was concerned that the island would regain its political independence and then slip back into a state of economic dependence on "the old country". Britain therefore proposed to fund a 10-year economic development program in Newfoundland, while keeping a tight rein on the island's finances. However, that plan fell apart in 1944, when the British government determined it could not afford to pay for Newfoundland's development. By 1945, it appeared clear to Britain's Government that, under these circumstances, Newfoundland's best hope lay in union with Canada.

The Imposed Future Course for Newfoundland.

With the end of the war in 1945, and Newfoundland now on a self-supporting basis, on December 11, 1945 the British Government announced that a "National Convention" would be established in Newfoundland in 1946. That Convention would examine the country's financial and economic situations, to review and recommend possible constitutional alternatives.

The National Convention itself voted in favour of a return to Responsible Government, but was instructed by Britain to put the question to the public. A referendum was held on June 3, 1948. Only 14.3 per cent voted for retention of the existing Commission of Government. By contrast, 44.5 per cent favoured a return to Responsible Government as it existed prior to 1934, and 41.1 per cent desired Confederation with Canada.

The British Dominions Office called for another vote between the two most popular, earlier choices. In a second referendum held on July 22, 1948, the choice was between Responsible Government and Confederation. The latter won with 52.3 per cent of the votes cast.

On March 31, 1949, Newfoundland entered the Canadian Confederation as the tenth Province.

The Debate about Newfoundland's Dominion Status.

Questions never resolved, but often vehemently debated since 1932 revolved around Newfoundland's Sovereign Rights as an established Dominion in the British Commonwealth of Nations.

One school of thought has considered that Commission was a reinstatement to Newfoundland's previous Colonial status. The fact that the Commission permitted the United Kingdom to conduct Newfoundland's external affairs was seen as evidence of that Colonial status. Although Newfoundland was included as a Dominion in the 1931 Statute of Westminster, Newfoundland had requested the United Kingdom not to have sections 2 to 6 confirmed until the Newfoundland Legislature approved the Statute. That formality had not been dealt with before the last sitting of the House of Assembly. The Commission of Government did not protest when the British Government entered into treaties with foreign countries on Newfoundland's behalf. Nor did the British Dominions Office.

The opposite viewpoint, as expressed in a very strong 1937 opinion by prominent St. John's lawyer J.B. McEvoy, was that Newfoundland was "A Dominion with its status as such in abeyance, and we are not by the advent of Commission of Government in Newfoundland relegated to the status of a Crown Colony". Taking the view that the Statute of Westminster in 1931 was a "declaratory act", McEvoy argued that the Letters Patent of 1934 establishing the Commission of Government merely suspended the Letters Patent of 1876 and 1905, which established the previous Responsible Government. McEvoy noted, "Nowhere is the term 'revoked' or 'repealed' to be found, suggesting abolition of the Constitution and reversion to some status other than that of a Dominion".

In 1975, another St. John's lawyer, Cabot Martin, asserted that the Commission was a "financial-administrative arrangement." In its factum for offshore minerals jurisdiction Supreme Court case with the Federal Government, the Newfoundland Government pointed out in 1981 that the Commission of Government itself reported to the Secretary of State for Dominion Affairs, not the Secretary of State for the Colonial Office. That fact definitely confirmed the applicability of Dominion status for the Commission of Government.

In his 1988 authoritative study of the Commission of Government era, *Newfoundland in the North Atlantic World, 1929–1949* (p. 48), historian Peter Neary wrote that "while her self-government was suspended, she was juridically a Dominion, however hollow the distinction. The Commission of Government would perforce at times enjoy great latitude in bargaining internationally on Newfoundland's behalf, but it always acted on sufferance for, in practice as well as in theory, sovereignty over Newfoundland belonged to the United Kingdom during the Commission era".

Melvin Baker.

Biographical Sketch

A native of Catalina, Newfoundland, Melvin Baker is the University Archivist-Historian (President's Office) for Memorial University of Newfoundland. He is a graduate of Memorial University and the University of Western Ontario. He has written extensively on twentieth century Newfoundland History.

This article is based on the author's "The Tenth Province: Newfoundland joins Canada, 1949," *Horizon*, vol. 10, 111 (1987), pp. 2641-67; and "Commission of Government," in *Encyclopedia of Newfoundland and Labrador, Vol. 2* (St. John's: Newfoundland Book Publishers Ltd. 1984), pp. 627-31.

13

The Commission of Government, 1934–1949.

By: Jeff A. Webb.

On 16 February 1934 the Commission of Government was sworn in, ending responsible government, and beginning a new chapter in Newfoundland's constitutional history. The Commission consisted of seven persons appointed by the British government. No elections took place, and no legislature was convened, for the next 15 years.

Three Commissioners from Britain were given the senior departments that had the greatest relevance to reviving the economy and balancing the government's budget: Natural Resources, Public Utilities, and Finance. Newfoundlanders were appointed as Commissioners for Justice, Public Health and Welfare, and Home Affairs and Education. The governor acted as chairman. Each of the six Commissioners voted upon measures which the governor would sign into law.

Newfoundland remained a dominion in name, and continued to be a responsibility of the Dominions Office in London, but its constitution was now similar to those in force in the empire's Crown colonies. Though the Commission was Newfoundland's government, its powers were circumscribed: in practice it needed permission from the Dominions Office for any major policy initiative, including the budget.

The Commissioners brought in outside experts to run key departments of government and brought new efficiency and accountability to the administration, but changing the nature of Newfoundland's economy and society was more difficult. The Commission did have a set of recommendations for new industries in the Report of the Royal Commission on Newfoundland (the Amulree Report, 1933), and recognized that it should be preparing the people of Newfoundland and Labrador for the day that responsible government would be resumed. Thus the Commission attempted to reinvigorate and reform the local economy and society through an economic and social agenda. But it had no magic solution to the Great Depression. Despite the significant improvements in public health services and education for example, the levels of poverty and government relief remained extremely high throughout the 1930s.

The Commission sometimes faced opposition from local elites, which made reform difficult if not impossible to implement. For instance, the Commission wanted to eliminate the long-standing "denominational compromise" between the government and the major churches, seeing it as wasteful and inefficient. It could do this within the civil service, where the merit principle became the general rule. But when the Commission attempted to change the denominational education system it faced strong resistance from the churches. It was, in fact, unable to reform the administration of education because of the opposition it faced from powerful factions within Newfoundland society.

This case illustrated that while the Commission of Government was nominally designed to give the country a "rest from politics," in practice it was a rest from electoral politics only. The Commissioners did not have to fear losing office in an election, but they learned that if they wanted to achieve anything they had to get the cooperation of those with power and influence in Newfoundland society. When designing legislation or a government program, for instance, the Commission routinely asked the opinion of the churches and the Board of Trade. In this way economic and social elites continued to exercise influence over the state through unofficial channels, and sometimes petitioned the British government directly. In a few instances, groups appealed (without success) to the courts, claiming that the Commission had overstepped its authority.

Ordinary people were not consulted, and were unable to attract the attention of British Members of Parliament. As dissatisfaction with the Commission grew, citizens turned to other methods to express their views, and pressure the government for policy changes. Letters to newspapers mobilised public opinion, and petitions circulated. Organized groups of the unemployed took to the streets to protest the lack of work and the low level of relief payments. The business community also became dissatisfied with the Commission, believing that the government had missed the opportunity to build a third paper mill, for example. By the end of the 1930s the Dominions Office was looking for a way to restore some public confidence in the Commission and even considered creating an elected committee to advise on policy.

The Commission was well aware that the non-democratic nature of the regime was problematic, and did take some steps itself to keep in touch with public opinion. Newfoundlanders were sometimes placed on committees to advise on specific policies or administer regulations, such as the Woods Labour Board or the Newfoundland Fisheries Board. The Newfoundland Ranger Force was formed not only to enforce the law, but also to provide the Commission with information on conditions in rural districts. The creation of a government-owned radio broadcasting corporation grew out of a desire to publicise the work of the Commission, though radio was also seen as a way of educating the public. All the same, the Commission was perceived as being remote from ordinary life.

The Commission's efforts to create industries to supplement the fishery were on the whole disappointing. One of the most interesting of these was the Land Settlement Scheme. A number of farming communities were formed – Markland was the first – to give work both to the urban unemployed and to impoverished fishing families. In addition, since the Amulree Report had suggested that Newfoundlanders were both overly dependent on the government and too individualistic, it was hoped that the settlers would soon become independent of government support, and learn to cooperate with each other on community projects. However, these communities did not prosper, and cost the Commission much more money than anticipated. The Commission also supported the establishment of cooperatives for similar reasons, but with limited results.

How long the Commission would have lasted in normal circumstances is impossible to say. By the late 1930s it had become unpopular, largely because it had failed to live up to Newfoundlanders' unrealistic expectations, and there might well have been changes. But the outbreak of war in 1939 changed everything. Everyone agreed that serious constitutional debate would have to be postponed indefinitely, and that it would be unpatriotic to criticise British government when it was facing a possible German invasion. The Commission was safe for the duration.

Newfoundland and Labrador were very important strategically during the Second World War. Military spending and – to a lesser extent – improved prices for exports created a sudden prosperity. Instead of being under constant financial pressure, and dependent on grants from Britain, the Newfoundland government now became financially self-sufficient – and actually lent money to the British government.

There was no question, therefore, that the Commission of Government as it existed would disappear after the war ended. The question which began to be debated in the mid-1940s was what its replacement would be. Would the Newfoundland electorate want simply go back to the constitution it had agreed to suspend in 1933? Would it want to continue a possibly reformed Commission system? Or might the voters agree to their country becoming a Canadian province? The last actions of the Commission were designed to ensure that this last option was successful. In 1948, a small majority of Newfoundlanders and Labradorians voted to become Canadians, a decision which became official on 31 March, 1949.

Assessments of the Commission have varied. Some historians have applauded the Commission's innovations in providing services to rural Newfoundlanders and Labradorians and its bold social and economic agendas. Others have criticized the Commission for not standing up for Newfoundland's best interest when allowing the United States to lease bases on the island without trade concessions from the U.S. Others have argued the "dictatorship" acted unfairly when it favoured Confederation during the referenda campaigns of 1948. Despite its administrative successes, ultimately the Commission proved itself to be implementing British policy rather than behaving as the government of the people of Newfoundland and Labrador.

Jeff A. Webb.

Biographical Sketch

Jeff Webb is an Associate Professor of History at Memorial University. A native of Gander, he attended Memorial and the University of New Brunswick, at which he completed his Ph.D. in 1995. He has edited the journal *Newfoundland and Labrador Studies* and published widely on the political and cultural history of twentieth-century Newfoundland. His book *The Voice of Newfoundland: A Social History of the Broadcasting Corporation of Newfoundland, 1939–1949* was published by the University of Toronto Press in 2008.

References

Baker, Melvin. "Commission of Government, 1934–1949." (1994) http://www.ucs.mun.ca/~melbaker/COMGOV.htm (November 2007).

Blake, Raymond B. *Canadians at Last. Canada Integrates Newfoundland as a Province.* Toronto: University of Toronto Press, 1994.

Bridle, Paul (ed.). *Documents on Relations between Canada and Newfoundland.* 2 vols. Ottawa: Department of External Affairs, 1974–1984.

Cadigan, Sean. *Newfoundland and Labrador: A History.* Toronto: University of Toronto Press, 2009.

Candow, James E. "Document: An American report on Newfoundland's health service in 1940." *Newfoundland Studies* 5.2 (1989): 221-39.

Chadwick, St. John. *Newfoundland: Island into Province.* London: Cambridge University Press, 1967.

Clark, Richard Leon. *Newfoundland 1934–1949 – A Study of the Commission of Government and Confederation with Canada.* Ph.D. Thesis, University of California, 1951.

Fizzard, Garfield (ed.). *Amulree's Legacy: Truth, Lies and Consequences Symposium: March 2000, Papers and Presentations.* St. John's: Newfoundland Historical Society, 2001.

Gwyn, Richard. *Smallwood: The Unlikely Revolutionary.* Toronto: McClelland and Stewart, 1972.

Handcock, Gordon. "The Commission of Government's Land Settlement Scheme in Newfoundland." *Twentieth Century Newfoundland: Explorations.* Eds. James Hiller and Peter Neary. St. John's: Breakwater, 1994. 123-51.

High, Steven. *Base Colonies in the Western Hemisphere, 1940–1967.* New York: Palgrave Macmillan, 2009.

Hiller, J.K. (ed.). *Newfoundland and Labrador Studies* (Special Issue on Confederation) 14.2, (Fall 1998).

Hiller, James K. *Confederation: Deciding Newfoundland's Future 1934 to 1949.* St. John's: Newfoundland Historical Society, 1998.

Hiller, J.K. and M.F. Harrington (eds.). *The Newfoundland National Convention, 1946–1948. Debates, Papers and Reports.* 2 vols. Montreal: McGill-Queen's University Press, 1995.

Hollohan, Francis and Melvin Baker (eds.). *A Clear Head in Tempestuous Times Albert B. Perlin: The Wayfarer: observations on the National Convention and the Confederation Issue, 1946–1949.*

St. John's: Harry Cuff Publications Limited, 1986.

Horwood, Harold. *A History of the Newfoundland Ranger Force.* St. John's: Breakwater, 1986.

Lodge, Thomas. *Dictatorship in Newfoundland.* London: Cassell, 1939.

Long, Gene. *Suspended State. Newfoundland Before Canada.* St. John's: Breakwater, 1999.

MacKay, R.A. (ed.). *Newfoundland Economic, Diplomatic, and Strategic Studies.* Toronto: Oxford University Press, 1946.

MacKenzie, David. *Inside the Atlantic Triangle. Canada and the Entrance of Newfoundland into Confederation, 1939–1949.* Toronto: University of Toronto Press, 1986.

MacLeod, Malcolm. *Nearer Than Neighbours: Newfoundland and Canada before Confederation.* St. John's: Creative Printers, 1982.

McCann, Phillip. "The Educational Policy of the Commission of Government." *Newfoundland Studies* 3.2 (1987): 201-15.

McCorquodale, Susan. *Public Administration in Newfoundland During the Period of the Commission of Government: A Question of Political Development.* Ph.D. Thesis, Queen's University, Kingston, 1973.

Neary, Peter. *Newfoundland in the North Atlantic World, 1929–1949.* Montreal: McGill-Queen's University Press, 1996.

Neary, Peter. " 'A Mortgaged Property': the Impact of the United States on Newfoundland, 1940–49." *Twentieth-Century Newfoundland: Explorations.* Eds. James Hiller and Peter Neary. Breakwater: St. John's, 1994. 179-94.

Neary, Peter. *The Political Economy of Newfoundland, 1929–1972.* Vancouver: Copp Clark Publishing, 1973.

Newfoundland Historical Society. *A Short History of Newfoundland and Labrador.* St. John's: Newfoundland Historical Society and Boulder Publications, 2008.

Newfoundland Royal Commission 1933 Report. London: HMSO, 1934. *Newfoundland and Labrador Heritage Web Site* http://www.heritage.nf.ca/law/amulree/amul_title.html (February 2008).

Noel, S.J.R. *Politics in Newfoundland.* Toronto: University of Toronto Press, 1971.

Overton, James. "Poverty, Dependence and Self-Reliance: Politics, Newfoundland History and the Amulree Report of 1933." *Amulree's Legacy: Truth, Lies and Consequences Symposium: March 2000, Papers and Presentations.* St. John's: Newfoundland Historical Society, 2001.

———. "Brown Flour and Beriberi: The Politics of Dietary and Health Reform in Newfoundland in the First Half of the Twentieth Century." *Newfoundland Studies* 14.1 (1998): 1-27.

———. "Moral Education of the Poor: Adult Education and Land Settlement Schemes in Newfoundland in the 1930s." *Newfoundland Studies* 11.2 (1995): 250-82.

Webb, Jeff A. *The Voice of Newfoundland: A Social History of the Broadcasting Corporation of Newfoundland, 1939–1949.* Toronto: University of Toronto Press, 2008.

———. "The Way it was Done: How Newfoundlanders Chose Confederation." *Newfoundland Quarterly.* December (2002): 26-32.

———. "The Responsible Government League and the Confederation Campaigns of 1948." *Newfoundland Studies* 5.2 (1989): 203-20.

14

Great Britain and the Future of Newfoundland, 1939–1945.*

By: Peter Neary.

Though rightly identified with death and destruction, war can sometimes incidentally and unexpectedly improve social order. Newfoundland's experience during the second world war is an excellent case in point. Battered by the Great Depression, Newfoundland surrendered responsible government in 1934 in favour of administration by a British-appointed commission, responsible to the Parliament of the United Kingdom through the Secretary of State for Dominion Affairs. In practice this system, introduced after a royal commission headed by the Scottish Labour Peer Lord Amulree had produced a scathing indictment of Newfoundland political leadership and public administration, combined a governor and six commissioners, three British and three Newfoundlanders (see *Nfld. Royal Com. 1933 Report*; Noel 186-214).

During the first five years of its existence, with the help of grants-in-aid from London, the Commission of Government effected many administrative changes and attempted several important social and economic reforms; but on the eve of the second world war Newfoundland was still mired economically. The recession of 1937–38 hit the Island hard, as its major industries, fishing, mining and pulp and paper manufacturing, were all highly exposed to international market forces. The Commission of Government had recovery plans in the late 1930s but these involved a reconstruction of local society whose benefits would take a long time to achieve. The return to economic well-being for Newfoundlanders, it seemed, would have to be a slogging route-march rather than a rapid, mechanized advance.

In a worried despatch, Governor Sir Humphrey Walwyn reported in July, 1938, that among the St. John's hard-core unemployed there was "a more surly and 'bolshie' spirit than there was two years ago as the prospect of any improvement in their economic condition shows no hope of materializing."[1] At the same time, "sensible people," while not against Commission of Government as such, were of the view that it had "failed to produce employment for all, failed to achieve a general economic improvement and failed to establish labour producing industries" (DO 35/725/N8/12 25). A harsher judgment was rendered early the following year when Lord Beaverbrook's London *Daily Express* sent the reporter Morley Richards to Newfoundland as its "Commissioner"; to the dismay of Whitehall and official St. John's he concluded that Newfoundland's Administration was "overwhelmingly unpopular" (March 27, 1939: 10).

Happily, relief was at hand, though it owed nothing to the plans either of the Commissioners or their mandarin masters in the Dominions Office. This was the war that began in September, 1939, which had a redeeming effect. By the summer of 1942, just over three years after Morley Richards' gloomy report, Newfoundland was, relatively, on the economic high road with her people enjoying the greatest prosperity they had ever known. Contemporary statistical evidence speaks for itself. Between December, 1938, and May, 1939, Newfoundland's relief recipients numbered 75,144 (the 1935 population of the Island and Labrador was 289,588); by 1942–43 the relief total for the same months had been reduced to only 6,907 (*Report on Financial & Econ. Pos.* 42). Simultaneously Newfoundland moved from an adverse to a favourable trade balance (43); and, beginning with the 1940–41 fiscal year, the Commission of Government produced the first of a series of budget surpluses that by 1946 would total $26 million (5).

In a report on economic conditions during 1940, the Commission noted "a distinct improvement" in the local economy; the equivalent report for 1942 described the change that had occurred in that year as "phenomenal" (DO 35/1143/N409/1 5; N409/2 6). Employment was now available to all who wanted it. By this time, moreover, the financial relationship with Great Britain had been reversed. In the fiscal year 1939–40 Newfoundland still needed a grant-in-aid from London to balance her books; but in 1941 she began making interest-free loans to Great Britain (DO 35/723/N2/73 50; DO 35/749/N314/6 77-78). By 1946 these amounted to $12.3 million (*Report on Financial & Econ. Pos.* 5). Such was the transformation the war quickly wrought.

What had caused the turnaround? Recruitment into her own armed forces and those of Canada and Great Britain, together with the sending of a forestry corps overseas (as in the First World War) undoubtedly helped; but above all Newfoundland's good fortune was a function of her strategic position in the North Atlantic in the age of air and submarine warfare. To defend themselves Canada and the United States had to defend Newfoundland, and it was their defence spending on the Island and in Labrador which accounted for the economic breakthrough. Canada was first on the scene following Prime Minister Mackenzie King's statement in the House of Commons on September 8, 1939, during the special session called to deal with the outbreak of fighting in Europe, that the "integrity of Newfoundland and Labrador" was essential "to the security of Canada" (Canada, *Debates* 35). In the grim month of June, 1940, after the fall of France, Canadian forces arrived in Newfoundland to defend the airbases at Botwood and Gander, which Great Britain and Newfoundland had built before the war in connection with experimental flights aimed at the opening up of a regular transatlantic air service (Bridle 116-21).

Gander now emerged as an indispensable link in the ferrying of aircraft and supplies to Great Britain. On November 10, 1940, seven American-built Hudson bombers lifted off its runways and wheeled out over the North Atlantic, the first of many such deliveries on one of World War II's most celebrated runs (Air 38/20 5). In April, 1941, Newfoundland concluded an agreement whereby the facilities at Gander and Botwood, together with a smaller base at Gleneagles, were transferred to Canadian control for the duration of the conflict (Bridle 1409-13). In 1941 also Canada began work on a fighter base at Torbay near St. John's (462-63). Yet another big Canadian wartime aviation enterprise in the region was the building of a base at Goose Bay, Labrador, to serve as an alternate to Gander in ferrying operations and to enhance general North American air defence. This difficult construction job was pushed forward with great speed and Goose was operational (though its runways were not yet paved) by December, 1941 (xlv). One British visitor likened arriving there in 1943 to coming on the "Ritz Hotel in the middle of the Kalahari desert" (DO 35/1375/665/5 255).

American military involvement in the region dates from the famous Anglo-American "Exchange of Notes regarding United States Destroyers and Naval and Air Facilities for the United States in British Transatlantic Territories" of September, 1940 (Great Britain, *Treaty Series* 15-16). Completed within a month of the issuing of the Atlantic Charter, this exchange presaged the building of the grand alliance that ultimately defeated the axis powers. In Newfoundland's case, Great Britain promised the United States base sites "freely and without consideration" (15). A lease was subsequently negotiated between Newfoundland and the United States and approved in a general Anglo-American leased bases agreement signed in London on March 27, 1941 (17-19). By this time, American forces had already been assigned to the Island. Three sizeable United States bases were built in Newfoundland – at St. John's, Argentia and Stephenville, giving the local economy an important new wage-paying industry. In the summer of 1942, at the height of the base-building boom, approximately 20,000 Newfoundlanders were employed on defence construction (*Rep. of Labour Relations Officer* 13). Nothing like it had ever happened on the Island before, and Newfoundlanders – men and women – were getting a taste for North American life that would endure.

The political consequences of these military and economic changes were manifold. The war highlighted the Commission of Government's administrative strengths and, in the short term at least, enhanced its legitimacy. Conflict and bureaucracy go hand in hand in the modern world, and the Commission was at its best in planning and in day-to-day administration. Furthermore, enlarged resources permitted it to enact badly needed educational and social welfare reforms; in 1942 schooling was made compulsory between the ages of seven and fourteen and a Labour Relations Office was created under the Commissioner for Public Utilities (see *Acts of Honourable Com. of Government 1942* 135-42: Neary "Canada and Nfld. Labour"). The latter Office carried out a national registration for employment purposes and set the terms under which Newfoundland contract workers could be recruited for jobs in the booming wartime industries of Canada and the United States. Its work demonstrated a growing sophistication in Newfoundland's public service and exemplified the larger international role now required of the Commission of Government.

Newfoundlanders looked outward in the busy and creative decade of the 1940s, and their government was called upon to defend their interests not only in base negotiations but in complex diplomatic bargaining over civil aviation and the management of the oceanic resources of the North Atlantic region. Among the Newfoundland Commissioners, the most active players abroad were L. E. Emerson who, as Commissioner for Justice and Defence, represented his countrymen at the 1941 London talks leading to the leased bases agreement, and Albert J. Walsh, who attended the civil aviation conferences at Chicago in 1944 and Bermuda in 1946.

Yet if the war gave the Commission of Government fresh purpose and enhanced prestige, it also raised again the question of Newfoundland's long-term constitutional future. The Commission system could be defended while the war was in progress on the grounds that change would disrupt the military effort and be unfair to those serving overseas who would be denied a say in what was being done; but the post-war political situation in Newfoundland would clearly be very volatile. In the age of the Atlantic Charter, Newfoundland's constitution was an anomaly that became harder and harder to defend. As one British document put it in 1944, "the objections to the present form of Government on grounds of constitutional theory are greatly reinforced today. It is constantly stated both here and in the United States that this war is being fought 'for democracy' and 'the democratic way of life'. The more this note is struck, the more glaring becomes the exceptional form of Government in Newfoundland – a white community, on the very doorstep of the American continent, self-governing for the best part of a century, enjoying Dominion status at the time of the Statute of Westminster, yet today with no representative institutions and with its constitution in suspense" (DO 35/1342/N402/29 175-76).

When the Commission of Government had been introduced in 1934, it had been agreed that self-government would be restored to Newfoundlanders at their request once they could support themselves again (Great Britain, *Public General Acts* 10). No definition had been given to "self-supporting," and no mechanism had been specified for the request that would trigger a return to the *status quo ante*. These omissions had not mattered in the dismal 1930s but by 1942 it was obvious to the Dominions Office that they would have to be addressed, even though Newfoundlanders themselves, enjoying the fruits of their economic revival, never pushed very hard or very systematically during the war for constitutional change. In 1943 Governor Walwyn wrote that what they really wanted was "a comfortable grant-in-aid and little responsibility" (DO 35/1141/N402/11 9) but his view had long since been overtaken by events, the belief in London being that "a new and vigorous policy with regard to Newfoundland" had become imperative (DO 35/723/N2/73 5). In the making of this policy, it was assumed that the existing good times in Newfoundland were accidental and that the Island faced a difficult post-war adjustment, a view that persisted even though the base-building boom was followed by a period of high demand for Newfoundland's export staples and continuing improvement in her public accounts.

The issues at stake for Great Britain were brought sharply into focus after Clement Attlee, the leader of the Labour Party, became Deputy Prime Minister and Secretary of State for Dominion Affairs in February, 1942. In May, 1942, Grant Mackenzie, the new minister's personal assistant, produced a long memorandum on the "Problem of Newfoundland," together with a brief account of his "personal impressions" for Attlee's private information (DO 121/92). Heretical in approach, Mackenzie wrote favourably of former Commissioner Thomas Lodge's 1939 *Dictatorship in Newfoundland* and the complaining reports of Geoffrey Shakespeare, Parliamentary Under-Secretary of State in the Dominions Office, and J. J. S. Garner, a civil servant in the same Office, who had visited the Island in 1941 and been shocked by its backwardness. Whereas since 1934 the instinct of the permanent officials in London concerned with Newfoundland had been to smother all criticism of their policies (Lodge was their *bête noire*), Mackenzie, coming from the outside, had nothing to defend and nobody to protect.

The result was a scathing indictment of the British record. The Commission of Government had done useful ameliorative work but had "failed" overall because it had not tackled "fundamentals." Nor was the root of the trouble in St. John's. The "primary responsibility" for what had occurred was Whitehall's because the Commission was what Great

Britain had made it. Unwisely, the Commission had assumed that the fishery must remain Newfoundland's economic mainstay, the result being that the industry was expected to absorb more and more manpower, whether it could provide an adequate return per man or not. Likewise the Commission had avoided the obstacle to development posed by a too-scattered population. Until the Island's people were reorganized in fewer settlements, transportation costs would remain high, education would falter, and "deadly parochial inbreeding" would continue. What was to be done? Mackenze's prescient answer was typically Fabian: Newfoundland's future lay in planning and political education. Great Britain should restore responsible government but not before a long-term plan of social and economic reconstruction had been drawn up and carried out. The fashioning of this plan should be the job of a reorganized commission, presided over by a new governor, appointed for his gifts of knowledge and leadership.

In September, 1942, Attlee himself visited Newfoundland, recording his impressions of it in a witty and characteristically trenchant note (DO 35/723/N2/73 58-67). Politics, he wrote, was regarded locally as something of a "national sport," and the Commission system had not only ended self-government but "a form of amusement" (59). Newfoundlanders believed that government was something from which one took rather than to which one gave and, alas, the absence of democratic practice since 1934 had not been offset by an attempt to teach them democratic theory. The Commission had been remiss most of all in its failure to prepare Newfoundlanders to resume self-government. L. E. Emerson thought that the Commission should rule for twenty years but had no suggestions about how his countrymen could be made fit to govern themselves again. "He would," Attlee observed, "keep his football team all the season in the dressing room without even a punt about and expect them to be fit to win a match at the end" (64). On the other hand, it was doubtful if the pre-1934 Newfoundland politicians who had been so discredited had been any worse than their Canadian and Australian counterparts. What had really distinguished them was their "narrower margin" (62). The Commission of Government had been ill-conceived, the creation of the administrative mind. It was aloof and its members tended to work in "water-tight compartments," without general purpose: "the machine was running but it was not progressing to any clear goal and there was no one at the steering wheel. All were busy keeping the engine running" (63-64). Newfoundlanders were disappointed that the Commission had not attracted more British capital but "hardly anyone" thought responsible government could be restored during the war (62). There was, however, a widespread desire to find some constitutional "half way house," though the schemes Attlee had heard about "would clearly breed irresponsibility." Great Britain, he concluded, had these choices:

> We can with general assent continue the Commission till the end of the war. There will then be an irresistible demand supported by all the weight of democratic sentiment for a return to a self government. If we accede to this we shall probably have a Government which will spend the available balances in an effort to cope with depression with a consequent return to bankruptcy.
>
> We can refuse self government with the result that we shall have to meet all the odium of the post-war slump which will be laid to our charge because we refused to let the people run their own affairs.
>
> We can try to formulate some system less than full self government keeping the brake in our own hands. We shall then promote irresponsibility and probably get the blame for everything that goes wrong.
>
> We can concede self government now while the going is good and while war conditions impose a certain restraint on the Government.
>
> We can try to devise some different form of Government which, while democratic, does not conform to the Westminster model. We can put off the evil day by appointing a commission of inquiry. (66-67)

Attlee did not put off the evil day, taking the first step into the maze in a lengthy telegram to the Commission of Government dated November 25, 1942 (DO 114/103 1-2). So as not to be overtaken by events, he wrote, it was important that a policy be devised for constitutional change in Newfoundland at the end of the war. For the moment, Confederation had to be ruled out as unacceptable to public opinion in both Canada and Newfoundland. This left three possibilities: the continuation of the existing system; self-government; or a constitutional "half way house." Of these only the second and third were realistic since the existing approach to government would not be appropriate in post-war circumstances. What Newfoundlanders seemed to favour, to the extent that they had considered the matter, was not "self-government at a single plunge" but a two-stage process whereby Whitehall would at first retain some financial control. Great Britain was not, of course, an entirely free agent in the matter. A "contract" had been made with the people of Newfoundland in 1933 and, assuming they were self-supporting, a general demand from them for the restoration of self-government could not be refused. In a different vein, noting how "undesirable" it was to have "all political activity. . .focussed on St. John's," Attlee advocated the creation of regional citizens' committees along the lines of the West Coast Association already functioning in Corner Brook. These should not merely provide an outlet for existing grievances but animate the political life of the country through general discussion of both local and island-wide problems. Lastly, Attlee asked the Commission's opinion of the worth of a special enquiry into Newfoundland's post-war economic prospects.

In its reply, received on January 15, 1943, the Commission accepted that there were economic difficulties ahead for Newfoundland; the prevailing prosperity was "accidental" and was already being eroded (2-5). With public expectations rising, Newfoundland would need assistance "for a number of years" to meet her obligations. This being so, the Commission contended, a wider range of possible forms of government than that proposed by London should be examined. In particular the continuation of the existing system and Confederation should be considered. While there undoubtedly were some Newfoundlanders who desired to return to responsible government after the war, there were others, perhaps a larger group, who feared that such a change, in the absence of proof that the country could support itself, might be economically unfortunate. A majority would probably support change but many believed that Newfoundland could have responsible government *and* grants-in-aid. If the latter were deemed impossible, incorporation into a larger state would look more attractive and a constitutional vote might produce a different result. Here two possibilities suggested themselves: association with the United Kingdom on the model of Northern Ireland or Confederation. There was, of course, reason to believe that Canada might be more receptive to union than ever before. Her interest in Newfoundland was growing; she feared United States influence there; and she wanted Labrador. Newfoundland's bargaining position *vis-à-vis* Canada had never been so favourable. Accordingly, Confederation might "be explored in secret between persons in the highest quarters."

Procedurally, the Commission argued, one of two conditions would have to be met before any change, other than the restoration of responsible government, could be effected: either the people would have to be consulted and approve; or a royal commission would have to make such a recommendation. As for Attlee's regional council idea, the Commission balked. Local self-government was readily available for those who wanted it; all that was required was willingness to pay taxes. This was the sticky point, there being "a profound conviction everywhere, except perhaps St. John's, that the taxation which a man pays to the Central Government is all the taxation he ought to be asked to pay and there is no hope of breaking down this conviction by argument." Regional associations might well encourage political debate but it would be a mistake for the government to sponsor them. It would be better to "stimulate" their formation informally and encourage them once established.

The Commission was also critical of Attlee's suggestion of a further economic enquiry. Newfoundland had been the subject of many such investigations and another would be useful only if it brought together "men of high standing with national reputations" who would be willing to devote a year or two to this work so as to appreciate fully local circumstances.

Next Attlee decided to send three members of Parliament to Newfoundland. This typified an approach which also led him to initiate study groups on local and parliamentary government among Newfoundland soldiers and forestry unit personnel serving in the United Kingdom (DO 35/1343/N402/32 110-13, 126): the parliamentarians would educate and animate Newfoundland public opinion and inform their colleagues at home. "Nothing could be more dangerous," the Commission of Government was told in the March 17, 1943, telegram inviting its acceptance of the proposed mission, "than that the Newfoundland people, now for some nine years without representative institutions, and without even any system of local or district government to give them training and experience in the management of public affairs, should suddenly be called upon, as it were overnight, to resume a form of self-government. In other words, there should be some preparation without delay for possible developments" (DO 114/103 5). The proposed mission would not have a formal structure but would be "goodwill" in nature (6). Its members would survey the local scene "and form some idea both of the potentialities of the country and of the capacity of Newfoundlanders to take charge of their own affair." This approach would have the advantage of showing Newfoundlanders that their "special problems" were being considered by the United Kingdom, without distracting attention from the war effort (6). It would encourage constitutional debate while "helping the Commission guide it in a useful direction" (6).

When the Commission was consulted about this proposal, it argued for the appointment instead of a royal commission to examine the whole constitutional position (6). Conditioning its response was an agitation which had developed, principally among businessmen, against the imposition, retroactively of increased taxes on the inflated incomes realized in the boom year of 1942 (see DO 35/1333/N402/1/2 92-95, 105-07). On March 8, 1943, a special meeting of the Newfoundland Board of Trade had come out in favour of "some form of representative Government" and had appointed a committee to make specific recommendations (DO 114/103 9). For several reasons, however, Whitehall rejected the royal commission idea (7). Such an enquiry would be premature because the route to be taken constitutionally after the war would depend on the economic circumstances of the day and these could not yet be forecast.

Again, a royal commission would disrupt the war effort, while denying the many Newfoundlanders serving outside the country a voice in their own future. Ultimately, by showing just how divided Newfoundland opinion was, the protest which had led the Commission of Government to press for a larger enquiry only served to confirm London in the wisdom of its intended course. Thus, when the Board of Trade and the West Newfoundland Association passed resolutions, on March 29 and April 7 respectively, favouring a new royal commission (8-9), their proposal was immediately rejected by seven prominent labour leaders. The view of the latter was that, in keeping with the bargain made in 1933, the single requirement for the return of responsible government was the presentation to the King by the "electors of Newfoundland" of a petition requesting it (8). Until this was done the Commission should continue to govern.

On May 5, 1943, Attlee announced to the Commons the despatch of the Parliamentary mission, pointing out in subsequent debate that Newfoundlanders were "kinsmen" and that by emphasizing "personal contacts" the government was acknowledging this fact (15; DO 35/1333/N402/1/2 43). C. G. Ammon, the Labour Member for Camberwell, would lead the mission and would have as colleagues Sir Derek Gunston, the Conservative member for Thornbury, and A. P. Herbert, the senior member for Oxford University and an Independent. Arriving in St. John's on June 21, the three M.P.s, accompanied by G. W. St. John Chadwick of the Dominions Office as Secretary, travelled extensively about the Island and as far north on the Labrador coast as Hopedale (DO 114/103 17; DO 35/1336/N402/1/10 48, 78). By the time they returned to England in September they had canvassed the views of a wide range of people and developed clear and strong opinions of their own. The one bad moment for the mission came towards the end of its stay when Ammon presented Gunston and Herbert with a report he proposed to make on behalf of the whole group (DO 35/1334/N402/1/8 30-32). His initiative was rejected by his associates and individual reports were eventually given to the Secretary of State (30-32; see DO 35/1336/N402/1/10 48-84, 87-124 for the reports of Ammon and Gunston). These were circulated to St. John's for the private information of the Commission but the Dominions Office rejected the latter's suggestion that they be published (DO 114/103 18, 22, 25).

In 1944, however, to the shock of Whitehall, Ammon published a revised version of his report as a Fabian booklet entitled *Newfoundland: The Forgotten Island* (DO 35/1339/N402/1/13 53, 59-60, 63-64, 84). Ammon, Herbert and Gunston agreed that a vote should be held in Newfoundland after the war, though they differed about its timing and substance (see DO 35/1335/N402/1/9 for their constitutional recommendations). Ammon and Herbert also favoured a ten-year development plan, to be carried out with British support. There was altruism in their advocacy of this, a desire to see Great Britain live up to her overseas responsibilities, do well by a plucky ally, and ensure Newfoundland a place in the better tomorrow for which the war was being fought; but the development proposed also recognized that political and economic change in Newfoundland were inseparable and "there must be no Imperial slum on the back doorstep of the United States" (DO 35/1142/N402/1/12 10). In Ammon's scheme the development plan would be the subject of the election. If approved at the polls, it would be carried out by a Commission of Government modified to include elected Newfoundland members. A second vote would then be held in ten years. If the development plan and the constitutional changes it involved were rejected by the electorate, self-government would immediately be restored.

Herbert favoured the early announcement that a vote on the constitution would be held two years after the war, together with a commitment by Great Britain to help Newfoundland regain responsible government within the next year unless her people chose otherwise. One year after the announcement of the vote to be taken on the constitution, an election would be held for the three Newfoundland seats on the Commission of Government. Before the constitutional vote a citizens' council, soon universally referred to as a national convention, would be appointed to consider possibilities for future government. With the recommendations of this body before them, the people would then decide on the form of government they wanted and the date of its inauguration. For his part Gunston wanted a vote five years after the war to decide whether responsible government should be reintroduced or not. In the meantime the Newfoundland seats on the Commission would be filled by election and the Governor return to being the King's representative alone.

This latter change was also envisaged by Ammon and Herbert. While differing on timing and method of selection, the members of the mission further accepted that the Governor's place at the head of the Commission table should be taken by a chairman.

On November 8, 1943, with these recommendations in hand, Lord Cranborne, who had succeeded Attlee at the Dominions Office the previous September, submitted a lengthy memorandum on Newfoundland to the War Cabinet (DO 35/1337/N402/1/11 208-11). The parliamentary mission, he told his colleagues, had found local opinion on the constitutional question "very fluid and divided" (208). Still, there was general agreement in the country on three principal matters: that the Commission system should not be altered during the war; that when a change was made, it should not be to "full responsible government" on the pre-1934 model; and that confederation was "wholly out of the question" (208). Union with Canada might well be the best solution, Cranborne asserted, but it was "a matter in which His Majesty's Government in the United Kingdom could not directly intervene" (209). Opposition to it in Newfoundland had several sources: the fear of direct taxation was one; the belief that small regional business would be "swamped" by large Canadian enterprise another; and the worry that "Newfoundland's interests would be sacrificed to those of Toronto and Montreal" a third (209). Confederation was thought of as a "drastic" step and would not be possible while there was "money in the till" (209). On the other hand, union with the United Kingdom along the lines of Northern Ireland flew in the face of geography, advances in air travel notwithstanding. "What most Newfoundlanders would like to look forward to after the war," Cranborne submitted, "would be some form of self-government which, while leaving the Island free to manage its own affairs, would provide for the retention by the United Kingdom of a general supervision over its finances and would thus enable it to turn for assistance to the United Kingdom Exchequer in case of need. In other words, they would like both to eat their cake and have it" (209). While a "clear-cut solution" would be preferable, the United Kingdom had to be prepared to accommodate Newfoundlanders if they wanted to return to full self-government in stages (209). What Great Britain must avoid at all costs, however, was backing any future Newfoundland government free to borrow and spend as it saw fit.

From this analysis Cranborne recommended that a public announcement of British intentions be made forthwith to satisfy the expectations the parliamentary mission had aroused. Such a statement, he argued, would have a "steadying effect" (211) on Newfoundland and should reflect a five-point policy: no constitutional change during the war; the promise that "as soon as practicable" after the war in Europe, Newfoundlanders would be provided with "machinery" by which to consider their constitutional future, in the light of prevailing circumstances; a commitment to restore full self-government if that was what Newfoundlanders then wanted and if they were self-supporting; a commitment "to examine. . .sympathetically" proposals expressive of the "general wish" of Newfoundlanders, for either the continuation of the Commission or the introduction of a system that was less than "full responsible government"; and the promise that, pending the post-war review, local government would be advanced and general reconstruction plans devised (209-10). At the same time Cranborne rejected the idea that the Commission at once be made more representative through the election of its Newfoundland members. There were objections to this both in theory and practice. Such a change would not only confuse the existing chain of command, but by producing "unsuitable men" might breed "disharmony" and, possibly, the "premature break-up" of the established order (211).

On November 18, while Cranborne was consulting the Commission about the wording of the proposed parliamentary statement, an alternative plan for Newfoundland was put to the cabinet by Lord Beaverbrook, the Lord Privy Seal (DO 35/1337/N402/1/11 202). His position was that the Commission had lost its legal foundation, given that Newfoundland had become self-supporting. Moreover, it was now believed in Newfoundland that corruption had not caused the *débâcle* of the 1930s and that responsible government had been given up in the interest of the country's bondholders and the Canadian banks. With Newfoundlanders pushing for the restoration of self-government (seven local newspapers were said to be supporting the cause), Great Britain should respond generously, thereby strengthening her hand in relation both to Canada's unjust claim over Goose Bay (the lease to this site was still being negotiated) and demands which could be expected from the

Americans about the use of their bases in Newfoundland for civil aviation purposes. A self-governing Newfoundand would defend the Imperial position in the western Atlantic against any "ganging up" by Canada and the United States. Not surprisingly, the highly combative view did not prevail, the policy advocated by Cranborne being adopted by the War Cabinet on November 19 with only minor amendments. There was to be a preamble in the statement indicating that Great Britain's "whole policy" was governed by the commitment she had made in 1933 concerning the restoration of responsible government; and "soundings" were to be taken immediately to determine what particular constitution-making machinery would be acceptable to Newfoundland opinion (179).

On December 2, 1943, the announcement presaged in these discussions was made in the House of Commons by P. V. Emrys-Evans, who had succeeded Geoffrey Shakespeare as Parliamentary Under-Secretary at the Dominions Office (Great Britain, *Parl. Debates*, House of Commons, cols. 599-600). Constitutional means had now been spelled out for Newfoundland (however vaguely), but the British remained open-minded about constitutional ends and still envisaged themselves assisting a new administration in St. John's economically provided they could retain a political control commensurate with their financial responsibility. "I would like to add," Emrys-Evans told the House after outlining the main policy points, "that there is no desire on the part of the Government to impose any particular solution. The Government will be guided by the freely expressed views of the people. It is for Newfoundland to make the choice, and the Government, with the assent of Parliament, will be very ready to give effect to their wishes" (600). Subsequently, the British worked within the four corners of this declaration; but by the time they had to invoke the procedure for constitutional review promised in 1943, they had come to favour strongly and were promoting actively a decision by Newfoundlanders in favour of Confederation. What brought them to this position was the difficulty ultimately posed by the reconstruction they had now also promised. Financing this, they eventually came to see, was beyond them. Political change was unavoidable in St. John's but an independent Newfoundland would need a backer. If Great Britain could not play this role, Canada would have to shoulder the responsibility.

On December 16, 1943, all three members of the Parliamentary mission were heard in a full-scale debate on Newfoundland affairs in the House of Commons. Then, on January 6, 1944, in a lengthy telegram to St. John's, Cranborne addressed the definition of the procedure to be followed after the war (DO 114/103 32-34). Having earlier informed the Commission that he was attracted by A. P. Herbert's suggestion of a national convention, he now dealt with the problem of selecting its members, listing three possibilities: nomination by the governor; election by popular vote on a district-by-district basis, perhaps using the pre-1934 constituencies; and appointment by the Governor of associational representatives together with nominees of his own, the whole to form a "complete cross-section" of local society (20, 32). Of these Cranborne preferred the third, but he invited the Commission's views, while suggesting further that a British constitutional lawyer be attached to the convention to advise and perhaps chair it. On the crucial question of what would happen after the convention had completed its business, Cranborne insisted that Great Britain must keep a free hand. The recommendations of the convention would have to be considered in London. How the Newfoundland people would then be called upon to decide would depend on the nature of the proposals put forward and the extent of the support for them in the convention.

Simultaneously, Cranborne asked the Commission to submit a comprehensive long-term program for reconstruction to be considered jointly by the Dominions Office and Treasury. Assuming their negotiations went well, this program would be approved in principle and published in Newfoundland with a statement indicating Great Britain's willingness to assist financially in carrying it out. Because of Newfoundland's existing prosperity, such assistance, it was assumed, would not be needed at first, while the help to be given later on would be decided in accordance with the decisions Newfoundlanders made about their constitutional future. Equally, the plan would be adopted on the understanding that it could be reviewed by any Newfoundland government that took office before its completion. From London's perspective this approach had two advantages: it would forestall criticism that the economic development of Newfoundland was being held back by the procedure that had been adopted on the constitutional issue; and it would get reconstruction going while leaving the United Kingdom free to determine its contribution as the constitutional situation changed. The carrying out of the plan was to proceed at once in the case of projects which would not detract from the war effort.

The request for a master economic plan was favourably received in St. John's, where a great deal of work had already been done along the lines suggested. In January, 1942, the Commission had formed a committee to plan for the return of servicemen to civilian life and for general economic reconstruction (see DO 35/1156/N718/1 10-13 for information on Newfoundland's planning for the post-war period). Sub-committees of this group had studied fisheries rehabilitation, vocational and technical training and interrupted education, employment assistance, forestry and forest products rehabilitation, and agriculture and land settlement. In 1942 also an Industrial Development Board had been formed to assist in the expansion of existing industries, foster new ones, and undertake independent economic enquiry (see *Acts of Honourable Com. of Government 1942* 1-5). As a result of the Commission's own planning work, the Dominions Office had already approved in principle projects for fisheries, land settlement and agricultural development (DO 114/103 34). In effect, therefore, Cranborne's new economic proposal was the logical extension of what had already been achieved.

Though it would fuss as always, the Commission was clearly ready to march forward on the planning side, but it bristled over what London was now proposing constitutionally, fearing it would be tried or usurped by a national convention. In keeping with such worries, the Commission argued in its February 23, 1944, reply to Cranborne's proposals that, though public opinion in Newfoundland had been relatively quiet since the Parliamentary statement in December, opposition might yet well up against what was intended (35-37). The groundwork for such a protest had been laid in various letters to the editor that had appeared after L. E. Emerson had chided Newfoundlanders for their seeming indifference to the big decisions presently being made about their future. The Commissioners foresaw two possible lines of attack. A pact, opponents of the national convention could argue, had been made in 1933 between the United Kingdom and Newfoundland which allowed only two constitutional choices: commission of government or the *status quo ante*. This pact could not be changed unilaterally and on the Newfoundland side could only be altered by "the same kind of body" which had originally accepted it – a responsible government (36). Much might also be made of the argument, already being advanced, that Great Britain would be guilty of "a breach of faith" if she did not offer Newfoundlanders their old constitution back once they had shown definitively that they could support themselves (36). If there had to be a convention, however, it would have to be territorially based. A body formed in this way would at least have the strength of democratic theory behind it and could be deemed the legitimate heir of the elected assembly which had made the 1933 arrangements. Members might be returned to the convention – the idea for this procedure originated with J. C. Puddester (another Newfoundland Commissioner) – in a two-stage process: primary elections would return town and settlement delegates for a given area who would then meet to decide the representation of the whole region. In this despatch also Newfoundland's government returned to its earlier advocacy of a commission to enquire into the country's financial and economic situation and, on the basis of its findings, to frame constitutional recommendations. Practically, the Commission submitted, there were only two options: responsible government or, substantially at least, the existing system. If Whitehall wanted the people to vote on other constitutional possibilities, an enquiry would be necessary to define them, as a national convention, being a representative body, could not produce the clear-cut choices a vote would entail. Given all that was at stake, the Commission suggested that one or more of its members go to London for talks with Cranborne before he completed his plans.

Two dissenting views complicated this report from St. John's. P. D. H. Dunn, the British Commissioner for Natural Resources, argued that in late 1944, after the reconstruction plan was drafted and funded, a vote should be held on the restoration of responsible government. He detected "a strong though as yet unexpressed desire for a change in the form of Government" (37). If Great Britain did not satisfy this, she would, given an economic downturn, face a political crisis and have to give way under pressure. The longer Newfoundlanders were kept in the "cotton wool" which had protected them since 1934, the more difficult it would be for them to resume self-government (37). An electoral verdict in favour of continuing the Commission system would also be beneficial. The Commission's weakness was that it lacked a popular mandate. If it were given one, it would be able to take the "drastic action against vested interests" that reconstruction might involve (37). Otherwise its work would be impaired and badly needed reforms delayed.

Governor Walwyn thought that Dunn was "unsettled" and "rather fed up" but his own views were no less outspoken, though they changed nothing in Whitehall (DO 35/1338/N402/1/11 202-03). According to Walwyn the constitutional outcome would have to be "in the nature of a half way house" (199). The Commissioners, he reported, rejected this solution because of their belief that "having once enjoyed self responsibility you can't step down"; but only a "noisy minority" in Newfoundland wanted old style responsible government (200). In any case the whole debate hinged on the meaning of self-supporting. "The country," Walwyn wrote, "could no doubt carry on in a Robinson Crusoe style and standard now, but with the present standard, which is far in advance of what it was several years ago, definitely *no*; with the reconstruction in sight, schools, sanitoria, cottage hospitals, settlements, roads, etc., in fact nearly up to English standard, it is too obviously impossible to contemplate without heavy or continuous grants-in-aid" (200). Great Britain should launch the general enquiry the Commission was advocating, but should not call it a royal commission lest it "be greeted with hoots of derision, because we have had so many missions." Though the Commission of Government could itself best guide the proposed national convention, it could not command public acceptance in this role.

The Dominions Office readily agreed to receive a delegation from St. John's but, for the moment at least, dismissed the policy objections heard from there. Dunn's case for an immediate vote was rejected because the arguments against a wartime election of any kind were "decisive" (DO 114/103 38). Equally, the worries of the other Commissioners about the national convention proposal were dismissed as insubstantial. To say that by accepting the Amulree recommendations, Newfoundlanders had limited themselves, when the moment for constitutional change arrived, to either the restoration of responsible government or the continuation of the Commission system, seemed to the Dominions Office to be absurd. It was "only reasonable" that before deciding their constitutional future the people "should be given the opportunity through their representatives of taking stock of the position in all its aspects" (38). Whitehall was, however, willing to be "guided by the advice of the Commission" on the "means" by which the convention should be called together and accepted that that body would need expert and independent economic and financial advice (38).

A negotiation followed over which Commissioners should go to England. A party of three, including two Newfoundlanders, was readily decided upon, and Dunn, Puddester and Emerson were chosen for the mission, which was to arrive in London late in July (41, 45). When the British suggested that H. A. Winter (another Newfoundlander) replace Emerson, who was expected to resign shortly to become Chief Justice, the Commission insisted that the latter be included because of his greater knowledge of constitutional and legal questions (42-43). In early June, after the Commissioner of Finance, Ira Wild, had visited London, more detailed instructors were sent to St. John's about the preparation of the reconstruction program. Specifically, the Commission was told that the plan should emphasize "measures for expanding the economy of the country and adding to its earning power" (44).

The talks which followed in London in August, 1944, between Lord Cranborne and Commissioners Dunn, Emerson and Puddester produced significant advances both constitutionally and economically. On August 8 Cranborne told the Commissioners that, while he had not yet broached the matter with his government colleagues, he favoured the passing of a special act of Parliament to fund over ten years the capital costs of development schemes in Newfoundland which he and the Chancellor of the Exchequer might approve (DO 35/1142/N402/31 7). The United Kingdom might also, he now indicated, take over Newfoundland's sterling debt if she in turn would put an amount equal to the annual charges on this towards the recurring costs of the development projects to be undertaken. This would be generous assistance indeed, and the Commissioners were quick to point out that its announcement before

Newfoundlanders voted in a referendum on their constitutional future would guarantee "an overwhelming vote in favour of a return to responsible Government" (9). This being so, Great Britain would need to establish a "controlling Corporation" which would remain independent of any future Newfoundland responsible government (9).

Cranborne agreed and on August 10 proposed that a joint development board be established when Parliament approved the development grant for Newfoundland and while the Commission of Government was still in office (3-4). This board would be chaired by a judge of the Newfoundland Supreme Court, and Great Britain and Newfoundland would each nominate three members to it. Future United Kingdom members might be the Comptroller and Auditor General of Newfoundland, who would remain a British appointee for the development period, the United Kingdom Trade Commissioner in Newfoundland and "one prominent Newfoundlander outside political life" (DO 35/1342/N402/29 185). The board, which would also have a secretary seconded from the United Kingdom, would consider and approve all schemes put forward for funding before they were submitted to London. Proposals to alter schemes approved before the board came into existence would have to be submitted through it to Whitehall for approval. The board would supervise the carrying out of funded projects and report to both the Newfoundland government and the Secretary of State for Dominion Affairs. Newfoundland would be required to produce for publication both locally and in the United Kingdom an annual report, including audited statements, on all funded items. Likewise, it would not be allowed to borrow externally without British agreement while the assistance program was in effect.

The advantages of these arrangements to Great Britain were manifest; and the proposed timing of the establishment of the board was also in her interest (see DO 35/1342/N402/31 3-4). If the board was functioning and accepted when Newfoundlanders decided their constitutional future, Great Britain would avoid a direct and potentially embarrassing link between the reintroduction of responsible government and the imposition of new financial controls. Again, by the time a decision could be made in favour of responsible government the reliability of the board would be known. Finally, the membership of the board would enlarge Newfoundland representation under the Commission of Government and thereby answer local complaints on that subject.

After Dunn, Emerson and Puddester arrived back in St. John's, the reconstruction proposals made in London were accepted in principle by the whole Commission (DO 114/103 46). But the Newfoundland Government questioned both the practicability, given its administrative resources, of emphasizing schemes of economic growth; and the wisdom of appointing a development board while the existing constitution was in force (46-47). Economic growth schemes, the Commission argued, would require time to develop and in some cases would necessitate a trial-and-error approach. It would be a mistake in a published program even to outline projects that had not been thought through. To do so would only "excite public hopes" and perhaps encourage waste (47). Further, it would be unwise to have two local bodies responsible to London. Nor would Newfoundlanders take the coincidence of the establishment of a development board and the reintroduction of elected government as a sign of British distrust. The opposite would be true: "The fact is," the Commission ventured, "that in all discussions of return to responsible government with or without financial aid from the United Kingdom, the hope is universally expressed that 'financial controls' will be established" (47). In reply the Dominions Office informed the Commission that only "a general outline" of the reconstruction program would be needed for publication (48). On the other hand, detailed estimates, giving priority to development over social services, would be required for departmental use in London. Nor did the Commission win its point about the development board. The establishment of this body on the announcement of the reconstruction program, it was told, would encourage the idea that the economic plan stood "on its own merits" and would be carried out whatever happened constitutionally (48). In any case, while the Commission governed, the three Newfoundland members of the board would "doubtless" be drawn from its ranks, a procedure which in itself should obviate any problem *vis-à-vis* Westminster (48).

With these explanations the various strands of the Commission of Government's planning effort could at last be woven together; and on September 25, 1944, Governor Walwyn forwarded to London the comprehensive program which had been requested (49-51). It was one of the major documents of the Commission period and anticipated much that would happen in Newfoundland during the next two decades. It was above all a fund of ideas for the future and as such belies the notion that the origins of the "unlikely" revolution which would occur in Newfoundland in the 1950s and 1960s are to be found in these decades alone.

The Commission's proposals were organized under four headings: "Economic Development Schemes"; "Improvement of Communications"; "Social Improvement Schemes"; and "Government Buildings" (DO 35/1342/N402/29 54-55; see also 12-31). The amounts to be spent in these categories were, respectively, \$ 39,600,000, \$ 30,000,000, \$ 26,300,000, and \$ 4,100,000, for a grand total of \$ 100,000,000. Under economic development, the part of the program the Commission had most haggled over, \$ 10,500,000 was set aside for "Supplementary Schemes. . .and Contingencies." Of the remainder, \$ 9,500,000 was to be dedicated to fisheries research and development; \$ 9,100,000 to land settlement and research, and geodetic surveying and aerial photography; \$ 1,000,000 to forest research and operations; \$ 6,000,000 to industrial research and government participation in new enterprises; \$ 1,000;000 to mineral exploration on the Island of Newfoundland and in Labrador; and \$ 2,500,000 to tourism. Under improvement of communications, the largest appropriation was \$ 16,000,000 for roads and bridges, but \$ 6,000,000 was provided for railway improvement (including dock facilities and steamer services) and \$ 5,000,000 for air service. This category also featured wharves and breakwaters (\$ 2,000,000) and telegraphs and telephones (\$ 1,000,000).

In the area of social policy the Commission's plan included major changes in education, health and welfare, housing and local government services. For education the provision of \$ 8,500,000 included \$ 5,000,000 for school building and curriculum improvement and \$1,500,000 for the construction of regional high schools. A vocational institute was to be built in St. John's and Memorial College expanded. The expenditure proposed for the building and equipping of hospitals together with other health care improvements was $7,400,000, while $5,000,000 was to be devoted to housing schemes outside St. John's, the capital itself being provided for by the St. John's Housing Corporation launched by a July, 1944 Act (see *Acts of Honourable Com. of Government 1944* 132-41). Local government was to be fostered with a like sum, while $2,000,000 was to be spent on central government buildings in St. John's.

While the reconstruction plan was thus being completed, important developments were also occurring on the constitutional side. In July the Commission assigned Magistrate Nehemiah Short of Corner Brook to look into the mechanics of returning a national convention – by primary or secondary elections or otherwise as his findings indicated (DO 114/103 45). In taking this step, however, the Commissioners again disputed in principle Cranborne's entire approach, arguing that in Newfoundland's circumstances a national convention would not be able to distil "wide and complicated issues" into clear electoral choices; but the talks that followed in London in August, 1944, buried this criticism (42, 46). For his part, Magistrate Short quickly concluded that primary and secondary elections would be expensive, difficult to administer and unpopular (45). His alternative recommendation, communicated to London on September 7, was that members be returned to the convention according to the traditions of the House of Assembly – by secret ballot and for the electoral districts, altered slightly as population change required, described in the redistribution act of 1925 (47). In this scheme of things a candidate for the national convention would have to be a voter in and a bona fide resident of a district in order to be nominated for it.

Other proposals about the national convention generally agreed on between London and St. John's by September, 1944, were that it should be presided over by a judge of the Supreme Court of Newfoundland and that it should be assisted by a British constitutional lawyer (DO 35/1342/N402/29 179). While the convention would not be preceded by the full-scale enquiry into Newfoundland's situation and prospects the Commission had long advocated, its members would be provided by Great Britain with a survey of the country's financial and economic position (179). This would be prepared by two officials, one each from the Dominions Office and Treasury, who would go to Newfoundland not immediately as the Commission requested but once the calling of the national convention had been announced in Parliament (DO 114/103 46, 48; DO 35/1342/N402/29 221).

The completion of the reconstruction plan and the refinement by the Dominions Office of its national convention policy set the stage for a broader debate within the British government on the future of Newfoundland. On September 22, 1944, Cranborne sent a lengthy note to the Chancellor of the Exchequer explaining developments to date (DO 35/1342/N402/29 172-80). While Newfoundlanders, this document argued, would "choose their own course for themselves after the war," Great Britain could not "just leave it at that and wait and see what happens" (177). Left to themselves Newfoundlanders would probably opt for a constitutional "half-way house" but this, it was now stated, would be "most embarrassing" to the United Kingdom because experience had shown its impracticality (177). With the Commission system unlikely to be acceptable after the war and Confederation ruled out as "wholly averse" to Newfoundland public opinion, Great Britain had to prepare for the restoration of self-government (178). But self-government by itself would not work; an independent Newfoundland would soon reach another financial impasse. Since Great Britain "could not contemplate a repetition of the 1933 chapter of events," the only answer was to underwrite Newfoundland for a transitional period (178). Hence the policy the Dominions Office had worked out, with its interlocking political and economic elements.

Treasury responded to this appeal with a resounding no (see DO 35/1343/N402/32 91-92 for the Treasury view). Not surprisingly, its opposition was a function of Great Britain's dollar situation. Except for purchases in the United Kingdom, the expenditures proposed in the development plan would have to be paid for in dollars; and since Newfoundland's banking system was an extension of Canada's, this meant Canadian dollars. It would, of course, be possible to issue Newfoundland currency but this would inconvenience import trade, much of which was with Canada and the United States. Such a step might also be construed as ruling Confederation out once and for all. Great Britain could also attempt to borrow dollars from Canada to finance the planned reconstruction but she might thereby prejudice larger financial negotiations of her own with the Dominion. When American Lend-Lease and Canadian Mutual Aid ended, Great Britain would have to increase her exports by 50% over pre-war figures in order to feed people and supply them with essential raw materials. This meant that she must avoid dollar expenditures for anything but her own pressing and immediate needs. Additional and inessential borrowing would increase the danger of "unacceptable conditions" from her creditors and threaten her position "as one of the three great Powers" (92). The conclusion for Newfoundland was inescapable: "We have...to face the fact that the expenditure now proposed and many other forms of expenditure may be in themselves politically and economically very desirable, but it is a melancholy fact that we cannot afford them" (92). It was a measure of the separation of ministries in Whitehall that so much effort in the Dominions Office could lead to so swift, simple and stark a conclusion at the Treasury.

While admitting the dollar problem, the Dominions Office countered that the choice was not whether Newfoundland would have to be helped, but when. By standing aloof until Newfoundland had exhausted her own surplus, Great Britain would merely postpone her involvement and risk intervention in more difficult circumstances (92). Initially, Cranborne agreed both to consider the revision of his department's estimates so as to eliminate immediate British expenditure and "to make some informal and non-committal soundings of the Canadians" before discussions with Treasury continued; but he was soon fighting back as best he could (DO 35/1343/N402/32 14). Eliminating the aid package, he argued, would unbalance and fundamentally alter a laboriously constructed policy and expose the government to "very strong" parliamentary attack (73). "It would," he wrote, "... be an anomalous and hardly tenable position if Newfoundland, alone of the dependent Empire, were to be left to fend for herself from her own limited resources over the whole field of reconstruction and development" (73). Nor was the moment ripe for talks with Canada. Ottawa was preoccupied with Stage II of the transatlantic plan for financing the war – the period between the end of hostilities in Europe and the defeat of Japan – while the future of Newfoundland was a topic for Stage III, postwar planning. This being so, "the best course" would be to postpone any further Parliamentary statement on Newfoundland (75). This would cause disappointment both there and at home but it would also afford a "breathing space" in which the Canadians might be consulted as opportunity arose (75). On January 19, 1945, the Commission of Government was told of this development, Parliament being informed eleven days after that detailed proposals on Newfoundland would not be forthcoming until later in the year (DO 114/103 52-53, 55).

This standstill lasted for several months, though in June, 1945, the Dominions Office accepted a Newfoundland proposal that Magistrate Short quietly get on with the work of preparing for a national convention election on a district-by-district basis (56). Later in the summer, however, with their own financial negotiations with Ottawa settled for the moment, the British seized on various informal Canadian enquiries about the future of Newfoundland to launch a fresh initiative. After the change of government in the United Kingdom in July, Lord Addison, the new Labour Secretary of State for Dominion Affairs, and Hugh Dalton, his Treasury colleague, affirmed the decision of their predecessors that the next step with regard to Newfoundland should be taken in Ottawa and that P. A. Clutterbuck of the Dominions Office, who had served as Secretary to the Amulree Royal Commission and been in the forefront of policy-making towards Newfoundland ever since, should go there to assist the High Commission in discussions (DO 35/1344/N402/39 22, 28-31). Significantly, in accepting these arrangements, Dalton reiterated the previous view of his Department. "I fully agree," he told Addison on August 30, "that progress must be made with restoring Newfoundland's constitutional independence, but I see no prospect whatever of this country being able to provide the finance for the Reconstruction programme. After taking into account the proposed remission of the sterling debt, we should be committed to providing some $200 million. Quite apart from the effect on our own Exchequer, this presents us with an exchange problem which is quite insoluble. If the money is to be provided, it will have to come from Canada" (22). Clutterbuck's mission, he concluded, would have to take account of this reality.

How were the Canadians likely to react? Clutterbuck himself was reasonably optimistic, as evidenced by a November, 1944, joint Dominions Office-Treasury minute he had helped draft which surveyed the history of Canadian-Newfoundland relations. According to this document, part of which the High Commissioner in Ottawa questioned, Newfoundlanders and Canadians got on well together individually, but their collective dealings had "been marred by a long background of mutual suspicion and distrust" (DO 35/1343/N402/32 93, 101) traceable to Newfoundland's rejection of Confederation in 1869. Canadians had traditionally viewed Newfoundland with "detachment, condescension and even contempt," believing that their neighbour was too small to go it alone in the modern world and would one day "fall into. . .the Canadian lap" (93). On the other hand, there was no need to hurry the process of union as the Island would be a liability rather than an asset. Not surprisingly, the result of these views had been to strengthen the determination of Newfoundlanders to remain independent and to promote among them the view that "nothing could be so disastrous...as entry into the cold and comfortless Canadian fold" (93). The effect of the war had been to change Canadian but not Newfoundland attitudes. Canada had finally come to see that Newfoundland's "full partnership" was necessary not only for her own security but to round off Confederation (93). The American presence in Newfoundland had driven this lesson home and the Canadians had come to realize that their previous parochialism had not served them well. Canada's self-interest now dictated a policy towards Newfoundland which would "gradually...build up an atmosphere of comradeship and practical co-operation in which the union of the two countries could be seen to be in the common interest" (94). But it would take time to overcome the "golden opinions" American forces had won in Newfoundland as compared to the impression left by their Canadian counterparts (94). This in turn gave Great Britain an opening. Knowing that an offer to Newfoundland would certainly be rejected, the Canadians were confining themselves to "friendly expressions of interest" and to "assurances that if Newfoundlanders themselves should wish to turn to Canada they would be given a warm and sympathetic welcome" (94). Confederation was desirable but might not yet be palatable in Newfoundland. What therefore should Canada do? In Clutterbuck's view it was "something which was calculated to ensure reasonable stability in the Island until there had been opportunity for a policy of breaking down the barriers to take effect" (94). The plans Great Britain had devised met this requirement admirably and might thus command Canadian support. If a self-governing Newfoundland had to stand alone, the inevitable crisis would "arrive *before* there had been any change in outlook towards Canada and while Newfoundlanders were still under the glamorous spell of the lavish American war-time expenditure in the Island" (94). What Great Britain intended would eliminate this danger while lessening the expenditure Canada would face in Newfoundland should the union of the two countries be later realized.

It was against this background of opinion that Clutterbuck arrived in Ottawa on September 15, 1945 (DO 35/1347/N402/54 98). Three days later he and two High Commission officials met with four representatives of the Department of External Affairs: Norman Robertson, Under-Secretary of State; Hume Wrong, Associate Under-Secretary; R. A. MacKay, Special Assistant to the Under-Secretary and the Department's leading Newfoundland expert; and J. S. (Scott) Macdonald who had been High Commissioner to Newfoundland since 1944. Clutterbuck opened the meeting by explaining the agenda that had been worked out for Newfoundland and the financial impasse that had now been reached. Great Britain, he said, would have to reconsider her plans for Newfoundland and would be helped greatly in this task by knowing Canada's attitude. To Clutterbuck's surprise, the initial response of the Canadian negotiators was "almost entirely negative" (99). There was, he was told, little public or political interest in Canada in Newfoundland affairs. Accordingly, it would not be possible for Canada to provide Great Britain with the money needed to back reconstruction in Newfoundland. Nor could the government of Canada fund reconstruction directly, for fear of provoking her own provinces. When Clutterbuck countered with the American threat, he got a more "helpful" response (99). Specifically, he was asked how Great Britain would react if Canada said she would welcome a recommendation from the national convention in favour of Confederation. Such an initiative, Clutterbuck quickly replied, would be "warmly received" in London, union with Canada being Newfoundland's "natural destiny" (100).

Having thus cleared the preliminary hurdle, Clutterbuck moved on to talks with MacKay and Macdonald on the financial implications of Confederation. The focus here was on whether Newfoundland could function as a normal province or whether she would need special treatment, a potentially difficult point. Leaving debt charges aside and assuming the carry-over of the existing surplus, it was agreed that a provincial government in St. John's would be able to meet its current expenditures out of normal provincial revenue sources. When this was reported to the larger group of officials, Clutterbuck detected an improved attitude on the Canadian side. While it was true, they now conceded, that, taking social security payments into account, Newfoundland would not initially pay her own way, there was more at stake than a balance sheet, the benefits to Canada being "both tangible and intangible. . .through the rounding off of the Confederation" (100). Clutterbuck's triumph was made complete when Prime Minister King told Malcolm MacDonald, the High Commissioner, that he regarded the union of Newfoundland with Canada "as natural, desirable and inevitable" (101). If the national convention led Newfoundlanders to seek Confederation, the government of Canada "would do the handsome thing by them" (101). But the initiative had to come from Newfoundlanders themselves, and Great Britain and Canada had to avoid any suspicion that they were conspiring to achieve Confederation. Newfoundland public opinion changed slowly and King doubted whether "a move towards union" could really be expected (101). Still he hoped he was wrong, for the convention would offer "a grand chance, which might not recur for a long time, of getting the Confederation question settled without it being made an issue in party politics in Newfoundland" (101). Delay, he agreed, might bring an embarrassing drift towards the United States. In a different vein, Clutterbuck told the Canadians that while in his forthcoming statement to Parliament the Secretary of State for the Dominions could not make "any overt reference to union with Canada," he would no doubt want "to deal... with Newfoundland's reconstruction needs in such a way as not to impede the swing of opinion towards Canada" (101). The Canadian negotiators were less delicate. Great Britain, Clutterbuck was told in no uncertain terms, would have to make it clear to Newfoundlanders that they "should not count on receiving further financial assistance from the United Kingdom" (101-02). This would "accord with the realities of the position" and "assist" Newfoundlanders in turning "their thoughts to Canada" (102). How to influence Newfoundland opinion "behind the scenes" should be the subject of Anglo-Canadian discussions after the British Parliamentary statement was out of the way (102).

Once this understanding had been reached in Ottawa, events moved swiftly to a conclusion in London. On October 25 Addison submitted a memorandum with three appendices, including a draft Parliamentary statement, to cabinet (91-102). He told his colleagues that union with Canada should now be Great Britain's objective in Newfoundland but that no hint of this should be given either at home or abroad. Newfoundlanders must take the initiative themselves and Great Britain must not appear to influence them, though, equally, she must avoid words or deeds which clashed with her objective. The moment was propitious for Confederation, Addison argued, because the war had "greatly strengthened" Newfoundland's "numerous ties with Canada" (97). Another factor, "perhaps of overwhelming significance," was the attractiveness to Newfoundlanders of Canada's new social security programme, another wartime development (97). For "most Newfoundlanders," the Canadian family allowance scheme, approved by Parliament in 1944 and now in effect, "would make all the difference between poverty and comfort" (97). "Once the full implications" of such measures, Addison concluded, had "penetrated the consciousness of Newfoundlanders in their remote settlements," there might occur "a rapid swing of opinion towards Canada" (97).

On November 1, 1945, Addison's recommendations were discussed by cabinet and given general approval (DO 35/1345/N402/43 119-21). He was, however, asked to consider further the proposed method of election to the national convention and to address himself to the question of whether an imperial conference should be called to consider a change in Newfoundland's status. The first of these points was raised by Prime Minister Attlee, whose knowledge of Newfoundland was, of course, detailed and extensive. After leaving the Dominions Office, he had kept in touch with the policy-making towards Newfoundland and had welcomed the plan which Cranborne had devised in 1944 (see DO 35/1342/N402/29 19-20; DO 35/1343/N402/32 126). Churchill, he noted in a September, 1945, minute, had always favoured generosity towards Newfoundlanders, "the amount required for them being a drop in the ocean of our own liabilities" (DO 35/1344/N402/39 13). Attlee also commented in this minute, written after Clutterbuck's mission, about the recent "forthcomingness of the Canadians." Ottawa, he observed, would "have to make a very good offer to overcome the particularity and local prejudice of the Newfoundlanders to say nothing of the vested interests of the Water Street [St. John's] Merchants."

It was to the latter group that the Prime Minister addressed himself in cabinet on November 1. His worry was that even if, as Addison intended, a candidate for the national convention would have to be resident in a particular constituency to be nominated for it, the "business and financial interests" might still secure undue representation (DO 35/1345/N402/43 119). Reopening a debate the Dominions Office and the Commission thought they had concluded, Attlee wondered whether in Newfoundland's special circumstances it would not be better to have interest groups rather than districts return members. Alternatively, the two approaches might be combined to produce a convention which truly expressed "the interests of the islanders" (119). Having consulted St. John's, Addison put the Commission of Government's case against this and in favour of a geographically based election to cabinet in a memorandum dated November 21 (98-100). Vocationally based representation, the Commission believed, would be open to "grave objection" because many Newfoundlanders, the majority of fishermen included, were not organized (98). The groupings that did exist, moreover, were "very divided" in constitutional and political outlook (98). Again, it would be impossible to decide how many members each organization should have. Nor could the method of election within the organizations to be represented be effectively controlled, a defect conducive to "intrigues and manoeuvres" which might well pervert the popular will (99). Finally, a vocational approach would be "unfamiliar" to Newfoundlanders, who would expect the national convention to resemble in form the House of Assembly which had agreed to give up responsible government (99). Admitting the importance of ensuring that workers and fishermen received "full representation," the Commission asserted that this could be achieved by requiring that a candidate have two years' residence (war service included) in a constituency in order to be nominated for it (99). This in itself would prevent business or other special interests from dominating the convention. Addison accepted the Commission's position: "the geographical basis of election," he wrote, "has the great advantage of being unassailable in democratic theory, and I feel that, with the safeguards mentioned, it should give us the results we desire" (99-100). When cabinet considered the matter again on November 27, it was this view that carried (96). The wishes of the Dominions Office also prevailed in relation to the question of calling an imperial conference to consider the future of Newfoundland. Such an approach would negate the arrangements made in 1933 and be considered "derogatory" by Newfoundlanders (100). It might also be "highly embarrassing" to the other Dominions, especially Canada (100).

On December 11 the government's plans for Newfoundland were at last announced in the House of Commons and the House of Lords. Attlee himself made the Commons statement, which was a shortened version of the announcement read by Addison in the Lords (Great Britain, *Parl. Debates*, House of Commons, cols. 210-11; House of Lords, cols. 541-44). The national convention was to be elected on the basis of adult franchise and would be an advisory body only. The job of its members was spelled out as follows:

> To consider and discuss amongst themselves, as elected representatives of the Newfoundland people, the changes that have taken place in the financial and economic situation of the Island since 1934, and bearing in mind the extent to which the high revenues of recent years have been due to wartime conditions, to examine the position of the country and to make recommendations to His Majesty's Government as to possible forms of future government to be put before the people at a national referendum.
>
> (House of Lords, col. 542)

In keeping with the cabinet decision of November 27, a candidate for election to the convention would have to be a bona fide resident of the district he / she sought to represent. Once the national convention's recommendations had been considered in London, the constitutional issue could be put to the people in a referendum (543). In the meantime, the short-term reconstruction schemes which the Commission of Government had devised could be pressed forward without delay. On the other hand, the carrying out of the Commission's long-term economic plans would hinge on the constitutional decision, thereby leaving any new administration with a free hand in the development field. A new, post-referendum government in Newfoundland would have to be given "the fairest possible start" but Great Britain must not promise what she could not deliver (544). "The special difficulties of our own financial position over the next few years," both Houses of Parliament heard in a wonderful piece of British understatement, "may well preclude us from undertaking fresh commitments" (544; *Parl. Debates*, House of Commons, col. 211).

Subsequently, in keeping with other provisions of the Parliamentary announcements and earlier understandings with the Commission of Government, G. W. St. John Chadwick of the Dominions Office and Edgar Jones of the Treasury were sent to St. John's (from London and Ottawa respectively) to work on the "factual and objective survey of the Island's financial and economic situation" the convention and Parliament would be given; K. C. Wheare, Fellow of All Souls College, Oxford, and an expert on federalism, was named constitutional adviser to the convention (DO 114/103 68, 71). The result of the work of Chadwick and Jones was the publication in June, 1946, of the useful and informative *Report on the Financial and Economic Position of Newfoundland* (Cmd. 6849). For its part the Commission of Government passed a National Convention Act, dated May 21, 1946 (*Acts of Honourable Com. of Government 1946* 108-206). The stage was now set for the tumultuous political drama, which would end on March 31, 1949, as Great Britain had long hoped it would, in Newfoundland's union with Canada.

A key factor in the success Great Britain achieved in Newfoundland in the 1940s was undoubtedly the uncertainty of local public opinion about the constitutional questions facing the country. Such matters can perhaps only attract popular attention when they are attached to leaders and policies, and in Newfoundland, because of the

Commission system and what lay behind it, this was difficult, if not impossible. Good times, a lingering defeatism, and inherited attitudes to authority may also have been factors stifling constitutional debate. In any event, lacking political parties, Newfoundlanders did not in large numbers seize upon wartime prosperity to demand more representative institutions or a voice in planning their own future. If they had done so in the heyday of the Atlantic Charter, Great Britain could scarcely have resisted them, the exigencies of war notwithstanding. In his formative November 25, 1942, telegram, Attlee told the Commission of Government that "if Newfoundland could be regarded as self-supporting and there were a general demand in Newfoundland for the restoration of self-government, it would not be practicable to refuse it" (DO 114/103 1). But the attitudes of Newfoundlanders and the divisions among them left the initiative in the crucial constitutional field to Whitehall. By asserting without challenge her right to establish the timetable for political change in Newfoundland, Great Britain positioned herself to influence strongly what that change would be. The British began defining constitutional means for Newfoundland while still debating constitutional ends. Accordingly, when they eventually decided that Confederation, a solution they had long favoured, was at last practical politics, they had to work towards their objective within the framework of the promises made to Newfoundlanders in the Parliamentary statement of December, 1943. But if that statement had imposed limitations on their subsequent policy-making, its general wording had also left considerable room for manoeuvre.

Great Britain could not dictate a choice to Newfoundlanders, but in the arrangements she announced in 1945 for the national convention she retained the last word on what they would decide and how they would decide it. This showed great foresight, for the national convention did not recommend that Confederation be on the referendum ballot, despite having sent a delegation to Ottawa and determining that terms of union were possible (see Neary, "Newfoundland's Union" for the post-1945 events). At this juncture the British exercised the prerogative they had so carefully guarded, adding Confederation to the ballot and thereby giving its supporters in Newfoundland, led by J. R. Smallwood, a chance they did not miss.

The margin of the Confederate victory in Newfoundland in 1948 was very narrow but from Whitehall's point of view it was a triumph nonetheless. In 1950 P. A. Clutterbuck, since 1946 High Commissioner to Canada, was able to write after visiting the new Province of Newfoundland with a detachment that belied his previous involvement in local affairs. He was obviously relieved, his country having been discharged from a duty it neither wanted nor could any longer perform. In the best traditions of the British civil service, Clutterbuck's name was scarcely known to those whose destinies he had helped shape.[2] Great Britain had arranged her departure from Newfoundland with a hard logic and clinical precision she would not always manage in other parts of her far-flung but now crumbling empire.

Peter Neary.

* This article was originally published in *Newfoundland Studies*, 1.1 (1985), 29-56, and is reprinted here with minor changes. The author thanks Dr. Melvin Baker for his assistance.

Biographical Sketch

Peter Neary was born on Bell Island and is now a Professor Emeritus at the University of Western Ontario, where he was Dean of the Faculty of Social Science, 1995–2002. His scholarly interests include the history of Newfoundland and Labrador, the history of political parties in Canada, and the history of Canadian veterans of the two world wars. He is the author of *Newfoundland in the North Atlantic World, 1929–1949*, co-author of *Part of the Main: An Illustrated History of Newfoundland and Labrador*, editor of *White Tie and Decorations: Sir John and Lady Hope Simpson in Newfoundland, 1934–1936*, and co-editor of *The Veterans Charter and Post-World War II Canada*.

Endnotes

1. Dominion Office series 35, file 725/N8/12, p. 23, Public Record Office. All subsequent parenthetical DO references are to material in the Public Record Office. Transcripts of Crown-copyright records in the Public Record Office appear by permission of H. M. Stationery Office.

2. Clutterbuck left Ottawa in 1952. He was then successively High Commissioner to India (1952–55), Ambassador to the Republic of Ireland (1955–59), and Permanent Under-Secretary of State in the Commonwealth Relations Office. He died on December 1975, at the age of 78 (*The Times*, December 31, 1975: 12).

References

Acts of the Honourable Commission of Government of Newfoundland 1942 to 1946. St. John's: King's Printer, 1942–1946.

Air 38/20, Public Record Office, "Summary of information covering the organization of the Atlantic ferry bomber service by the Canadian Pacific."

Canada, House of Commons, *Debates*, 5th Session, 18th Parliament. Ottawa: King's Printer, 1939.

Great Britain, *Parliamentary Debates*, House of Commons, fifth series, Vol. 395. London: His Majesty's Stationery Office, 1943.

———. House of Lords, fifth series, Vol. 138. London: His Majesty's Stationery Office, 1946.

———. *The Public General Acts*, 1933–34. London: King's Printer [1934].

———. *Treaty Series No 2* (1941), Cmd. 6259. London: His Majesty's Stationery Office, 1941.

Neary, Peter. "Canada and the Newfoundland Labour Market, 1939–49." *Canadian Historical Review* 62 (1983): 470-95.

———. "Newfoundland's Union with Canada, 1949: Conspiracy or Choice?" *Acadiensis* 12 (1983): 110-19.

Newfoundland Royal Commission 1933 Report, Cmd. 4480. London: His Majesty's Stationery Office, 1933.

Noel, S.J.R. *Politics in Newfoundland.* Toronto: Univ. of Toronto Press, 1971.

Report of the Labour Relations Officer for the Period June 1st, 1942, to February 8th, 1944. St. John's: Newfoundland Government, 1944.

Report of the Financial & Economic Position of Newfoundland, Cmd. 6849. London: His Majesty's Stationery Office, 1946.

"The Difficult Little Island" That Must Be Taken In: Canadian Interests in Newfoundland During World War Two.[1]

By: John E. FitzGerald.

Sir Alan Patrick Herbert was a famous British author, a playwright, the Editor of *Punch* Magazine, and the independent member of Parliament for Oxford University. In this last capacity he was sent to Newfoundland during the summer of 1943, at the height of World War II, as part of a mission of MPs tasked to make recommendations to the British government about the constitutional future of Newfoundland. Herbert later wrote:

> A little before we left London, I asked a high Canadian official: "Do you want Newfoundland?" He said, "No." "Do you want Labrador?" [I asked.] He said, "Yes." When we got back, I met him by chance, outside the Dominions Office and [again] put the same questions. This time he firmly answered "Yes" to both. In other words, it now seemed so important to get Labrador, that *the difficult little island must be taken in....*[2]

The reason why this "little island" was so "difficult" was because in 1933, facing bankruptcy to the tune of $100 million, Newfoundland's Parliament accepted the recommendations of the Amulree Royal Commission and self-government was suspended, the only self-governing Dominion of the British Empire ever to do so. It did so as a condition of receiving British financial assistance. Britain promised that when the country was again financially self-supporting, and at the request of the people, self-government would be restored. The problem was, with no House of Assembly, and no elections, there was no recognized mechanism for making such a request, and none was provided. The question was not debated in the Newfoundland House in the dying days of 1933, and hardly addressed by MPs in Westminster in their haste to return

Newfoundland to crown colony status. From February 1934 until April 1949, Newfoundland was governed by an appointed Commission of Government, consisting of six commissioners and a governor, all chosen by London, all answerable to the British Dominions Office.

With World War II came gradual agitation in Newfoundland for the return of responsible government. In 1941 the Dominions Office responded by sending out MP Geoffrey Shakespeare. But all Shakespeare did was sip cups of tea with the chosen few at Government House, and incite wild speculation among the natives of St. John's about British intentions towards Newfoundland. In 1942 Clement Attlee, the Secretary of State for Dominions and Deputy Prime Minister in the Churchill coalition government, arrived in St. John's. He took soundings, but ultimately decided very little. Agitation reached a climax in early 1943 when the Newfoundland Board of Trade passed a resolution asking for another Royal Commission to investigate the possibility of returning to self-government. So Attlee replied by sending a "Goodwill Mission" of three parliamentarians to Newfoundland – Charles Ammon of the Labour Party, Derrick Gunston of the Conservatives, and the independent MP Alan Herbert – to investigate conditions in the island and Labrador, and make recommendations as to the constitutional future. Newfoundland newspapers were critical: what the "*sans culottes*" in Newfoundland had asked for, surely, was the bread of responsible government, but Attlee had responded with the cake of an inquiry.[3] After a tortuous return to London in the British navy destroyer *Orwell*, zig-zagging across the submarine-infested North Atlantic, Herbert delivered a report to Parliament that fall which proved that Big Brother really was watching. Reflecting an idea of R.B. Job's which had some currency in the St. John's newspapers that summer, Herbert ultimately recommended that Newfoundland have a Citizen's Council to recommend future types of government to be put to the people in a referendum. But because the MPs reports were not "official", the Dominions Office decided that they were not to be published, and the first thing most Newfoundlanders knew was that two years later, on 11 December 1945, Britain announced that Newfoundland was to have a National Convention.

But what did the 1943 Goodwill Mission find? They found a Newfoundland transformed. They found the most heavily militarized war zone in the western hemisphere, teeming with American and Canadian servicemen on enormous army, naval and air bases, busy patrolling the North Atlantic, and in ferrying aircraft, supplies, vessels, and servicemen from the New World to the Old. When war had been declared in September 1939, scores of patriotic Newfoundlanders rushed to volunteer and join up with the RAF, the Canadian army, and other services. In planning for their own country's defence, Canadian military planners realized that one-third of the iron ore used at Sydney came from Bell Island, Newfoundland, so therefore Canada was going to have to defend Conception Bay. Then Britain informed the Commission of Government that it had no money to provide for the defence of the largest airport in the world, the Newfoundland Airport at Hattie's Camp, Gander. Ironically, Britain had already spent $40 million building Gander.[4] The Commission went to Canada, and Canadian troops assumed the defence of Gander Airport in June 1940.

While Newfoundlanders were watching the ballet of the war, the Canadians were trying to re-write the music. By July 1940 Canada was planning for a continental war effort. A briefing paper, prepared for Canadian Prime Minister Mackenzie King by a self-styled Group of Twenty Canadians, argued that Canada should take over the entire defence of Newfoundland. In August, King met with the American President, Franklin Delano Roosevelt, in Ogdensburg and announced the creation of a Canada-United States Permanent Joint Board on Defence (the PJBD), composed of members from the military and civil services of each country, and eventually, two representatives of Newfoundland, which would "consider in the broad sense the defence of the north half of the Western Hemisphere."[5] All its decisions had far-reaching implications for Newfoundland, and the first item of business on the PJBD agenda was the defence of the island and Labrador, and this ultimately brought the Canadian and American servicemen to these shores. In late 1940, PJBD surveyors arrived in Newfoundland and started looking for appropriate sites for military bases.

On 3 September 1940, American President Franklin Delano Roosevelt announced to the American Congress, and to Newfoundlanders listening in on the radio, that a deal had been reached between the U.S.A. and Britain. Britain would "authorize the use of Newfoundland, Bermuda, the Bahamas, Jamaica, St. Lucia, Trinidad, and British Guiana as naval and air bases by the United States in the event of attack on the American hemisphere" by means of purchase or through 99-year leases.[6] In exchange, Roosevelt said, Britain would receive fifty over-aged destroyers and a variety of airplanes and marine vessels, provided that the American people and the U.S. Congress could be assured that "the national defence and security of the United States would be enhanced." Newfoundland seemed to be on the tip of Roosevelt's tongue, a condition perhaps predisposed by the president's frequent summertime fishing trips to the Island. Churchill had agreed with the Bases-for-Destroyers deal, but informed the president that "It will be necessary for us to consult the Governments of Newfoundland and Canada about the Newfoundland base in which Canada has an interest. We are proceeding at once to seek their consent."[7]

This immediately placed the Commission of Government on the defensive. Newfoundland's Commissioner for Defence, Sir Edward Emerson, reported to Churchill that Newfoundlanders were incensed that their country was being given away without their consent by a temporary, unelected, appointed government. Churchill replied by playing the patriotic card, calling on Newfoundlanders to defend the Empire. And Emerson had little choice but to agree. On 27 March 1941, Emerson trotted out an American-born Newfoundland businessman with an Oxbridge accent, Leonard Outerbridge, to sell the Bases-for-Destroyers deal. He spoke on radio station VONF, brow-beating stubborn Newfoundlanders into taking "a long and a broad view of it," telling them to realize that their country was playing "a vital role in uniting the great English speaking democracies" in nothing less than "the defence and preservation of civilization."[8]

Outerbridge needn't have worried about Newfoundlanders accepting the deal, or the Americans. At the end of January 1941, after four days trying to enter the fog-bound Narrows of St. John's harbour, the U.S. troop ship *Edmund B. Alexander* was nudged into its berth on the south side. Newfoundland changed forever. Thousands of American servicemen poured off the vessel. Camp Alexander Tent City sprung up on Carpasian Road. Base construction at Argentia, Stephenville, St. John's and Gander began to boom. As she watched the lanky Yankees march down the gangplank, the svelte young St. John's *chanteuse* Nellie Ludlow spoke for many Newfoundland women when she exclaimed, "I'm having one of them!"[9] Newfoundlanders instantly accepted the handsome, well-dressed, young Americans, all boasting their own teeth, much to the chagrin of the jealous Canadian troops already stationed in St. John's.

Compared with the wealthy Americans, the Canadians were despised. Downtown restaurant owners and merchants of erstwhile sleepy St. John's were suddenly forced to insure their plate-glass windows against the flying bottles of drunken, brawling Canadian naval ratings. The Canadians did not have bases, with "one armed bandits" which paid generously, open to locals for entertainment on Friday nights. They did not have a Hollywood-driven USO, supplying the bases with stars such as Bob Hope, Joan Blondell, Phil Silvers, Frances Langford, or Les Brown and His Band of Renown. The Canadians weren't sending Edgar Bergen and Charlie McCarthy into the playgrounds of St. John's to entertain the children. The Canadians were blamed by Newfoundlanders for not adequately defending the SS *Caribou*, allowing it to be sunk in the Gulf of St. Lawrence.[10] Canada even took flack for the tragic Knights of Columbus Hostel Fire in December 1942. The U.S. Consul George D. Hopper reported that the hostel had been built with Canadian money primarily for the use of Canadian servicemen, and that over half the casualties had been Canadians, but that Canadian authorities turned down an American offer of a burn surgeon from Boston. Even City Hall was upset. The City Council was enraged that Canadian military vehicles were eating up the city's streets, but that Canada wasn't paying its share of the repair bill while the Americans were.

The City Council also charged that Canadian military authorities had virtually "taken possession of St. John's" and that all available vacant space was being occupied by flimsy Canadian "tar paper buildings", instead of taking example from the wiser American practice of building permanent structures on the outskirts of the town.[11] To almost everyone, then, compared with America the Beautiful, the Canadians were like vichyssoise: cold, half French, and difficult to stir.

Difficult to stir, that is, until self-interest got in the way. The Canadian and American presence in Newfoundland and Labrador during the war gave rise to great political contention between the two for supremacy. Canada was determined to win. In July 1941, a month before Roosevelt and Churchill met at Argentia to issue the Atlantic Charter, Roosevelt's son, Ensign Elliott Roosevelt, let it be known in Ottawa that he would lead an American surveying party in Labrador to search for a suitable site for a huge new airport. When Canadian military planners got wind of this, they notified Prime Minister King's office. Canada sent a surveying team, and beat Roosevelt by one day to a survey of the Labrador Plateau. Construction immediately began on the enormous Goose Airport, to be used by Atlantic Ferry Command to send ... aircraft to Europe. Its strategic importance meant that its existence remained secret, until a British newspaper let the cat out of the bag in 1943. During the summer of 1941 the American and Canadian governments also stepped up their diplomatic presence in St. John's. Jealous that the Americans were about to appoint "a senior and new Consul General to St. John's", wrote Norman Robertson of the Department of External Affairs, to his Prime Minister Mackenzie King, it was time for Canada to recognize that Canada "has more varied, more important, and more urgent business with Newfoundland than with all the self-governing Dominions in which we maintain High Commissioners put together."[12] To address this inequity, the Canadians appointed a high-powered High Commissioner to Newfoundland, Charles Burchell. A Halifax lawyer with a background in trade, Burchell was sent to St. John's with what soon became several specific missions: to promote Canadian trade with Newfoundland; to secure 99-year-leases on Goose Bay and Gander airports for Canada which, as Mackenzie

King noted, "we are already spending money on"[13]; to promote the friendly neighbour Canada; and to secure customs and tariff concessions and bait and catch landing privileges for Nova Scotian fish companies in Newfoundland. The Canadians had recognized that with the war, and the arrival of the Americans, Newfoundland's position had changed, and that they had better do something about it.

Without a doubt, the greatest impact of World War II on Newfoundland was financial and economic. On 4 July 1940, Newfoundland's Commissioner of Finance J.H. Penson announced that for the remainder of the war, Newfoundland would no longer ask Britain for financial assistance.[14] A year later, the embarrassing admission of a $700,000 budgetary surplus was tantamount to an admission that the country was financially self-supporting, which was the first condition to be met for self-government to be returned. But self-government was not returned. The standard explanation of economic impact of the war usually quoted by historians comes from a report prepared by G.W. St. John Chadwick of the Dominions Office and E. Jones of the British Treasury for the National Convention when it met in the fall of 1946:

> After remaining at an average level of $12 million per annum during the three years ending March 1940, current revenue...rose to over $16 million in 1940–41 and thereafter climbed year by year to reach a level of $33.4 million in 1945–46....with the increase in revenue there was a growth of internal lending in the form of war loans and the purchase of savings certificates. The government could now afford to expand its normal and reconstruction expenditure, but even after repaying certain outstanding debts and servicing the National Debt, the yield from taxation and borrowing was high enough to bring about a budget surplus year after year. The result of almost six years of wartime financing was to yield a cumulative surplus of about $26 million,

> to which must be added 6.5 million from public borrowing. Out of this total of $32.5 million, some $12.3 million was lent to the United Kingdom [Chadwick and Jones omit to note that this was an interest-free loan], and $½ million was provided as a free gift for the setting up of a Spitfire squadron, and the remainder was allowed to accumulate as bank deposits.[15]

But in actuality, this was a monochromatic picture of the situation, one carefully crafted by a conservative bureaucracy which was keenly aware of the need to answer to politicians who themselves were not eager to encourage talk of self-government in Newfoundland. As a result, the Chadwick-Jones Report failed to take into account a whole raft of financial and economic complications which the war brought to Newfoundland. Nowhere did it account for the hundreds of millions of dollars of Canadian and American expenditures in Newfoundland (more on this later), or even the expenditures of the British Admiralty, which in 1943 spent $6 million alone in Newfoundland. By 31 December 1942, there were 13,200 Americans and 19,200 Canadians in Newfoundland. Newfoundland's economy was thriving, and Water Street merchants demanded a 25% increase in the supplies they required.[16] At the peak of base construction and employment in December 1942, there were 22,000 Newfoundlanders working on American bases, and by July 1943 George Hopper reported to Washington that there had been labour shortages in Newfoundland in fisheries, mining, forestry, and that the base contractors were compelled to import workers from the States and Canada.[17]

It is a great irony that while Canada was suspicious about the American presence in Newfoundland, it also realized that it could benefit enormously from it. Newfoundlanders working on the bases, as well as servicemen, were paid in American dollars. They would then go and deposit those dollars in the bank, in one of the four Canadian banks operating in Newfoundland. But of course, Canada transferred these American funds to its Canadian banks in Canada, where the Government of Canada made healthy revenues by taxing the banks' profits,[18] a fact noted by Newfoundland Commissioner Sir John Puddester in 1940.[19] To keep an eye on these revenues, in April 1943, G.S. Watts of the Bank of Canada in Ottawa visited St. John's. He reported meeting with the sole Newfoundland Foreign Exchange Control Officer, Mr. Calver, who answered to Finance Commisioner Ira Wild and worked out of a 5 x 7 foot office in the Customs Building in downtown St. John's. Calver was diligent and had a "firm grasp" on the rules, but he needed "to be initiated into the finer points" of foreign exchange control.[20] Watts then reported:

> To anyone familiar with the attitudes of Newfoundlanders to Canada, which at its best is suspicion and at its worst the next thing to hatred, it is a matter for comment that our Exchange control relationships with [the] Newfoundland Government have not resulted in cries of 'intervention' or 'Confederation'. Actually, barring an incident while I was there, the subject has never been raised. ...P[eter] J. Cashin, a former minister of finance... declared that we were being supplied with $15 [million] U.S. per annum by Newfoundland to defray our deficit and that Newfoundland was in danger of being 'sold up the river'.[21]

In confirmation of Cashin's charges, Watts then reported that "One of the principal aims in visiting St. John's was to assess the effects of the reported completion of the U.S. Military bases on our net receipts of U.S. Funds from Newfoundland", which in 1942 amounted not to Cashin's $15 million, but to $33.5 million, and which for 1943 were expected to net another $17 to 18 million in U.S. funds for Canada.[22] Watts noted that Newfoundlanders hoping for the return of self-government harangued the Canadian Banks, and complained that only a fraction of their deposits were invested at home and that their assets have been drained off for investment elsewhere. He then noted that the manager of the Bank of Nova Scotia told him that "the real savings deposits of individuals are sacrosanct", for a

Newfoundlander "will starve before he commits the crime of drawing on his savings." Currency hoarding was the practice, not the exception, said the bank manager, and the steady trickle of old bills and antiquated gold pieces into St. John's convinced him that "there was a dollar hoarded in the outports for every dollar of individual savings deposits in the banks."[23]

The Canadians in Newfoundland keenly wanted Newfoundland to grow more dependant on Canada for its goods and supplies. And from the Canadian perspective, why not? If Newfoundland were in a balance of trade deficit position, she would be much more dependent on Canada, which increasingly would be able to call the shots. By December 1943, the Canadian and American governments created a Combined Food Board which in part was responsible for supplying Newfoundland (not being an agricultural country, Newfoundland was forced to import foodstuffs). In particular, both Watts of the Bank of Canada, and R.P. Bower, the Canadian Trade Commissioner in Newfoundland, expressed concern that Newfoundland was already getting, and might get more of its supplies outside Canada and the United States, thus reducing the chances of Canada and the U.S. getting its supplies from the same sources.[24] And if ever there was a case of identifying a problem and proposing a mutually beneficial solution, a letter on trade from External Affairs Undersecretary Norman Robertson to Burchell in February 1944 noted "low levels of Newfoundland nutrition", and then observed that Newfoundland "should be able to count on the sympathetic support, and, if necessary, on the material assistance of Canada."[25] In essence, Canada used its supply position and every other advantage it had over Newfoundland to force a balance of trade deficit on Newfoundland, making Newfoundland's economy more subservient to and dependent on Canada's.

Even Alan Herbert also recognized this. While he was in St. John's in 1943 he ran into Burchell on Water Street and got into an argument with the Canadian, warning him, "Keep your hands off Newfoundland!" When Burchell replied angrily that "Some of us were trying to build up the Empire while there were some in England trying to break it up", Herbert walked away, muttering, "Canadian banking in Newfoundland! Canadian life insurance companies!"[26] Unfortunately, Newfoundlanders didn't realize that they had been bitten until it was too late. It became clear in an article in the 31 December 1946 *Daily News* by Calvert C. Pratt, one of Newfoundland's most astute importers and businessmen. By then, the National Convention had begun meeting, Smallwood had proposed a motion to send a delegation to Ottawa to seek Canadian terms, and it had been defeated, and confederation was being discussed. Pratt asked how much Newfoundland would have to pay for Canadian services, and he stated that only after Newfoundland figured out what it needed from Canada should it go there to seek terms. He then savaged Canada's wartime trade practices. Before 1939, he charged, Canada used its exports to Newfoundland to top off its profits, essentially dumping goods in the Newfoundland market, selling it cheaper than it could be bought in Canada. But during the war, Canadian exports to Newfoundland cost more and the Canadians profiteered because local demand was up. From 1936 to 1939 Newfoundland's imports from Canada were only 36.9% of the total, but emergency controls and wartime restrictions ran Canadian imports up to 67% during the war years. Pratt then posed the fifty-cent question, which was never answered for Newfoundland before it entered confederation: to what extent would Newfoundland be subsidizing Canadian industry by relinquishing its own duties and as a Canadian province, buying in the Canadian market? Canadian purchases from Newfoundland were one-fifth of Newfoundland purchases from Canada, and Pratt issued the dire warning that even if Newfoundland bought everything from Canada, it could not hope to extend its exports to Canada and there was the very real danger of losing its export markets, which were in Europe and which paid Newfoundland in pounds sterling. Caught between two currencies, in order to keep the European markets for its fish, Newfoundland would need pounds sterling and would need to keep its trade facilities, and this would never be allowed under confederation.[27]

In 1943, Canada deployed a full-court press against Britain to grant it a 99-year lease on Goose Bay airport. British Commissioner P.D.H. Dunn warned the Americans through George Hopper that such a lease would give strong rights to Canada and that "they would insist on dictating the terms of post-war civil [aviation] rights and wish to freeze out all others."[28] Dunn also told Hopper that during the London talks, Hugh Keenleyside spoke with Newfoundland's Ray Gushue about the future of Newfoundland. When Gushue suggested that a referendum would be in the offing, and that a fair plebiscite would include the question of joining the United States, "Keenleyside was horrified at this suggestion and replied, "Certainly not!". When Gushue inquired how the voters could be prevented from stating their choice between the two countries, Keenleyside answered, "Oh, we would use pressure to stop that."[29] On 23 October 1944, a day that should live in infamy, after much badgering and threatening Britain with severe economic sanctions, Canada was granted a 99-year lease on military aviation at Goose Bay Airport, with a promise to talk about civil aviation after the war. In Newfoundland there was the usual futile public outcry that the trustees of the Commission had once again alienated part of their ward's inheritance. But Canada would not be satisfied until it could control post-war international *civil* aviation, and owning Newfoundland would be the key to this. Hopper wrote Washington in late 1944 and early 1945:

> Britain is in the position to delay indefinitely the return of responsible government; she is also in a position to "buy off" by money grants most of the opposition to continued dictation from London.... but...most Newfoundlanders believe that in granting to other interests these valuable rights a reasonable return in the form of annual rentals or equivalent economic concessions should be demanded.[30]
>
> ...
>
> I still believe that the British Government is in no hurry to grant resp[onsible] gov[ernmen]t to Newfoundland for another good reason, namely,

> the fact that as long as the present form of government exists the disposal of rights and concessions regarding civil aviation will remain under the control of Britain, and no chance is to be taken that an independent government in Newfoundland may alienate such rights to the prejudice of Imperial schemes in trans-Atlantic aviation.[31]

And in November 1945, Hopper's successor as American Consul in Newfoundland, Robert J. Cavanaugh, wrote Washington that the true "tragedy of Newfoundland [was] not that it surrendered self-government, but that it has obtained so little in return."[32]

By late 1944, the realization had long since dawned on Canadian civil servants, that the answer to Canada's problems was confederation. From his lair on Circular Road in St. John's, in October 1946 (it could just as well have been in 1943), Burchell's successor J. Scott Macdonald wrote a memo to his boss Norman Robertson, who circulated it to Mackenzie King and his cabinet, pressuring them to speed-up confederation. In part his memo read:

> The present is not a particularly propitious time to discuss terms of union with Newfoundland, for the tide of prosperity which came with the war, shows... little sign of receding.
>
> The accession of Newfoundland would increase the Canadian population by 312,889 people. [It would] enlarge the Dominion [of Canada] by 192,000 square miles, an area larger than Finland or Sweden and nearly four times the size of the Maritime Provinces, possessing very considerable mineral and forest resources as well as easy access to the finest fishing grounds in the world. It would solve, permanently, all questions of post-war military and civil aviation rights which are at

> present terminable after March 31st, 1949, on twelve months' notice. It would make possible a common jurisdiction over North Atlantic Fisheries.
>
> It should not be overlooked, in considering the advantages of Newfoundland to Canada, that those advantages are a good deal more substantial than in 1895 when [confederation] was last considered. Newfoundland is now larger by 110,000 square miles of territory commonly regarded at that time, in Canada at least, as forming part of the Canadian Labrador but since awarded to Newfoundland by the decision of the Judicial Committee of the Privy Council [in 1927].
>
> Moreover, [Newfoundland] is richer by the investment of at least $100 million by Canada and at least $300 million by the United States primarily for defence but much of which was spent on roads, wharfs, telephone lines, warehouses and similar buildings, radio ranges, airfields, the training of Newfoundlanders in various technical jobs, etc., and has redounded to the general development of the country.

Then, Macdonald exploited the fear of what might happen to Canada if Newfoundland was not encouraged to join:

> [Newfoundland] will be driven, by the force of events, to take measures to emphasize and strengthen its position as a separate economic and political unit. Such measures would doubtless include... the appointment of Trade Agents to push the sale of Newfoundland fish in the United States, Cuba, the West Indies, Brazil, Spain, Portugal, Italy, Greece, and other areas in which Canadian fish [from Nova Scotia] are also

> marketed.... [Newfoundland might negotiate] Trade Agreements with the countries who are the chief purchasers of Newfoundland products, offering them in return, a market for their products to the detriment of our exports; the withdrawal of permission to Canadian fishing vessels to store fish and salt in bond [in Newfoundland] while operating on the [Grand] Banks; [Newfoundland might raise] royalties on iron [ore] and other minerals to buttress falling revenues; and the termination of defence rights except on payment of heavy rentals. [Newfoundland's quest for] diversification would be stimulated involving further development of local manufacturing which already includes paint, nails, rope, tobacco, biscuits, beer and soft drinks, oilskins, clothing, etc. cutting down our [Canadian] market and progressively adding to the vested interests that would be opposed to closer relations with Canada. Newfoundland might even, in view of the fact that it sells so largely to the countries allied with sterling, be led to attach itself to the sterling bloc [that is, the countries whose currency was the British Pound Sterling] and terminate the special position accorded to Canadian financial institutions [in Newfoundland].[33]

Macdonald then sought Ottawa's permission to assure two Newfoundland confederates, J.R. Smallwood and his associate, F. Gordon Bradley, "the men who would organize the [National Convention] delegation to Ottawa", that "the Canadian government is very aware of the special position of Newfoundland and would be prepared to discuss the question of terms on that basis."[34] It is instructive to note that Macdonald's letter was written 11 days before the Convention first heard Smallwood's motion to send a delegation to Canada.

Eight months later, Macdonald's colleague, J.R. Baldwin, the secretary of the Canadian Cabinet committee on Newfoundland, informed the Cabinet that because Newfoundland's imports from Canada rose from almost $10 million before the war to $40 million annually by 1946, if Newfoundland joined the United States, Canadian trade with Newfoundland would be reduced to "a small proportion of its present volume". Furthermore, he wrote,

> Should Newfoundland remain outside of Canada, the present United States ascendancy in the Newfoundland-Labrador region will almost certainly increase and might very well lead to a virtual withdrawal from the area by Canada in favour of the United States. Although it may be argued that Canada would have little to lose by such a development from the point of view of defence, this would inevitably point to the absorption of Canada within the United States orbit.[35]

And becoming American was what Canada wished to avoid like the plague.

The discovery of natural resources in Labrador during the war served as a powerful magnet for attracting Canadian interest in Newfoundland. After 1944, Canada became aware of enormous iron-ore reserves on the Quebec-Labrador boundary, an estimated 300 million tons. Emerging from the cabinet meeting at which it was decided to meet a delegation from the National Convention and offer terms, C.D. Howe, the Minister of Reconstruction and Supply, also known as the "minister of everything", remarked "That iron ore in Labrador looks good. Let's do it."[36] Or to put it another way, when Jack Pickersgill was asked why Newfoundland couldn't have been given back her self-government before joining Canada, and why the confederation was done the way it was, he replied: "Canada got Newfoundland cheap, and we knew we'd never get her as cheap again."[37] Canada saw that the natural and strategic resources which had emerged and developed in Newfoundland during the war had completely changed the water on the beans. And it was clear that their worth was not going away with the end of the war. That Canada pursued their acquisition is not surprising, but it gives the lie to the argument that post-war prosperity would have been temporary for Newfoundland. It is by no means certain that Newfoundland would have returned to poverty had it gotten back self-government. Such what-ifs and what-might-have-beens belong to the realm of speculation. Yet for Newfoundlanders, that was exactly what the discussion of their country's future was about in the late 1940s.

What might Newfoundland have done if it had managed to get back self-government? National Convention member Charles Bailey had a few sharp ideas. He suggested that the first things would be to "...adjust our currency to our markets by putting in a national bank, and tak[e] the load off the fishermen who had to carry the weight of selling in a cheap currency market and buying [in] a dear money market. We have to get divorced from the dear Canadian dollar. If markets can't be found in Canada for our products, then we have got to have a currency either tied to the pound where we sell, and where we can buy, when things get to normal, or else with the U.S., where we can buy and sell."[38]

Yet it was not to be. The documents of the Canadians, the Americans, the British, and the even the Commission of Government's Newfoundland Ranger Force are full of reports that Newfoundlanders were not at all interested in confederation throughout the 1940s. Canada realized this, and knew that confederation would be a hard sell. It did not want to be seen as prejudicing the outcome of any referendum against responsible government, but Canadian interests desperately wanted Labrador. At the end of December 1947, the American Embassy in Ottawa noted that Jules Timmins, the president of the Labrador Mining and Development Company, of Montreal, had told him that Labrador had 600 million tons of iron ore, and that Timmins had only given this information to a few key others – his friends C.D. Howe, Hugh Keenleyside, and his company's directors which included Liberal

Senator Hartland Molson, because "full revelation" to the Newfoundland public "might affect the outcome of the Newfoundland constitutional referendum and arouse stock market speculations."[39] Then, long after Canada had decided what it wanted and what the value was, came Joe Smallwood's confederation campaign, funded by the Liberal Party of Canada, and as the late Greg Power maintained, by Molson, Timmins and his brother,[40] who were reported to be vigorous, almost athletic, in their endorsement of the Liberal Party.[41] So the "somewhat squawking baby" of Newfoundland, as one British official put it, was forced to abandon economic independence, sovereignty, and control over its own resources and its destiny, and enter the lair of the Canadian wolf shielded only by the safety-blanket of the Canadian social welfare state.

The year after confederation, Alan P. Herbert wrote that:

> Labrador may become another Alaska, because it has the largest iron ore deposits in the world waiting to be exploited.... Whoever runs them, Labrador will be an old-age pension for Newfoundland for a very long time....
>
> Few Canadians seem to realize that the possession of vast iron resources is going to have a profound effect on the whole Canadian economy.
>
> With great expansion planned for Ontario iron mines and the tremendous deposits along the Labrador-Quebec boundary just waiting to be developed, Canada is due to become one of the world's major producers and exporters of the heavy metal on which our industrial civilization is based. In a few years' time, Canada's Iron Ore would be an important means of earning U.S. dollars and improving our balance of trade. Eventually it will provide the firm foundation on

> which Canada can expand her whole industrial economy....Labrador Iron Ore [c]ould be the deciding factor in getting the St. Lawrence Seaway completed at long last... [there are] Labrador-Quebec iron ore deposits in the heart of the Ungava Peninsula, ...reserves of some 400 million tons of high grade ore have already been proven, and an initial output of 10 million tons a year is already planned.
>
> The U.S. needs iron ore reserves to replace or spin out the dwindling Mesabi reserves....
>
> [Back in 1943] I had never heard of the dwindling Mesabi iron-ore reserves in the United States. I had no notion that within five years, people would be boasting of 400 million proven tons of haematite ore ... on the Quebec-Labrador boundary. I simply smelt a rat or two; and I think my untrained nose was pretty good. ...one day, as well those great Falls [the Grand Falls on the Hamilton, now the Churchill River] will be harnessed. One day, I dare say, that timber will be cut; a railway will run from the mines to the St. Lawrence, and Labrador will laugh at the frozen sea.[42]

To that, it might be added, Canada laughed at Newfoundland. On 1 April 1949 the tariff wall came down which protected Newfoundland's small manufacturers. Cheaper Canadian goods flooded into Newfoundland. It has been conservatively estimated that 4000 jobs were instantly lost.[43] But Canadian minister C.D. Howe remained indifferent to this challenge to Newfoundland manufacturing, allowing Newfoundland's best interests to be sacrificed on the altar of confederation, doing nothing to ease the situation.[44]

The Newfoundland per capita debt, which was about $160 dollars the day before confederation, jumped to about $1300 dollars the day after,[45] but much to the chagrin of Newfoundland's leading intellectual and speaker of common sense, A.B. Perlin, the new province received no debt equalization compensation which it should have been due, which could have greatly assisted in the transition to provincehood. Canada quickly used its new control over Newfoundland's airports while it still could (before the era of the jet aircraft) to force its way into American civil aviation markets. The 502 vapour trails eight miles above St. John's every day testify to the continued existence of the Great Circle Route, and the wealth which continues to accrue to Canada as a result of controlling what once was Newfoundland's airspace.

Writing of the uses of the past in French politics and culture, the historian Robert Gildea has noted that "What matters is myth, not in the sense of fiction, but in the sense of a construction of the past elaborated by a political community for its own ends."[46] Certainly, Newfoundland's confederation with Canada is replete with myths. The historical myth about Newfoundland during the war has been the myth about pre-confederation Newfoundland: that it would be eternally impoverished, that it didn't have a hope of making it on its own, or as the Toronto *Globe and Mail* prefers, that Newfoundland was a basket case until it was rescued by Canada. But these myths simply are not supported by the evidence. Either Canada was the most altruistic nation in history, or more likely, it actually stood to gain from Newfoundland's confederation, and took steps to "take in" Newfoundland because it wanted Newfoundland and Labrador's resources. The war brought the Newfoundland state back from the dead, and the war, coupled with the absence of the democratic scrutiny of public policy in Newfoundland, provided the ideal circumstances for Canada to quietly circle around and carefully size up its prey. Some historians have argued that Canada began the process of "integrating" Newfoundland into confederation with the drafting of terms of union late in 1948. But this was ten years too late. Long before the referendums and the Ottawa delegation of 1948, Newfoundland and Labrador came substantially under Canadian economic influence, and well on the road to confederation. Confederation for Newfoundland was about gaining the Canadian social welfare state. But confederation for Canada was about securing its own best economic interests, even if most Newfoundlanders at the time didn't know the difference. The Canadian responses to the opportunities presented by the war in Newfoundland beg the question: if Canadians couldn't afford to lose Newfoundland, could Newfoundlanders afford to lose Newfoundland?

John E. FitzGerald.

Biographical Sketch

Dr. John FitzGerald has conducted research on Newfoundland's political and constitutional history at archives throughout Newfoundland and Labrador, Canada, the United States, the United Kingdom, France, Ireland, and Italy. He has been a Post-Doctoral Fellow, Lecturer, and Adjunct Professor of History in the Department of History, Memorial University, and has published articles on aspects of 19th and 20th century Newfoundland and Labrador history in The *Newfoundland Quarterly*, *Newfoundland Studies*, *The Beaver*, and *Historical Studies*. Active in the heritage and cultural sector provincially and nationally, he has served on the board of many historical societies and boards, has advised the provincial and federal governments on historical matters, and has frequently commented on the social, political, and cultural history of Newfoundland and Labrador in local, national, and international media. In May, 2006 he was appointed Provincial Representative in the Newfoundland and Labrador Office of Federal-Provincial Relations in Ottawa.

Endnotes

1. An earlier version of this essay was read to the Newfoundland Historical Society's Encounters With the Wolf Confederation Symposium on 26 February 1999 during the session entitled "The

Impact of World War II on Newfoundland". This essay is based on research funded by the Social Sciences and Humanities Research Council of Canada, the Institute for Social and Economic Research, Memorial University, and the J.R. Smallwood Centre for Newfoundland Studies, Memorial University.

2. A.P. Herbert, *Independent Member*, 272. The italics are mine.

3. National Archives and Records Administration, Washington, D.C. (hereafter NAW), Record Group 84, Box 53, Foreign Service Posts of the Department of State (hereafter FSPDS), St. John's, Newfoundland Consulate (hereafter SJNF), General Records 1943, vol. 9. Charles S. Reed II, St. John's, to the Secretary of State, Washington, 5 June 1943.

4. Paul Bridle, *Documents On Relations Between Canada and Newfoundland, Vol. I* (Ottawa, 1974), 98, memo by the Secretary of State for External Affairs, 29 August 1940.

5. Ibid., 24.

6. Francis Lowenheim, Harold D. Langley, and Manfred Jonas, Eds., *Roosevelt and Churchill: their secret wartime correspondence* (New York, 1990): 108-9, Roosevelt to Churchill, 13 August 1940.

7. Ibid., 109-10, Churchill to Roosevelt, 15 August 1940.

8. NAW, RG 84, FSPDS, SJNF, box 82, file: "St. John's, NF Prominent Persons, 1951–1952, 050-", Lt. Col. L.C. Outerbridge, "Broadcast on the subject of the agreement leasing military bases in Newfoundland to the United States."

9. T.J. Cahill (a friend of Ludlow's) to the author, 18 February 1999.

10. Bridle, *Documents I*, 1310, Report of G.S. Watts, 1 April 1943.

11. NAW, RG 84 FSPDS SJNF Box 48 Gen Recs 1942 vol. 11. George D. Hopper SJNF to SSW, 16 January 1943.

12. Bridle, *Documents* 1, 195, Robertson to King, 15 July 1941.

13. Ibid., 98, note by SS. Ext Aff, 28 August 1940.

14. NAW, RG 84 FSPDS, SJNF, Gen Recs 1941, Box 43, vol. 8, copy of *Daily News*, 4 July 1941.

15. James K. Hiller and Michael Harrington, *The Newfoundland National Convention 1946–1948, Vol. II* (Montreal and Kingston, 1995), 19.

16. NAW RG 84 Box 48 FSPDS, SJNF Gen Recs 1942, vol. 11, George D. Hopper to the Secretary of State, Washington, 31 December 1942.

17. Ibid., Box 56 FSPDS, SJNF Gen Recs 1943, vol 13, George D Hopper to the Secretary of State, Washington, 26 July 1943.

18. Bridle, *Documents II* (Ottawa, 1984): 921, Bridle to the Secretary of State for External Affairs, 12 July 1948.

19. Bridle, *Documents I,* 1186, JC Puddester to King, 28 November 1940.

20. Ibid., 1310 and ff., Report of Watts on Newfoundland visit, April 1943.

21. Ibid.

22. Ibid.

23. Ibid., 1319.

24. Ibid., and NAW, RG 84 FSPDS, SJNF, Box 53, Gen Recs 1943, vol. 9, R.P. Bower to Director, Commercial Intelligence Service,

Ottawa, 18 December 1943.

25. Bridle, *Documents I*, 1222, Robertson to Burchell, 12 June 1944.

26. Ibid., 79, Burchell to Robertson, 13 September 1943.

27. *Daily News*, 31 December 1946; also see Bridle, *Documents II*, 505.

28. NAW, RG 59 Box 22 Goose Bay 1942–7, George D. Hopper to the Secretary of State, Washington, 13 November 1943.

29. Ibid.

30. NAW RG 59 Box 22 Goose Bay 1942–7, Hopper to the Secretary of State, Washington, 26 October 1944.

31. Ibid., Hopper to the Secretary of State, Washington, 6 January 1945.

32. NAW RG 84 Box 66 FSPDS SJNF, R.J. Cavanaugh to the Secretary of State, Washington, 29 November 1945.

33. Bridle, *Documents II*, 299-300, Macdonald to Robertson, 17 October 1946.

34. Ibid.

35. Ibid., 496-8, Memo of JR Baldwin to the Canadian Cabinet, 16 June 1947.

36. Public Archives of Canada, Sound and Moving Image Archives, Charles Granger Collection, Paul Bridle to Charles Granger, 27 June 1980, CA 1980–79/1.

37. J.W. Pickersgill to the author, 11 August 1992.

38. Hiller & Harrington, *National Convention I*, 1273, Captain Charles Bailey to the National Convention, 20 January 1948.

39. NAW RG 59/843A.6351/12-2247, Ray Atherton to the Secretary of State, Washington, 22 December 1947.

40. Gregory Power to the author, 27 March 1989 and 27 January 1992.

41. Richard Geren and Blake McCullogh, *Cain's Legacy: The Building of the Iron Ore Company of Canada* (Sept-Iles, Québec, 1990), 33.

42. A.P. Herbert, *Independent Member*, 272, 275.

43. Doug Letto, *Chocolate Bars and Rubber Boots* (Paradise, NF, 1998), 99.

44. Raymond B. Blake, *Canadians At Last: Canada integrates Newfoundland as a province* (Toronto, 1994), 97.

45. Bridle, *Documents II*, 356, JS Macdonald to the Secretary of State for External Affairs, noted on 11 December 1946 that Newfoundland's per capita debt was $238 while Canada's was $1068. By 26 May 1948, Bridle would be able to report (Bridle, *Documents II*, 877) to the Secretary of State that the independent McDonald Currie Report commissioned by the *Western Star* estimated that Newfoundland would have a deficit of $4.5 million at the outset of confederation, while the provincial per capita debt would jump from $160 to $1340.

46. Quoted in Kevin Whelan, *The Tree of Liberty* (Cork, Ireland, 1996), 133.

This article appears in the *Newfoundland Quarterly*, Vol. 35, No. 3 (Spring 2001), pp. 21-28, and is used with permission.

16

Mackenzie King's Attitude Towards Newfoundland's Entry into Confederation.

By: Raymond B. Blake.

Introduction by Paul J. Johnson.

This chapter is about Canada's Prime Minister Mackenzie King's "Attitude" about Newfoundland's possible Confederation with Canada. It reveals the enthusiasm and concerns of Canada's senior politicians and officials, as they struggled with all the considerations, to decide on whether and how to influence, and ultimately facilitate, a union of Newfoundland with Canada. It is a fascinating, remarkably detailed, and true "inside story".

I

Prime Minister William Lyon Mackenzie King's role in completing Confederation with Newfoundland is frequently overshadowed by Louis St. Laurent's. Although St. Laurent was Prime Minister during the final negotiations with Newfoundland, King had presided over the initial steps that laid the foundation for the victory of Confederation in 1948. It was also King who made the momentous decision to accept Newfoundland as a province despite the narrow victory for the Confederate forces.

The final decision for King was not an easy one. In fact, the whole Confederation issue of the late 1940s was difficult for him. Undoubtedly, King wanted Newfoundland to become a part of Canada, but he feared the political repercussions of such an occurrence. He realized that most of the provinces were hostile to the federal government giving generous financial subsidies to

Newfoundland. On the other hand, King realized that if Canada did not complete union with Newfoundland, it could easily come under the influence of the Americans, creating an eastern Alaska. Furthermore, the United Kingdom was constantly exhorting King, as were many officials at the Department of External Affairs. King also realized that many in his Cabinet wanted Newfoundland as the tenth province. Certainly King knew how historians would judge his tenure as Prime Minister if he completed Confederation. He was aware that history was harsh in its judgment of those who had confronted the issue but had failed to bring it to fruition. He did not want to be seen as another failure.

When King finally made the decision to accept Newfoundland into Confederation, he had obviously considered all the possible repercussions. After much hesitation, which characterized his whole approach to the issue, he decided to act in the best interests of the country. After 1939, King had seen the strategic importance of Newfoundland and he knew that Canada could not afford to lose the colony. To achieve his objective, King adopted a simple policy: he never gave the Newfoundlanders reason to believe that Canada was over-zealous or aggressive in its approach but at every opportunity he tried to improve relations with the colony. His policy proved to be effective and one that pleased him immensely because he had succeeded where his predecessors had failed.

II

When the governments of Canada and the United Kingdom passed the appropriate legislation to consummate the union of Newfoundland and Canada, the London *Times* reported it as "the final phase of an evolutionary movement."[1] In many respects the *Times* was accurate. Once the British had defeated the French in North America, relations between Newfoundland and the other colonies improved. Newfoundland was party to the proceedings when the mainland colonies confederated in 1867, but the Newfoundland advocates of union were resoundingly defeated when they took the issue to the electorate. Despite several unsuccessful attempts to bring Newfoundland into the union after 1869, contact between Newfoundland and Canada grew and the relations between the two continued to improve, except for a few notable exceptions.[2]

Newfoundland was, in many respects, a domain of Canada by the Second World War. Canada's hegemony in the financial affairs of Newfoundland was clearly established. There were important economic, educational and religious bonds between the two,[3] but following the outbreak of hostilities Canada's interests in Newfoundland were largely strategic. King recognized the strategic importance of Newfoundland and Labrador to the defence of Canada and before his declaration of war, he said that Newfoundland would be included in Canada's defence preparations. In the House of Commons on 8 September 1939, he reiterated its importance when he announced that the "integrity of Newfoundland and Labrador were essential to the security of Canada."[4]

When he learned that the United States wanted the right to establish military bases in Newfoundland in exchange for sending destroyers to aid the British war effort, King wanted assurances from British Prime Minister Winston Churchill that he would be consulted about matters pertaining to Newfoundland. King was characteristically vacillating throughout the negotiations, but perhaps with good reason. By June 1940, with the fall of France imminent, he realized that the United Kingdom was the only remaining obstacle for Hitler to overcome before he began his assault across the Atlantic. He hastily cabled Churchill, urging him to expedite matters that would permit the Americans to establish bases along the Atlantic coast.[5] King felt correctly that the strong military presence of the Americans in Newfoundland ensured the security and safety of Canada.

Before an agreement could be concluded, however, King had a change of heart. He informed Churchill on 18 August of Canada's commitment to Newfoundland, adding "there will probably be necessity for co-operation between the three governments in matters pertaining to that island."[6] Some of the officials in the Department of External Affairs wanted him to improve on Canada's special relationship to bring Newfoundland into the Canadian fold. One such official was Norman Robertson, Under-Secretary of State for External Affairs from 1941–46, who warned King that granting the Americans a base of operations in Newfoundland would compromise Canada's position there. He feared "that the United States would not. . .take Canadian interests in Newfoundland as seriously as Canada felt they ought to be taken." At the time he saw Confederation as one alternative for Newfoundland, but he was worried that the American presence would jeopardize its eventual realization.[7] However, with German U-Boat activity increasing in the North Atlantic, King was not about to delay the agreement to protect Canada's interest. On 26 August, he wrote Lord Cranborne, Britain's Secretary of State for Dominion Affairs, that he was ready "to have the United States lease of bases granted without delay" pointing out that "our coasts are left bare of defence to help the British at a critical moment."[8] Obviously King considered the defence of Canada and the United Kingdom more important than the protection of Canada's interest in Newfoundland. All was not lost, however. A protocol attached to the destroyer-for-bases agreement recognized Canada's special interest there.[9]

Despite the protocol's recognition of Canada's interest in Newfoundland, its privileges there were secure only during the war. But as soon as the Americans were given long-term leases for defence purposes, King hastened to strengthen Canada's position. He recorded in his diary that "we should secure. . . rom Newfoundland ourselves, a lease similar. . .to that being given to the United States by the United Kingdom." The Canadian War Committee acted immediately, authorizing $1 million for an airport at Gander. By the time of the cessation of hostilities, over $65 million had been spent to fortify Newfoundland and Labrador against the threat of invasion,[10] an expenditure that clearly demonstrated Canada's interest and commitment there.

Although his suggestion in 1943 was not accepted by King, Robertson continued to press for Confederation. He realized, of course, that Confederation would take time to complete, but he also believed that it deserved "better handling and franker exchange than it was getting" from the King government. He was obstinate about the necessity for Canada to maintain a profile comparable with the Americans and the British in Newfoundland. He also believed that Canada should be represented there by a permanent official. He suggested to King that after the war Newfoundland would be considering a return to self-government and Confederation would certainly be discussed. A permanent representative "could help to straighten out some of the snarls in which our trade and fishing relations. . .are now entangled." Furthermore, he argued that the newly appointed American Consul General would foster better relations between the United States and Newfoundland at Canada's expense.[11]

Within three months of Robertson's letter to King, Nova Scotia native Charles J. Burchell was appointed Canada's first High Commissioner to Newfoundland. When King informed Burchell of his appointment, he alluded to Canada's military, strategic and long-term interests in the colony. King also reminded him of the special importance attached to his position:

> During the next year or two the question of Newfoundland's relation to Confederation is quite likely to become an important issue. In the circumstances, we think it desirable to emphasize Canada's special relationship with Newfoundland and propose to do so by appointing a High Commissioner there.[12]

King's early interest in Newfoundland came from his friendship with Sir Wilfred Grenfell, founder of the International Grenfell Mission, and Norman Duncan, King's roommate at the University of Toronto who subsequently spent many years writing about Newfoundland. Duncan's love for Newfoundland was not lost on King. Furthermore, Grenfell considered Newfoundland as the "utmost limits of Canada's far-flung territories." He thought Canada to be the most Christian country in the world and he considered the leadership provided by Sir Wilfrid Laurier, the Honourable W. Mackenzie King, and Sir Robert Borden reason for anyone being "proud of a close link with that great country."[13]

Robertson was undoubtedly pleased with the Burchell appointment and with King's long-term interest in Newfoundland. Throughout the war he continued to express his eagerness to see Newfoundland a part of Canada. In March 1943, he wrote to King that "somehow, sometime, Newfoundland should become a part of the Canadian Confederation. I think that, in the long run, both political and strategic considerations make this inevitable."[14] In a debate shortly after with J. W. Noseworthy, a former Newfoundlander representing York South in Parliament, King announced his government's policy towards Newfoundland. The door was always open, he said, and "should they make that decision clear and beyond all possibility of misunderstanding, Canada would give most sympathetic consideration to the proposal."[15] But for Robertson, a policy statement was not enough. Two years later, he told King that the demand for Confederation would not arise spontaneously, but support could be anticipated if generous terms were offered.[16] Robertson also suggested that Canada prepare for the possibility of Confederation. In a memorandum to King he suggested that if Canada were interested in Newfoundland and were willing to inform the United Kingdom of its interest, then "a small committee of officials under a senior official of the Department of External Affairs be set up to examine in detail the various aspects – constitutional, financial, and administrative – that would require consideration if Newfoundland accepts the proposal and enters into Confederation."[17]

Whether it was upon the urgings of Robertson or King's genuine interest in Newfoundland, the foundation for Confederation was being laid in 1945. In that year a report was prepared for External Affairs entitled "The Financial Cost of Incorporating Newfoundland in the Dominion" by Robert A. MacKay, a Dalhousie University professor who had become Special Assistant to the Under-Secretary of State for External Affairs during the war. A year later, other officials were actively encouraging the government to prepare for Confederation.[18] J. Scott Macdonald, then High Commissioner to Newfoundland, informed External Affairs that Newfoundlanders would soon meet to decide their political future and union would be discussed. He suggested Ottawa be prepared and External Affairs agreed. Within Cabinet, Brooke Claxton, Minister of National Defence, played a vital role in creating a serious interest in Newfoundland, suggesting to Hume Wrong, Associate Under-Secretary of State for External Affairs that:

> If we have any interest whatsoever in entering negotiations with Newfoundland then surely to goodness we ought to do it now and do it very informally through someone who has no official connection whatever either in this country, in Newfoundland or in the United Kingdom. What we would want would be someone who already had some standing there to open this up in active discussion with their people completely outside of politics. With encouragement he might then come here. With proper discretion it would take some time for this activity to leak out and I would not think that there would be any way in which news of it could adversely affect this government.[19]

Wrong had been instrumental in establishing MacKay's informal interdepartmental committee "to put together a Cabinet memorandum on the likely effects that union with Newfoundland would have on Canada." Although the committee met on only a few occasions, it prepared a comprehensive report on virtually all aspects of union, ranging from the financial and legal implications to the beneficial effects of union.[20]

While some officials at External Affairs were pursuing the possibility of union, Newfoundland itself was demanding the return to self-government which had been revoked in 1934. Following the recommendations of Lord Amulree who had been appointed to investigate the colony's financial and economic problems, Newfoundland had surrendered her Dominion status and reverted to the status of a crown colony. Since then Newfoundland had been administered by a Commission of Government, a six-man appointed body with equal representation from the United Kingdom and Newfoundland and with a Crown-appointed Governor as chairman.[21]

On 11 December 1945, British Prime Minister Clement Attlee, who had earlier visited Newfoundland, announced in the House of Commons the formation of a National Convention in Newfoundland "to consider and discuss. . .the changes that have taken place in the financial and economic situation. . .since 1934. . .and to make recommendations to His Majesty's Government as to possible forms of future government to be put before the people at a national referendum."[22]

King was not surprised at this. London had seized every opportunity that arose to counsel him of its intentions to help make Newfoundland a Canadian province. In the fall of 1945, Malcolm MacDonald, the British High Commissioner to Canada, informed him that his government would soon take steps "towards having Newfoundland seek to come into Confederation." Of course, King was cautious, suggesting that Newfoundland not be forced to join, that "we should let them know we would be willing to have them consider favourably their coming into the Confederation at any time."[23] When King travelled to London later that fall, he found Lord Addison, then Secretary of State for Dominion Affairs, eager to discuss the Newfoundland situation. According to King, the British were afraid that Newfoundland would fall into American hands.[24]

At home, King's interest was nurtured by officials at External Affairs who continued to warn him of just such a danger. He agreed, but he was not consistent in his distrust of the U.S. and its anxiety to acquire Newfoundland. In early March 1947, when External Affairs was pushing to have Newfoundland brought in immediately, King urged caution. Despite the warnings of Lester Pearson, Under-Secretary of State for External Affairs, that the Americans could get control of Newfoundland through their air bases, King was not perturbed. He wondered if Canada would not gain by having the Americans "assume a responsibility for the protection of this continent."[25]

It is difficult to ascertain the precise cause of King's change of attitude towards the American threat. His earlier worries had faded. Perhaps the implications created by the Igor Gouzenko affair that exposed a Soviet spy network in Canada in September 1945, continued to reverberate in his thoughts, arousing his suspicions of the Soviets. Concomitant with the growing international tension between the West and the Soviet Union, King conceivably saw greater security for Canada under the protective wing of the Americans. He had certainly entertained that belief during the war, lauding Britain's decision to lease bases to the Americans. Possibly he had remembered President Franklin Roosevelt's assurances that the Americans had no interest in Newfoundland. Whatever the reason, King's fear of the American threat in Newfoundland had nearly vanished.[26]

When the National Convention convened in 1947, there was, however, little reason for optimism among the Confederate forces. They constituted the smallest faction, a mere "handful of delegates from outpost constituencies," in a Convention, dominated by the mercantile and professional elements, that favoured a return to responsible government. Even the group wanting to retain the Commission of Government outnumbered the Confederates.[27]

Yet, the Confederate forces had powerful allies. Lord Addison suggested that if the Convention wished to explore the possibility of Confederation, a delegation should be sent to Ottawa. But with the overwhelming majority hostile to Confederation, the Confederates found it exceedingly difficult to even discuss the issue. The task became the crusade of Joseph R. Smallwood, a former farmer and journalist, who was the only member elected to the Convention as a Confederate. Smallwood attributed his conversion to Confederation to Gordon Bradley, a former cabinet minister and convention delegate, who had realized much earlier than Smallwood that Newfoundland's welfare could be improved only through union with Canada.[28]

Smallwood admitted that he knew very little about Canada. Thus, in 1946, he travelled to Ottawa on a fact-finding mission. Although Frank Bridges, Minister of Fisheries, told him that an interdepartmental memo had been circulated about Newfoundland's possible entry into Canada and his support for it, Smallwood noted that everyone in Ottawa tried to avoid him because they wanted to avoid giving the impression that Confederation was a plot engineered by Canada. In characteristic style, he wrote, "I expected to have a warm welcome in Ottawa. If the plague had descended on them, I don't think they would have been any more scared. They were scared. They were really scared; I was almost untouchable."[29]

He was perhaps accurate in his assessment of the situation because External Affairs feared a similar perception. J. Scott Macdonald and MacKay, who both knew of Smallwood's plan to visit Ottawa, agreed that the visit could be viewed as a collusion between Ottawa and Newfoundland Confederates. Wrong shared their view, but he also realized that Canada needed a man with Smallwood's enthusiasm if the colony was to be brought into Confederation. Thus he informed Macdonald that if Smallwood insisted, they would have to comply with his wishes because he "may be too valuable a friend to risk antagonizing." Obviously worried over the interpretation of Smallwood's visit, he suggested that Smallwood take a 'round-about' route through New York. And, to allay any further suspicions, Wrong also suggested that Smallwood not be given introductions to government officials except MacKay, who shared with him a mutual interest in Newfoundland writing.[30]

When Smallwood arrived at Ottawa in August 1946, however, there is little evidence to suggest that he was shunned. He met various ministers including Louis St. Laurent, the acting Prime Minister, and J. W. Pickersgill, the Prime Minister's Special Assistant. Although External Affairs had tried to discourage the visit, perhaps in keeping with King's strategy not to appear anxious, it proved crucial to the eventual outcome of the National Convention. After making a favourable impression on Canadian political leaders, Smallwood returned, convinced that Canada would accept Newfoundland on satisfactory terms; and a Confederation movement was born in Newfoundland.[31]

As the time approached for Canada to decide if she would meet a delegation from Newfoundland, External Affairs assumed an important role. Pearson suggested to Robertson, then High Commissioner in London, that if the United Kingdom withheld financial assistance, union with Canada would be more palatable to Newfoundland. Pearson was later informed by Sir Alexander Clutterbuck, High Commissioner to Canada, that the United Kingdom would comply with Canada's request and would withhold "generous financial assistance" if Newfoundland chose to become a self-governing dominion. Pearson realized immediately that this would greatly enhance the opportunity for Confederation.[32] Shortly after, during a Cabinet debate on the matter, King said it had to make a decision because the British government was ready to abandon Newfoundland if Canada were willing to admit it to the Confederation. He noted that Canada's long-term objective was to bring Newfoundland into the federation, but he wanted to settle the contentious federal-provincial agreement on taxation before another province was added.[33]

Although King had agreed by October 1946 that Canada would receive a delegation from the National Convention to discuss union, he was never confident that he had made the right decision. Even when negotiations began, he continued to harbour doubts and, on more than one occasion, he considered breaking off talks with the Newfoundland delegation.

By 30 October 1946, King had agreed to receive a delegation from the National Convention should a request be received.[34] At the same time, a Cabinet Committee was chosen by King "to consider and advise government on questions relating to Newfoundland and to supervise the work of the interdepartmental committee." If the calibre of the ministers that he appointed was an indication of the value he attached to the project, he certainly wanted results. Most of his trusted, influential, and high-profile ministers such as St. Laurent, Brooke Claxton, J. L. Ilsley, C. D. Howe, and D. C. Abbott were on the committee.[35] By December, however, King was vacillating. He believed that union was the long-term objective for Canada, but he did not wish to exasperate the already tense relations with the provinces by allocating federal funds to a new province.[36] When the National Convention finally passed a resolution on 20 March 1947, requesting the Canadian government to receive a delegation to discuss "what fair and equitable basis may exist for the federal union of Newfoundland and Canada," King reluctantly agreed to receive the delegation.[37]

Pickersgill attributed King's reluctance to fatigue. He wrote to him that "the overwhelming fatigue from which you suffer may have had the effect of magnifying the difficulties, not absolute but in relation to the advantage of bringing in Newfoundland." Pickersgill added that if Newfoundland fell into American hands, it would diminish Canada's defence budget and guarantee the country's security. However, such an occurrence would be disastrous for the national psychology. If the Americans acquired Newfoundland, it would reduce Canada's international importance. Thus, Pickersgill saw Newfoundland as a touchstone for Canada; if the King government accepted responsibility for Newfoundland, this would indicate Canada's desire to pursue an independent foreign policy, but if Canada failed to assume responsibility for Newfoundland, Canada would be relegated to a position of dependence. Furthermore, Pickersgill prognosticated domestic turmoil if Canada pursued the latter course. He believed that international crises like World War I and World War II spawned nationalism and unity in Canada, but

> if we seek shelter within the outstretched and seemingly protecting arm of the United States and thereby avoid most of our external responsibilities. . . Canada would become a mere collection of quarrelling ultimately divided provinces and communities without national will or national purpose.

He further suggested that the admission of Newfoundland would become a national objective, unifying the nation as it pulled together to bring Newfoundland into the Canadian family. He also tried to impress upon King the value to his career of completing union with

Newfoundland. He wrote that achieving Confederation "may be the crowning triumph of your unparalleled career."[38]

Pickersgill's memo must have had some effect upon King. When the Newfoundland delegation arrived in Ottawa in June 1947, the *Financial Post* reported that the government went out of its way to make the delegation welcome.[39] King was perhaps more excited than anyone about the arrival of the delegation. He had discussed the possibility of union with Addison, Roosevelt, and Attlee, but he had not played an integral role in what had transpired since the matter had first been pursued with some vigor. When the delegation arrived, he was host at a dinner given for it and presided over the meeting that began the negotiations. He took the opportunity to express his feelings on the issue, noting that union was not "a course to be undertaken lightly," but one which merited "serious and unhurried examination" by both parties. He was unequivocal when he stressed that "the question of the colony's future was one for the people of Newfoundland to decide and not a matter in which the people of Canada or the government of Canada would wish to interfere." And he was extremely pleased with the compliments he received on his speech at the dinner: "Many of our men and others spoke of me and my speech. They seemed to think it was one of the best I ever made. I know it produced a fine effect."[40] The event, undoubtedly, had a beneficial effect upon King. He immediately saw himself as a Father of Confederation and contemplated remaining in his position as Prime Minister a little longer to oversee Newfoundland's entry into Canada:

> It is a strange thing that among the many other things which now fall into my lot, I should be called upon to complete the union of all British possessions in the North American Continent. . .I should not indeed be surprised if it might be that my part would help bring about the rounding out of Canada as a nation in a manner which would take in all the territory from the waters of the Atlantic to those of the Pacific. To this end I would be tempted to remain a little longer in public life than otherwise I would wish to be.[41]

Although King's enthusiasm for staying in public life and the imminent union with Newfoundland grew as summer approached, he was not without his moments of doubt. By 11 July 1947, St. Laurent and his Cabinet Committee realized that union would cost Ottawa an additional $15 million annually over and above the normal financial obligations to Newfoundland. Although the expenditure was a mere fraction of federal spending, it was considerably more than the government could justify spending on the Maritime Provinces. King realized that to proceed under such circumstances would be politically disastrous. Consequently, St. Laurent was to tell Gordon Bradley, chairman of the Newfoundland delegation, that successful negotiations were impossible at this time.[42]

This suggestion, however, was not followed. The King Cabinet decided a few days later to continue negotiations. Perhaps King changed his mind because of his party's by-election victory in Halifax on 14 July. It was the third such victory for him and his party after three earlier defeats. He recorded his excitement and pleasure in his diary:

> Today's victory in Halifax places an additional obligation to stay in public life for a while longer. . . It makes me happy to think of how these results will read in the United Kingdom and the United States as well as in Canada. It is a marvelous thing on top of the record of the Liberal Party in office at a moment when the world is in the state of unrest that it is at this time.[43]

King's good fortune continued to grow with the passage of his government's Reconstruction Bill a few days later. Again, he basked in the rays of victory as his party expressed its pleasure, giving him a standing ovation in the House of Commons.[44]

With King's electoral and Parliamentary successes, and recovering strength, it was inevitable that he would agree to proceed more vigorously with negotiations to achieve union. He would have preferred to have had all outstanding matters with the provinces settled, but he concluded that the long-term objectives were more important than a probable short-term backlash from the Maritimes. He reasoned that if Confederation were aborted and if Newfoundland subsequently ignored Canada in favour of the Americans, future generations would blame him and his government.[45] Since he was concerned with how history would judge him, he did not wish to jeopardize what he considered a remarkable career by bungling the union issue. Thus, on this rare occasion, he pushed aside political considerations and noted "the feeling in Cabinet was that there were larger National and Commonwealth considerations of which full account should be taken." Of course, St. Laurent's insistence on the "value it would be to [King's] name and to the future to have Newfoundland come into Confederation while [King] was Prime Minister" helped propel him into supporting a concerted effort to complete Confederation.[46]

III

King's enthusiasm for Confederation during the summer of 1947 was indeed uncharacteristic. Throughout the whole Confederation debate he was usually much more cautious and hesitant. There was little doubt, however, that he favoured Confederation, but the political problems sometimes nullified any movement in that direction. Smallwood and Pickersgill were both conscious of the lack of enthusiasm on the part of the Cabinet, Smallwood later writing that the "Canadian Cabinet was by no means falling over itself to have Newfoundland join Canada." Pickersgill later noted that there were "grave doubts in the minds of nearly all, well, I think all the ministers in Ottawa. Not about the desirability of having Newfoundland as a part of Canada, but about the viability of fitting Newfoundland into the federal-provincial picture in Canada."[47]

Some ministers, nevertheless, expressed a greater desire than King to secure Newfoundland. According to Smallwood and Pickersgill, Howe was, from the start, favourable towards union because he knew the potential of Labrador's resources. St. Laurent was perhaps most instrumental in the Cabinet in influencing King's decisions towards Newfoundland. It was not surprising that Claxton, given his desire to have Newfoundland join, suggested that Canada receive the delegation and assume the public debt of Newfoundland to impress its people, however unpopular such action might be in some parts of Canada.[48]

King, however, was hesitant about offering Newfoundland attractive financial inducements. He realized that it would be extremely difficult to propose generous financial terms to Newfoundland without creating adverse reaction from the richer provinces and precipitating demands from the poorer ones for increased subsidies.[49] Although King had earlier thrust this issue aside as he pushed ahead with his dream of completing Confederation, he had returned to his characteristically cautious approach by the end of July.

By August St. Laurent and his Cabinet Committee were ready to release the proposed terms for the entry of Newfoundland into Confederation. But, at the same time, Frank Bridges, New Brunswick's representative in the Cabinet, died. With an impending by-election and the absence of a New Brunswick representative in his Cabinet, King was not prepared to release the terms. Perpetually conscious of the political repercussions he was not about to have Newfoundland become an issue in a by-election, especially in the Maritimes where he anticipated the strongest opposition because the region would resent Newfoundland receiving better terms than they. Even claims by St. Laurent that 80 percent of the country would support Newfoundland's entry failed to convince King to proceed. Although he admitted there was some validity in St. Laurent's assertion, he suggested it was only "until they know the terms. Once the terms are known, the different provinces would begin to take exception to them. . .we would be asked why we were treating strangers better than our own people and supporters." In his diary King recounted a similar incident that had sealed the fate of a predecessor. According to King, 90 percent of the electorate favoured reciprocity when Sir Wilfrid Laurier first advocated it, but he was nonetheless defeated in the election of 1911. Well-versed on Laurier's career, King was determined not to suffer a similar fate.[50]

King was unsettled by the death of Bridges. In his diary he did not reveal any sympathy for the Bridges family, but the death created a political problem for him. Earlier in the year he had been excited, enthusiastic, and confident with his success, but the approaching by-election obviously worried him. He was afraid that it would prevent "bringing the Newfoundland issue to a satisfactory conclusion and also mean the loss of a seat". Although he promised to go ahead and confront the situation and "meet it the best way we can," he refused to release the proposed terms with Newfoundland during the by-election. He feared that both Angus L. Macdonald, Premier of Nova Scotia, and J. B. McNair, Premier of New Brunswick, would oppose the terms and he feared this would be disastrous for his party. King, however, saw much wider ramifications:

> We would have utter chaos in Canada and the Government would be beaten and we would be further away from federation with Newfoundland than ever. Unless we could make perfectly sure of winning the forth-coming by-election, I felt it would be much better to let the present delegation go back and tell their people that we could not agree to their terms.[51]

Eventually, King got his way in Cabinet, the ministers finally agreeing that the terms would not be released until New Brunswick had its representative in the Cabinet. King was determined not to have the Newfoundland issue debated in a by-election, wanting the debate in Parliament where "opponents could be met in arguments in the open and bound to answer, and not on the hustings." When McNair arrived in Ottawa to discuss the matter, he supported King. St. Laurent and Ilsley, among others, wanted the matter discussed and a decision made, but King wanted negotiations to cease. It seems that King had lost his enthusiasm for the matter and he wanted the whole Confederation issue postponed until Newfoundland had returned to self-government. His change in attitude may have been prompted by rumours that Newfoundland merchants were financially supporting the Progressive Conservative candidate in the New Brunswick by-election to demonstrate their hostility towards King for meeting the Newfoundland delegation to discuss the possibility of union.[52]

King was also aware of the feeling of several of the provinces. With the exception of Quebec, however, no province objected, on principle, to having Newfoundland become a province of Canada. Premier Maurice Duplessis and many Quebecois were still smarting over the 1927 ruling of the Judicial committee of the Privy Council that awarded Labrador and its resources to Newfoundland. St. Laurent hoped that union would "help to rectify the situation, or at least reduce its consequences." Duplessis had warned him bluntly that he expected to be consulted before any agreement was reached. Of course, King was aware of Duplessis' demand and it was obvious that the Premier would not agree to admitting Labrador into Confederation as a part of Newfoundland. Certainly, King was also aware of Duplessis' description of the union as a "plot to bring three hundred thousand more Britishers into Canada."[53] And in a conversation with McNair, King learned that if Newfoundland received better financial terms than the Maritimes, it would create problems for his party there.[54]

Thus he realized the formidable task that confronted him in August 1947. Earlier in the summer when everything seemed to be going well, he was not faced with such a dilemma. But the death of Bridges and the pending by-election compelled King to consider all possibilities. If the Newfoundland matter became an issue in the by-election, it could mean defeat for the Liberals. This King feared the most. Since he did not want to retire a loser, he used this as an excuse to delay a final decision on Newfoundland, a decision he knew would not be popular with some of the provinces.

He realized from the outset that Newfoundland would be a financial liability. Because he did not want to incur any further antagonism from the provinces, he believed that the union with Newfoundland should be a "national matter, not a party one." Thus, he wanted to include the Opposition parties and the provinces in any negotiations with Newfoundland.[55]

When the possibility of receiving a delegation was initially discussed in Cabinet, he urged his government to be cautious. He stressed that careful consideration had to be paid to the reaction of the Opposition parties and the provincial governments. Because he realized the political ramifications of admitting Newfoundland, he stressed that the matter was not one for the Liberal Party alone. He suggested that all parties in Parliament work together to complete Confederation. Later, St. Laurent discussed the matter with the Opposition leaders and they agreed.[56] Although King said that the provinces would also be consulted, there is little evidence to suggest that any initiative was taken in this regard. He did, however, discuss the matter with the Governor-General who offered his assistance, but it appears King decided to act alone.[57]

He was reminded by External Affairs that it was not necessary to consult any other party or the provinces before Newfoundland was admitted. There was no evidence to show that the existing provinces had been consulted prior to the admission of British Columbia and Prince Edward Island. Neither was there any evidence to suggest that the provinces were consulted prior to the 1871 amendment to the Constitutional Act, 1867 which authorized Parliament to create new provinces out of the North-West. Furthermore, the Constitutional Act, 1867 which provided for the admission of Newfoundland, made no mention of consulting the existing provinces. King, however, placed political expediency before constitutional rights. He reminded Pearson, who had suggested the federal government had the constitutional right to act unilaterally, that this "would not meet the situation at all". King added that the federal government had jurisdiction over taxation, but the provinces did not look at constitutional rights. They only saw the federal government taking away their rights, and to bring Newfoundland into Confederation by resolution "would only emphasize all of that kind of reasoning and would be very dangerous."[58]

Although King initially took the Opposition into his confidence, he soon decided against proceeding further in this direction. When the delegation arrived, the Opposition leaders were invited to the dinner given for the delegation. They were informed of the background meetings on the Newfoundland issue and, King suggested, "We might let leaders know we are anxious that the matter should not be a party affair. That we might call them into conference later. That there would be an official committee to gather data, etc."[59]

Within a month, however, King had changed his mind. He had decided that he could not be hurt politically by the issue. Of course, his political successes of July 1947 had restored his confidence and it was obvious to him that he and his party could complete Confederation alone. Furthermore, he came to the conclusion that he could not trust the Opposition to assume responsibility for anything that went wrong. He decided that he would continue negotiations with Newfoundland and when completed, a resolution would then be introduced in Parliament. For King, characteristically, there was political expediency in this approach:

> The effect of that would be to put each political party on the spot. If the parties voted against the resolution, they would have to share responsibility for not having Newfoundland come in. I am not at all sure that to take that attitude would not make a first class national issue in the campaign. I am sure that the Canadian people will wish to see our Dominion rounded out from the outward waters of the Atlantic to those of the Pacific. Of course it may be that the delegates here will wish something too exorbitant. That would alter the situation.[60]

Although King had finally decided on a parliamentary procedure for the admission of Newfoundland, he was very uncertain when or how to release the proposed terms. When the Cabinet first discussed them in August, he suggested that "we had not agreed to any terms thus far." St. Laurent, however, reminded him that by permitting the negotiations he had implicated the government.[61]

King was frightened that the proposed terms would give the impression that Newfoundland's every desire was accommodated while Canada received little. Because of this, King remained noncommittal. He finally came to the conclusion that the Newfoundland people would have to debate the terms first. If they were acceptable to them, then the terms would be introduced in Parliament. However, if they were unacceptable, the matter would end there. King judged this to be a safe political route. If the Newfoundland people accepted the terms, he was certain that Canadians too would favour their acceptance. This *modus operandi* would not put his government in the position of acting first which carried the possibility of both the Newfoundland and Canadian people rejecting the terms. Such an outcome would be disastrous for the government and for King.[62]

King did not act, however, until the Liberals won the by-election in New Brunswick. Shortly after Milton Gregg's victory, the proposed terms were released. King had decided that the matter would be handled only by his party and that the provinces would not be consulted. He had decided that the representatives in Parliament would be sufficient to speak for the provinces.[63] In his letter that accompanied Canada's offer, King reiterated his determination not to influence the Newfoundland decision on Confederation:

> The Government of Canada would not wish in any way to influence the National Convention nor the decision of the people, should they be requested to decide the issue of Confederation. Should the people of Newfoundland indicate clearly and beyond all possibility of misunderstanding their will that Newfoundland should become a province of Canada on the basis of the proposed arrangements, the Canadian Government, subject to the approval of Parliament, would for its part be prepared to take the necessary constitutional steps to make the union effective at the earliest practicable date.[64]

The proposed terms did not create a wave of enthusiasm in the National Convention. With the exception of Smallwood and Bradley and their small band of Confederates, most of the Convention remained hostile to Confederation. Yet, King did not attempt to bolster the support for Confederation. He continued to see the question of the colony's future as one for Newfoundland alone to decide. It was not a matter for the Canadian government. This approach, however, created some problems for the Confederates in Newfoundland. There were charges that the Canadian government was lukewarm or indifferent to Newfoundland's choice. MacKay informed the High Commissioner there that the government was neither "lukewarm nor indifferent but it wanted Newfoundland to decide its future without influence from Canada."[65] King hoped that a cautious policy towards Newfoundland, tempered with non-interference would achieve the result he desired. Perhaps it came as a surprise to him that his approach suffered a temporary set-back when the National Convention voted on 23 January 1948, to keep Confederation with Canada out of the referendum that would decide Newfoundland's political future.

When the National Convention's recommendations were known, Pearson informed King that it had no authority to decide what constitutional alternatives would be placed before the people. The members of the Convention had been elected on personal qualifications, not known political views. Thus, its purpose was only to make recommendations to the United Kingdom. Pearson added that the British Government was fully aware of the powers of the Convention and "it had been intimated on more than one occasion that [it] may accept recommendations from minorities in the Convention as well as from majorities with respect to forms of government."[66]

The British government was bitterly disappointed that Confederation had been rejected in the Convention. Throughout the whole decade, it had repeatedly expressed its private desire to see Newfoundland become a province of Canada. Despite the Convention's recommendation, the United Kingdom remained adamant. However, it was faced with a dilemma: if it included

Confederation without any apparent reason, it would be accused of trying to push Newfoundland into Confederation, an accusation it dearly wanted to avoid. Two events transpired that permitted the United Kingdom to achieve its objective and still appear neutral.

The first occurred in Newfoundland. Immediately following the rejection of Confederation, Smallwood and Bradley mounted a massive public campaign against the 29 members of the Convention who had voted against Confederation. The response was overwhelming. Within days, St. John's was deluged with telegrams, letters, and petitions demanding the inclusion of Confederation in the referendum. It is interesting to note, however, that the petitions were never sent to the United Kingdom.[67]

The second encouraging signal was an ambiguous policy statement from the King government. Confederation could not be included if it were not agreeable to Canada. When External Affairs asked King for advice on the matter, he had to listen to two conflicting arguments in Cabinet. Some were opposed to offering any advice to the United Kingdom, arguing that Newfoundland should first win responsible government and then negotiate with Canada. King later wrote "that is the position I have taken from the beginning." St. Laurent and others disagreed, arguing that Canada should ask to have Confederation placed on the ballot.[68] Although King did not actively participate in the discussion, he appears to have accommodated both factions. Officially, the government replied that it did not wish to be consulted on the matter so as to appear neutral on an exclusively Newfoundland matter. Yet, unofficially, Canada welcomed the decision to include Confederation on the ballot. King, of course, had doubts about the contradiction in Canadian policy. He did not think it was proper to say that it would not interfere, and then, in the same statement, welcome the inclusion of Confederation. Later, he wrote, "I pointed out that sooner or later, it would be known that Canada had mentioned things; that would defeat the very thing that those in Newfoundland wished to achieve in the way of Confederation."[69] For him to permit the adoption of such a policy when he had reservations about it, implies his predilection towards union with Newfoundland. Because such action was contrary to his non-interference stance, it may suggest, too, his respect for St. Laurent who argued so vehemently for union.[70]

With the barrage of telegrams supporting Confederation and Canada's 'unofficial' authorization, the United Kingdom decided to include Confederation on the ballot. On 2 March 1948 Philip Noel-Baker of the Commonwealth Relation Office informed Newfoundland of the options: Confederation, return to responsible government, or the continuation of Commission of Government. To rationalize the inclusion of Confederation, he said "it would not be right that the people. . .be deprived of an opportunity of considering the issue at the referendum."[71]

Although the United Kingdom, with Canada's unofficial blessing, had found the rationale for the inclusion of Confederation, the outcome of the vote rested solely with the Newfoundland people. Although King had ample opportunity to intervene in the campaign, there is no evidence to suggest that he did. The task of bringing Newfoundland into Confederation fell to Smallwood, Bradley, and the Confederate Association together with quiet but substantial financial support from some Liberals in Canada.

The Confederate Association had been inaugurated on 26 March 1948. Although Bradley was elected President, Smallwood provided the leadership. Under him, the Confederates were better organizers, better campaigners, and better propagandists than their chief rivals who advocated a return to responsible government.[72] Noel has concluded that the Confederates "skillfully cultivated the image that they were the party of the little man, bravely confronting the vast wealth and power of 'Water Street', but, in fact, they were better financed than their opponents." Apparently, Smallwood had two important contacts in the Liberal Party, Howe and Senator Neil McLean, party treasurer in the Maritimes and owner of a large fish cannery in Newfoundland. Through them, he was introduced to Nova Scotia Senator Gordon Fogo, the National Liberal Federation president. Smallwood, however, realized that if he were implicated in a fund-raising campaign with the Liberals, it would douse the flames of Confederation. It would furnish his opponents with the evidence they sought to charge that Confederation was a conspiracy engineered by Canada and the United Kingdom. Thus, the task of fund-raising fell to Ray Petten, a close associate of Smallwood and later a Newfoundland Senator. The Liberal Party, of course, was in a similar predicament and, instead of funding the Confederates directly, it gave Petten a list of pliable Liberal donors. Harold Horwood, an executive member of the Association, has since claimed that Liberal supporters contributed nearly a quarter of a million dollars to Smallwood's campaign. However, Noel has argued that the outcome was decided not by money, but by organization.[73]

King was obviously more concerned about what appeared to be an increasing American interest in Newfoundland and a Newfoundland interest in the United States than about the financial support for the Confederates. Just as the Canadians and Newfoundlanders had met to discuss the possibility of union, Wainwright Abbott, a senior American diplomat, was appointed Consul-General in Newfoundland. Immediately, he began receiving informal but official instructions from Washington. As the referendum debate commenced, a party advocating economic union with the Americans was organized. Abbott subsequently informed the State Department that it cannot be doubted "it will rally considerable support." Later, he advised that "popular sentiment here favours United States over Canada and Great Britain."[74] King and his Cabinet discussed the possibility of union with the U.S. being added to the ballot and predictably advised the United Kingdom that such an addition would be undesirable.[75]

Despite assurances from diverse sources[76] that the U.S. had expressed little interest in Newfoundland, King was irritated about the persistent remarks of some American officials that gave credence to his suspicions. The St. John's *Sunday Herald*, an anti-confederate newspaper, reported that 51 American Senators were willing to meet and discuss the possibility of economic union with Newfoundland if a delegation were authorized to do so. King resented such pronouncements which were often used by the opponents of Confederation. He felt that the Americans should adopt the Canadian stance and refrain from active participation in the referendum debate.[77]

Since the option for union with the Americans was not on the ballot, King had little need for immediate concern. What perturbed him, however, was the possible defeat of Confederation and the return of responsible government which could conceivably usher in closer economic ties with the Americans. As the campaign drew to a close, King recorded in his diary that if Confederation won, Newfoundland would be a source of trouble in the future, but for him, "the only thing to do is save the Island from drifting into the hands of the Americans. . .Specially important to Canada."[78]

IV

When King heard that neither of the three choices polled a majority in the referendum held on 3 June 1948, he was somewhat disappointed. Despite what he had said a few days before the vote, he would have preferred to see responsible government returned, and Confederation completed between two governments. He was not at all disappointed that Confederation trailed responsible government by three percent. In fact, he was pleased that he and his government had brought Confederation closer than any other: "We at least have moved the whole matter forward. When Confederation does come, it will have been our Government which has taken the great step to bring this about." King realized that he had advanced Confederation but, by not completing it, he had not created any problems for himself or his party.[79]

In the second referendum King was not so fortunate. With the exception of the addition of a number of prominent politicians, leading businessmen, and former Commissioners to the Confederate side, the campaign was remarkably similar to the initial one. The voting pattern, too, remained very similar. When the final ballots were counted on 22 July, Confederation had won with 52.34 percent. The narrow victory created a problem for King – it was not the substantial majority he had said was necessary, but it was, nevertheless, a majority and the final decision on Confederation now rested with him.

He realized that a substantial minority in Newfoundland had opposed Confederation. If he proceeded with union, nearly half the population of Newfoundland would be hostile towards it. If he failed to complete union, perhaps it would destroy forever the vision of Canada held by the Fathers of Confederation. He was certainly in a dilemma, but proponents for the conflicting sides were quick to offer him their advice.

Undoubtedly more influential on King than the correspondence he received from Newfoundland, was the verdict of MacKay's investigation of the post-referendum state of opinion in Newfoundland. His report largely prompted King to act swiftly and in a positive manner. MacKay's first impression was that the public, including many anti-confederates, had accepted the outcome. The anti-confederate *Sunday Herald* had publicly accepted the verdict of the people as had Chesley Crosbie, a wealthy St. John's businessman who had opposed Confederation in favour of economic union with the Americans, but who now implied that he could be willing to be part of the delegation to complete final negotiations in Ottawa. MacKay also informed King that many others who had supported responsible government were ready to concede defeat and accept Confederation.[80]

Furthermore, he informed King, Confederation had won 18 of 25 electoral districts, an increase of two over the initial vote. A comparison of votes cast by districts revealed that "in almost every district where Confederation led Responsible Government on the first occasion, it increased its lead on the second, and. . .in every district but one, where it trailed Responsible Government, it closed the gap." St. John's was a perfect example of the latter point where votes for Confederation increased from 24 percent to 31 percent over the two ballots.[82]

Pickersgill's perceptive observation for King on the day following the vote made the problem of the slim majority no problem at all. By the time he received King's telephone call seeking his opinion of the result, he had some quick calculations. He had compiled the percentages of the popular vote that King had received in each election since 1921. It revealed that King had received 50 percent only in the 1940 election. When he received this information, King realized that the vote for Confederation was quite impressive, and he said, "Well. . .that puts a different light on it."[83] The matter of the slim majority never thereafter surfaced as a problem.

External Affairs had also prepared a report for King on the editorial comment in Canadian newspapers regarding Confederation. It informed him that 11 of 18 welcomed Confederation while only five voiced opposition. Two were non-committal. An avid reader of editorial comment, King was undoubtedly pleased with the support he for moving positively.[84]

The Prime Minister was also influenced by the United Kingdom. Before the second referendum, London had informed him that they would regard the slimmest majority as sufficient. After the vote, Noel-Baker said that the vote was a "fine achievement. . .it is well distributed in the different sections of the people." He advised a rapid completion of union and urged his High Commissioner to try and influence the Canadian decision.[85]

When King finally decided to accept Newfoundland into Confederation, it seemed the logical thing to do; Newfoundland had voted to join after Canada had made its position known. King feared union would only add to Canada's troubles as well as create problems for him and his party in the Maritimes. Yet, he understood that the

> bringing in of Newfoundland is the logical end to it, and probably in the course of time it will be among the accomplishments of the Administration of which I am the head. It will be that of the rounding out of Confederation by the addition of a tenth province. This will be completing the nation in its physical boundaries as it has already been completed in its complete autonomy and its position as a nation within the British Commonwealth of Nations.[86]

Once again he pushed political considerations aside and he did what he considered best for Canada. In addition to nationalistic motives, he derived some personal pride when he saw himself as a Father of Confederation:

> I had never dreamt that my name would probably be linked through years to come with the bringing into Confederation of what will be the 10th province and quite clearly the last. Having relation to my grandfather's part in laying the foundation of responsible government, it is interesting that it should be left to me as practically last of the completed task before giving up Leadership of my Party. To have been the one, as Prime Minister, to announce the entry within a few month's time, of Newfoundland into Confederation. It is wholly probable that, if spared, I shall have something of significance to do with the event itself when it comes to pass. Might even be listed as one of the Fathers of larger Confederation.[87]

When the Canadian decision was made public on 30 July 1948, King told the people that the plebiscite in favour of union was "clear and beyond all possibility of misunderstanding" and it was attained "without any trace of influence or pressure from Canada."[88] In his public broadcast, he alluded to the Fathers of Confederation and how gratified he was to complete their dream while he was Prime Minister and leader of the Liberal Party.[89]

The rest was anti-climatic and indeed, disappointing, for King. Before the final terms of union were debated in Parliament, he had relinquished the Prime Ministership to St. Laurent. Thus, it was he and not King who led the debate on Newfoundland. King merely watched and conceded in his diary that St. Laurent and his ministers were the ones entitled to the credit.[90] When he played a minor role in the official ceremonies marking the union, he did not attempt to conceal his remorse and disappointment: "I was happy to share the day's ceremony; a little disappointed that I had not found it possible to hold out to see the Parliament through."[91]

It was indeed an inauspicious denouement to the issue for King. He had cautiously pursued union since 1939. His policy was one of restraint and sympathetic interest. Although his approach often irritated some of his officials and ministers, he always did what he considered best for his country, his party, and for himself. He was careful to avoid giving Newfoundland the impression that he was overzealous towards union, but he always transmitted the message that when the colony was ready to join, Canada would be pleased to accept it. In the end his approach proved to be quite effective because Newfoundland voted to join Canada. It was, indeed, unfortunate for King that he did not see the matter to its final conclusion. If he had, he would have received the credit he deserved for his handling of the matter. His role would not have been overshadowed by Louis St. Laurent's.

Raymond B. Blake.

Biographical Sketch

Raymond B. Blake is a professor of history at the University of Regina but for 2009–10 he was appointed the Craig Dobbin Chair of Canadian Studies at University College Dublin in Ireland. He is the author of several books, including *Canadians At Last: The Integration of Newfoundland as a Province* which was re-issued by the University of Toronto Press in 2004 as well as *From Rights to Needs: A History of Family Allowances in Canada, 1929–1992* and *Beyond National Dreams: Essays on Canadian Citizenship and Nationalism* with Andrew Nurse, both of which were published in 2009.

Endnotes

1. *Times* (London), 19 January 1949, p. 5.

2. See S.J.R. Noel, *Politics in Newfoundland* (Toronto, 1973), pp. 36-37 and Peter Neary and S.J.R. Noel, "Newfoundland's Quest for Reciprocity, 1890–1910" in Mason Wade, (ed.), *Regionalism in the Canadian Community* (Toronto, 1969), pp. 210-226.

3. Robert MacKay (ed.), *Newfoundland: Economic, Diplomatic and Strategic Studies* (Toronto, 1946), p. 132 and A. Lacey, "Canada's Tenth Province?", *University of Toronto Quarterly*, 12: 435-45.

4. Hugh L. Keenleyside, *Memoirs of Hugh L. Keenleyside, On The Bridge of Time*, Volume II (Toronto, 1982), p. 200 and David MacKenzie, "Canada and the Entrance of Newfoundland into Confederation, 1939–1949", Unpublished Ph.D. Dissertation, University of Toronto, 1983, pp. 38-41.

5. King Diaries, Transcript 150, p. 640.

6. Ibid., Transcript 151, pp. 785-86 and Stetson Conn and Byran Fairchild, *The Western Hemisphere: The Framework of Hemisphere Defence* (Washington, 1960), pp. 55-56.

7. J. L. Granatstein, *A Man of Influence: Norman A. Robertson and Canadian Statecraft, 1929–68* (Toronto, 1981), pp.118-19.

8. King Diaries, Transcript 152, p. 828.

9. Robert A. Mackay (ed.), *Canadian Foreign Policy, 1945–54. Selected Speeches and Documents* (Toronto, 1970), p. 248.

10. Mackenzie, "Canada and the Entrance of Newfoundland into Confederation", p. 137.

11. Library and Archives Canada (LAC), W. L. Mackenzie King Papers (Notes and Memorandums, MG 26 JR), Volume 308, File 3270, C213281-6. Hereafter cited as KP.

12. MacKenzie, "Canada and the Entrance of Newfoundland into Confederation", p. 103. See C. P. Stacey, *Canada and the Age of Conflict. A History of Canadian External Policy*, Volume II (Toronto, 1981), pp. 415-425.

13. Wilfred T. Grenfell, *Forty Years for Labrador* (Boston 1932), p. 315 and J. W. Pickersgill and D. F. Foster (eds.) *The Mackenzie King Record*, Vol. IV (Toronto, 1970) p. 52.

14. KP, Vol. 308, File 3269, C213237.

15. Paul Bridle (ed.), *Documents on Relations Between Newfoundland and Canada*, Volume II (Ottawa, 1984), pp. 74-75.

16. KP, Volume 308, File 3269, C213342.

17. Bridle, *Documents,* Volume II, p. 171.

18. Ibid., pp. 240-41, 219; LAC, R.A. MacKay Papers (MG 30 E159), Volume 6, file: Semi-official and Personal Correspondence, re: Newfoundland, 1944–50; and KP, Vol. 308, File 3270, C213342.

19. LAC, Brooke Claxton Papers (MG 32 B5), Volume 114, File 2 and J.R. Smallwood, *I Chose Canada* (Toronto, 1973), p. 571.

20. MacKay Papers, Vol. II, File: "General Correspondence, March-November, 1946".

21. Frederick Rowe, *A History of Newfoundland and Labrador* (Toronto, 1980), pp. 413-404.

22. MacKenzie, "Canada and the Entrance of Newfoundland into Confederation," p. 206. See, Peter Neary, "Clement Attlee's Visit to Newfoundland, September 1942," *Acadiensis*, XIII, No. 2 (Spring 1984), pp. 103-106.

23. King Diaries, Transcript 222, p. 923.

24. Ibid., Transcript 223, p. 994.

25. Pickersgill, *Record*, Volume IV, p. 50.

26. King Diaries, Transcripts 158, p. 335 and 181, p. 1043.

27. Noel, *Politics in Newfoundland*, pp. 246-47 and Richard Gwyn, *Smallwood: The Unlikely Revolutionary* (Toronto, 1972), p. 83.
28. Claxton Papers, Vol. 14, File 2 (1945–47).

29. Smallwood, *I Chose Canada*, p. 565.

30. Bridle, *Documents*, Vol. II, p. 264.

31. R.A. MacKay, "Smallwood in Ottawa", *Dalhousie Review*, Summer 1970.

32. MacKenzie, "Canada and the Entrance of Newfoundland into Confederation", p. 313.

33. King Diaries, Transcript 237, 27 December 1946.

34. MacKay Papers, Vol. II, File: General Correspondence, March-November, 1946. See, C.P. Stacey, *Mackenzie King and the Atlantic Triangle* (Toronto, 1976), p. 68.

35. KP, Vol. 308, File 3270, C213359.

36. King Diaries, Transcript 237, 27 December 1946.

37. Ibid., Transcript 240, pp. 260-61.

38. KP, Vol. 308, File 2352, C165586-89.

39. *Financial Post*, 7 June 1947, p. 2.

40. King Diaries, Transcript 243, p. 566.

41. Ibid., Transcript 243, pp. 566-68.

42. Ibid., Transcript 244, p. 619.

43. Ibid., Transcript 244, p. 628.

44. Ibid., Transcript 244, p. 632.

45. See, Rowe, *History of Newfoundland and Labrador*, pp. 444-45.

46. King Diaries, Transcript 244, pp. 643-44.

47. MacKenzie, "Canada and the Entrance of Newfoundland into Canada," p. 278.

48. Claxton Papers, Vol. 114, File 1.

49. Pickersgill, *Record*, Vol. IV, p. 53 and J.W. Pickersgill, *My Years with Louis St. Laurent: A Political Memoir* (Toronto, 1975), p. 77.

50. King Diaries, Transcript 245, pp. 795-801.

51. Ibid., Transcript 245, p. 797. See, Dale Thomson, *Louis St. Laurent. Canada* (Toronto, 1967), p. 214.

52. Pickersgill, *Record*, Vol. IV, pp. 79-81.

53. Thomson, *St. Laurent*, pp. 208-9, 234.

54. King Diaries, Transcript 246, p. 830 and Claxton Papers, Vol. 114, File 3, 1947–48.

55. Pickersgill, *Record*, Vol. III, p. 35.

56. MacKenzie, "Canada and the Entrance of Newfoundland into Confederation," p. 32.

57. Pickersgill, *Record*, Vol. IV, p. 50.

58. Claxton Papers, Vol. 114, File 1.

59. Pickersgill, *Record*, Vol. IV, pp. 50-51.

60. King Diaries, Transcript 244, p. 644.

61. Ibid., Transcript 246, p. 830.

62. Ibid., Transcript 247, pp. 932-38, 943-48.

63. Pickersgill, *Record*, Vol. IV, p. 81.

64. KP, Vol. 308, File 3270, C213497.

65. Canada, House of Commons *Debates*, 11 March 1948 and MacKay Papers, Vol. VI, File: McEvoy, J. B., Personal Correspondence, re: Newfoundland, 1947–48.

66. KP, Vol. 308, File 3270, C213499.

67. MacKay Papers, Vol. III, File: ICCNR – General Correspondence and Memoranda, January-August, 1948.

68. King Diaries, Transcript 252, p. 146.

69. King Diaries, Transcript 252, p. 146-48. See, Bridle, *Documents*, Vol. II, pp. 823-24.

70. See, John W. Holmes, *The Shaping of Peace. Canada and the Search for World Order, 1943–57*, Volume II (Toronto, 1979), p. 120.

71. KP, PMO, Vol. 456, File N-19.

72. Gwyn, *Smallwood*, p. 97 and Noel, *Politics in Newfoundland*, p. 256.

73. Harold Horwood, "Newfoundland and Confederation, 1948–49", in Mason Wade (ed.), *Regionalism in the Canadian Community, 1867–1967*, pp. 250-51 and Gwyn, *Smallwood*, pp. 99-100.

74. Paul Bridle, "Canada, the United States and Newfoundland, 1946–48," in *International Perspective*, November/December, 1983, p. 21.

75. Bridle, *Documents*, Vol. II, p. 821.

76. Claxton Papers, Vol. 114, File 1, 1947–48.

77. Bridle, *Documents*, Vol. II, p. 871.

78. King Diaries, Transcript 255, p. 479. See, Bridle, "Canada, the United States and Newfoundland," p. 20.

79. Ibid., Transcript 256, p. 484.

80. KP, Vol. 308, File 3272, C213537.

81. Ibid., Vol. 246, File 2352, C165628-29.

82. Bridle, *Documents*, Vol. II, pp. 949-51.

83. Smallwood, *I Chose Canada*, p. 580.

84. Bridle, *Documents*, Vol. II, pp. 956-61.

85. Ibid., pp. 918-19, 961-62.

86. King Diaries, Transcript 258, p. 716.

87. Ibid., Transcript 258, pp. 713-24.

88. MacKay Papers, Vol. III, file: ICCNR – General Correspondence and Memoranda, January-August, 1948 and King Diaries, Transcript 258, p. 725.

89. King Diaries, Transcript 258, p. 739.

90. Ibid., Transcript 264 (no page number given).

91. Ibid., Transcript 265 (no page number given but entry was made on 1 April 1949).

This article appears in the *Newfoundland Quarterly*, Vol. LXXXII, No. 4 (Spring 1987), pp. 26-37 and is used with permission.

17

We Love Thee Newfoundland.

By: Paul J. Johnson.

In Newfoundland and Labrador, you are at the farthest east part of the Western World. On Signal Hill, on a clear day, you can be the first to see the sun rise, seemingly right out of the ocean, to shine all across Canada. When you visit Cape Spear Lighthouse near St. John's, you are as far out in the Atlantic Ocean as you can be within North America.

In Newfoundland and Labrador, we have a unique, remarkable geological history. It spans virtually the entire evolution of Planet Earth. The majestic Torngat Mountains in Labrador, the highest mountains east of Western Canada's Rockies, contain radio-metric aged rocks that are nearly four billion years old; as old as the oldest rocks found anywhere else on Earth. For comparison, the Rocky Mountains are a mere 100 million years old. The rocks of Signal Hill in St. John's are more than five times as old as those of the Rockies.

Ancient volcanoes, continents that drifted around the earth, earthquakes, and the relentless abrasion by glaciers, wind, rain, frost, and raging seas, have carved out our hundreds of spectacular bays, harbours, coves, and "tickles". They make up our tremendously varied coastal scenery. The stark escarpments and stone layers of our towering seaside cliffs offer dramatic testament to Newfoundland and Labrador's cataclysmic past, in contrast with today's tranquility.

Magnificent Gros Morne National Park in Western Newfoundland is a true wonder that depicts the Earth's history. That huge, particularly exciting UNESCO World Heritage Site can be accessed by road or by cruiseship. Along our coastlines you can see clearly visible "geological faults", where drifting continents joined together. Underfoot in St. John's, right at the surface, there are three distinct geological formations.

Western Newfoundland also offers the beautiful Humber Valley, Deer Lake, and Marble Mountain with the best skiing east of the Rockies. We have over 20 challenging golf courses, with tree-lined fairways professionally sculptured into the surrounding hills, lakes, seashores, and even waterfalls.

Our Sea.

Our Province has an astonishing 29,000 kilometres (18,000 miles) of coastline. That equals almost *ten* times the distance from Newfoundland to Ireland, or more than 70 percent around the complete circumference of the earth.

Out in the Atlantic, not far off our East Coast there are two, huge, colliding ocean currents, one cold and one warm. They merge and move eastward as one. When the humidity between the warm Florida Gulf Stream and cold Labrador Current triggers an environmental reaction, massive fog banks are generated.

Fog banks, at their most imposing size, can be 305 metres (1,000 feet) high - - twice the height of Signal Hill. When fog banks are near to shore, they often move in over the land. Whether on land or at sea, fog is usually cool, and can severely restrict visibility. For early explorers, with no chart to follow and only a compass and the sun and stars by which to navigate, thick fog posed a dreadful threat.

Offshore, to the east of Newfoundland and Labrador, are huge, underwater "continental shelves" known as the "Grand Bank" and "Labrador Bank". Each is about as big as our island. At the time of the last ice age they were islands (above sea level). With a present depth generally less than 100 metres (330 feet), the Grand Banks are shallow enough to catch the energy of the sun and be the breeding ground for billions of minute creatures called "plankton". Plankton are the plentiful foodstuff for many, many millions of fish and shellfish. Although the Grand Banks are excessively fished today, they are still one of the world's most prolific fishing grounds.

Our Archaeological Past.

The earliest humans who lived in Newfoundland and Labrador left archaeological sites dating back over 9,000 years - - four and a half times as far back as our modern calendar goes. These cultures include the Maritime Archaic people, the Palaeo-Eskimo, and the sadly-extinct Beothuk Indians.

Near L'Anse Amour, in Labrador, is North America's oldest known burial mound. About 7,200 years ago, the remains of a boy were buried there, with some of his people's tools and weapons.

A Legend, and Our Recorded History.

Legend tells us that in the sixth century A.D. St. Brendan and his monks sailed here from Ireland in a sturdy boat sheathed with animal-skins. That would have been 400 years before the Vikings settled, and 900 years before John Cabot's epic voyages.

In 1000 A.D., 500 years before John Cabot "discovered" Newfoundland, or Christopher Columbus sailed to the Caribbean, the Norsemen (Vikings) settled for several years at L'Anse aux Meadows in northern Newfoundland. Their Viking village was the earliest confirmed European exploration and settlement of North America. The site has now been faithfully excavated and rebuilt. L'Anse aux Meadows was not only the earliest European presence in the "New World": it was also the world's first contact between two branches of humankind from opposite sides of the earth.

During the 1500s, in history's hundred-year "Age of Discovery" every one of the brave European explorers who sought a shorter sea-route to the fabled riches of the Orient sailed into the waters of a "New-Founde-Land". Cabot, Corte Real, Verrazzano, Cartier, Champlain, Hudson, and others all found themselves confronted by our often fog-shrouded, iceberg infested waters, and an impenetrable coastline that blocked any passage to China.

Today, we can only try to imagine the hopes, dreads, and bewilderment of the adventuresome, wealth-seeking explorers and their crews as they sailed into the unknown. They were in constant dread of running onto rocks, coastlines, or even encountering fabled sea-monsters. Those voyages are amongst the most intriguing of tales.

In 1583, Sir Humphrey Gilbert took possession of Newfoundland for Queen Elizabeth I, thereby establishing the “Cornerstone of the British Empire”. Newfoundland became Britain’s first overseas “possession” and its “Oldest Colony”. As Gilbert was reading his proclamation, fishing boats from different European nations were present in St. John’s Harbour, as they had usually been for possibly 100 years. Those fisherfolk were peacefully co-existing in Newfoundland, even though their countries were often at war with one another.

Newfoundland and Labrador, mostly under British rule, were the scene of many savage battles between the English and French. On direction from their monarchs, the military fought and died for conquest and control of the riches of these lands and seas. During different periods, the island had both French and English capitals and military garrisons. To this day, the tiny islands of St. Pierre and Miquelon off our south coast remain “possessions” of France.

Newfoundland and the American Pilgrim Fathers.

In 1620 when the ship *Mayflower* was on its way with the first “Pilgrims”, to what became “Plymouth Rock” (Massachusetts), it stopped en route at Renews in Newfoundland for water and food. By 1620 (an early date in American history) Renews was in its second century of participating in the transatlantic cod fishery.

It is also recorded that many of the *Mayflower* Pilgrim Fathers would have perished during their first winter except for the advice and assistance in planting vegetables which they received from “Squantum”, a Cape Cod Indian who had earlier learned to speak English in the pioneer Newfoundland settlement of “Cupids”.

About St. John's.

St. John's is the oldest English settlement in Canada, with the oldest business street. St. John's is also the nearest North American port to Europe, being closer to Ireland than it is to Winnipeg, Manitoba. St. John's was attacked and burned several times by the Dutch and the French. Also, St. John's buildings were destroyed three times by "great fires" - - the last one in 1892. St. John's always rose from its ashes.

Signal Hill National Historic Site is likely Canada's most historic place. On Signal Hill, first the French, then the English won battles to seize control of the colony. On Signal Hill in 1901, Marconi received the first transatlantic wireless message. Signal Hill is crowned by the world-famous Cabot Tower, with the "Lookout" panoramic views of the Atlantic; a colourful military tattoo; and the "Wonder Underground" Johnson GEO CENTRE (opened in 2002), which exhibits our Province's four-billion-year-old geological history and offers five other Earth and Space attractions. GEO PARK Historyboards® interpret the geological and botanical natural heritage of Signal Hill and the remarkable handiwork of Newfoundland's Traditional Stoneworkers.

In World War II, in the "Battle of the Atlantic", St. John's, Newfoundland became a fortress, as the main defence position for North America. The "Atlantic Charter" was negotiated between Churchill and Roosevelt off the East Coast of Newfoundland. The principles of the Atlantic Charter eventually led to the establishment of the world's "United Nations Organization".

The Settlement of Newfoundland and Labrador.

Europeans settling in Newfoundland and Labrador, came mostly from England, Ireland, and Scotland. The English language is almost universal. Because so many of our hundreds of coastal communities (outports) have been comparatively isolated for centuries, you will hear words and phrases that "hark back" to the "olden times" in our "old countries". Visitors today are often charmed to hear the lilt of our conversations, much as they would have heard centuries ago in "Olde England", the "Emerald Isle", or "Bonnie Scotland" - - from whence most of us came.

After many generations, this province has seen the almost complete merging of its original settlers into a nearly seamless, composite culture. Many of our natural inheritances from our English, Irish, and Scottish ancestors are preserved in our language, music, and storytelling. Newfoundland has developed its own fanciful folklore, much of it quite wistful and beautiful.

We are famous for tall tales, poetry, songs, art, and crafts, now found in our captivating music, theatres, art galleries, book stores, and gift shops. Our people are as pleasant as can be found anywhere. Amongst the most vivid recollections of our visitors is that people are so approachable, kind, and humorous. Lively conversation and a quick wit are considered by Newfoundlanders to be an easy, enjoyable, and natural pastime and entertainment, and also a great way to learn "what's happening".

Newfoundlanders and Labradorians are not pompous or presumptuous. Visitors may have to be the first to "speak up". Our people and our local shopkeepers are honest. They always try to give enthusiastic help and good value. Here, price-haggling is virtually unknown.

Newfoundland and Labrador has inherited and refined a "traditional" cuisine, based on local home-cooked chicken, pork, lamb, game, seafood, vegetables, and berries. Very popular are "Old Country" favourites such as a roast of beef, sausages, Irish stew, chops, steak-and-kidney pie, puddings, cakes, cookies, breads, buns, "toutons", and tea biscuits. Fish and brewis is a unique dish, made from unleavened, "Hardtack" baked bread. Fish and chips is an "eat-out" special.

Independence and Interdependence.

It was common for several members of a family to leave England, Ireland, or Scotland together, to settle in Newfoundland. But, it was more likely for a single person to come here on their own. Either way, it certainly took fortitude and initiative.

Once here, a settler could not be independent for very long. To go into the fishery necessitated arranging a fishing ground with other fishermen, and a place on shore to set up a wharf, a boat, fish flakes, and building a house. That took goodwill, and teamwork. In an outport, sharing in work and in thinking, was natural and inevitable.

A major aspect of interdependence was between the fishermen and the merchant or planter (fish buyer). To find money to exist while procuring a season's catch, or building a new on-shore property, inevitably required setting up credit with a planter or merchant. With that, the final vestige of independence flew away.

Many views are expressed about the complete dependence of our fisher families in their way of life. But to look at the situation in a positive and realistic way, not one of our 1,450 settlements could have been built from scratch without extraordinary goodwill and teamwork. That is a tremendous testament to the decency and determination required for overcoming their many difficulties.

There Are Some Good Things about Adversity.

While you will have read in this *Anthology* about many problems involved in living in isolation in one of our hundreds of very small outport communities, we should realize that those hardships are what has created our "hardy" people. Those people can "stand up" against far more adversity than people brought up in an easier lifestyle. That is only one of the good sides of outport life.

Our long winters were used to make or mend nets and gear. But they also provided "family time" which was scarce in the "work time". The cold months were when the parents knitted, crocheted, and sewed clothing, made furniture, and taught themselves how to fashion toys, games, woodcarvings and models, big-and-little wheelbarrows, and wood-whistles and wind-pipes.

The average outport adult has been raised to become a "jack of all trades". With the Second World War, there came the "friendly invasion" of Newfoundland and Labrador by Canadian and American military and the need to build all manner of army, navy, and air force bases. Over 20,000 of our "hardy, handy men" (and women) were lured out of the fishery and did a highly commendable job of completing all kinds of trades-work to build the bases. Our "ready-willing-and-able" people simply "turned to" and "did everybody proud". They earned never-before "cash wages" to buy things their families had never ever dreamed of giving or owning.

The Great Blessing of Music.

Before World War II, the average outport had no electricity, few radios, no sports field, and virtually no community services. Many towns had several religious denominations, each with its own church, hall, and school. Over many, many years, the holding of seasonal school and hall concerts, and the practicing of church choirs, fostered a huge amount of "natural talent" in singing, storytelling, plays, and folk dancing, in Newfoundland.

It is thanks in large measure to isolation that the extraordinary cultivation and born-in love of music is present to such an astonishing degree. It is found in our weekend dances ("times"), singsongs, house parties, and sea shanties. Music, jokes, and play-acting are inherent, often spontaneous, and truly enjoyable in all sorts of gatherings.

"Making our own fun" has been both a necessity, and a great treasure and pleasure, born in part from isolation and Newfoundlanders' need and determination to make the best out of life.

The Miracles of Our One-Room Schools.

In our smallest communities, where there were only one-room schools, it is easy to understand the extreme problems of teaching (and learning) all subjects, in all grades, in one classroom. The problems afflicted both the students and the teacher. When the students were old enough to help the family, having learned to read and write, there were strong tendencies to "quit" school.

But, the gifted student, having the same inspired teacher in the same room for possibly eight or ten years, often turned out to be a remarkably able, strongly determined individual. They developed the ambition and confidence to move mountains or tame the seas - - and many of them did just that.

There is much to cherish about Newfoundland, and admire about our people. And much to learn about their determination and resourcefulness for making the most out of their circumstances.

Our Search for "Doing Good".

There is reason to believe that there was a natural "screening-process" at work in the settling of Newfoundland. Almost every person who decided to strike out for a better life in coming here, contributed to the selective breeding of our resolute and industrious Newfoundlanders. Nothing says more to prove that, than our laudable compulsion to find ways of "doing good".

This chapter provides examples of many community service organizations, which, for thousands of our people, have satisfied a major part of their longing for doing and being good.

Some of Our Oldest Community Service Organizations :

Benevolent Irish Society.

Craft Association of N & L.

Church Lads Brigade.

Loyal Orange Association.

Knights of Columbus.

Masonic Lodges.

Newfoundland Outport Nurses Industrial Association.

Newfoundland Board of Trade.

Newfoundland Historical Society.

Newfoundland Historic Trust.

Society of United Fishermen.

Star of the Sea Society.

YW / YMCA.

Various Service Clubs.

What Motivates Newfoundlanders To Join and Work ?

Purpose.
Meaning.
Goals.
Outreach.
Service.
Strength.
Achievement.
Identity.
Teamwork.
Friendship.
Belonging.
Hope.

Our Patriotic Symbols.

Next we will look at nine symbols representing Newfoundlanders' irrepressible yearning for patriotism, identity, and "belonging". Despite the lack of kind consideration from our Kings or Queens, the Colonial or Dominions' Offices, or other governing authorities, these symbols have been especially important to us for many year:

The Newfoundland Coat of Arms: Granted to Newfoundland on January 1, 1637, they were not legally assumed until 1928. The heraldic description is: Arms – Gules, a cross argent, in the first and fourth quarters a lion passant guardant regally crowned or, in the second and third quarters a unicorn passant argent, maned and unguled of the third, and gorged with a crown, thereto a chain affixed passing between the forelegs and reflected over the back, also or. On the right and left are two Newfoundland native Beothuk. The motto is *"Quaerite prime dei"* ("Seek ye first the Kingdom of God").

Cabot Tower: Erected in 1897 to commemorate the 400th anniversary of John Cabot's voyage to Newfoundland, and as a memorial of the 60th year of Queen Victoria's reign. Built of sandstone and standing 500 feet above sea level atop Signal Hill, Cabot Tower has a commanding view of the Harbour, the City of St. John's, the Atlantic Ocean, and Cape Spear (North America's most easterly point). Always important for communications, Signal Hill was the Lookout that used to fly the merchants' flags when their ships were arriving.

Newfoundland Dog: The origin of the now world-famous Newfoundland Dog is not certain. There are different theories. "The Newfoundland" is an important symbol of Newfoundland's early history. Characterized by their loyalty, intelligence, and life-saving capabilities, Newfoundland Dogs were dependable, strong, and willing working dogs. They were also faithful and affectionate companions and excellent family pets.

The Caribou Emblem of the Royal Newfoundland Regiment: Formed as a unit of British Imperial Forces on August 21, 1914, the history of the Regiment goes back as far as 1775, when hostilities of the American Revolution spread into Canada. The Regiment played a significant role in the overseas battles of World War I, suffering tremendous losses at Beaumont Hamel, Gallipoli, Gueudecourt, and Monchy-le-Preux. In World War II the Regiment became two Newfoundland Artillery Regiments.

The Union Flag: Known since 1606 as the "Union Jack", it is comprised of a "union" of the superposed flags of Saint George (England), Saint Andrew (Scotland), and Saint Patrick (Ireland). It remains the national flag of Great Britain. First raised in Newfoundland at Cupids in the early 1600s, it was officially adopted as Newfoundland's flag in 1931, and re-adopted as the provincial flag in 1952. Although no longer the provincial flag, it holds special meaning for Newfoundlanders: our soldiers fought under it in three wars, and it symbolizes our ties to the British Empire.

The Irish Newfoundland Flag: Also referred to as the "native flag" or the "tricolor", the pink, white, and green was developed in the 1880s, merging two rival groups: the "natives", or well-established citizens of St. John's (who were largely Roman Catholic); and newly arrived immigrants from Ireland. Although some considered it a "national flag", it was never proclaimed.

The Flag of Labrador: Designed in the 1970s by the Labrador Heritage Society, the flag is intended to symbolize the heritage of Labrador and its people. The white bar represents the snows of Labrador; the green, the green-and-bountiful land; and the blue, the waters of the rivers, lakes, and ponds. The black spruce twig shows that this tree is common to all parts of Labrador. The three branches of the twig represent three races of Labrador people: the Inuit, the Innu, and the European.

The Flag of Newfoundland and Labrador: Designed by Newfoundland artist Christopher Pratt and adopted officially by the Provincial Flag Act, passed on May 27, 1980. The white represents snow and ice; the blue the sea; the red human effort; and the gold our confidence in ourselves. The blue section on the left side of the flag is reminiscent of the Union Jack and our British heritage; the red and gold section on the right, represents our future. The two red triangles represent the island and Labrador portions of the Province. The golden arrow points the way ahead.

The Pitcher Plant: The Pitcher Plant has been the floral emblem of Newfoundland and Labrador since 1954, but had been engraved on Newfoundland's penny-coin half a century earlier. This carnivorous plant grows in marshes and swamps. Its large, single flower has wine-red petals around a wine and gold centre. Its leaves, shaped like a water pitcher, collect water into which insects fall. Enzymes in the water change the insects into nutrients for the plant. A stylized Pitcher Plant is now used in provincial identification.

THE ODE TO NEWFOUNDLAND.

Newfoundland's National Anthem.

The Ode To Newfoundland.

When sun rays crown thy pine clad hills,
And summer spreads her hand.
When silvern voices tune thy rills,
We love thee smiling land.

We love thee, we love thee,
We love thee smiling land.

When spreads thy cloak of shimm'ring white,
At Winter's stern command.
Thro' shortened day and starlit night,
We love thee, frozen land,

We love thee, we love thee,
We love thee, frozen land.

When blinding storm gusts fret thy shore,
And wild waves lash thy strand.
Thro' sprindrift swirl and tempest roar,
We love thee, wind-swept land,

We love thee, we love thee,
We love thee, wind-swept land.

As loved our fathers, so we love,
Where once they stood we stand,
Their prayer we raise to heav'n above,
God Guard Thee, Newfoundland.

God Guard Thee, God Guard Thee,
God Guard Thee, Newfoundland.

Sir Cavendish Boyle.

**SIR CAVENDISH BOYLE,
1849–1916.**

British Governor of Newfoundland, 1901-1904.

Born England, educated at Charterhouse, joined the Colonial Service and was the Colonial Secretary in Bermuda, Gibraltar, British Guiana before becoming Governor of Newfoundland.

While here, wrote many poems about the rugged beauty of our island.

His most famous work was set to music and became our much-loved "Ode to Newfoundland", officially adopted as our National Anthem on May 20th, 1904.

Where In The World Is Newfoundland ?

Ten Things To Think About :

1. Despite what some believe, St. John's is not near the Arctic Circle. St. John's is farther south than any part of Manitoba, Saskatchewan, Alberta, or British Columbia.

2. St. John's is obviously farther south than the large cities of Winnipeg, Regina, Edmonton, Calgary, Vancouver, or Victoria.

3. St. John's is also south of 90 per cent of the Provinces of Ontario or Quebec.

4. St. John's is farther south than England, Ireland, or Scotland.

5. St. John's is farther south than Norway, Sweden, or Finland.

6. St. John's is farther south than Amsterdam, Brussels, Paris, Berlin, Warsaw, or Moscow.

7. St. John's is closer to Ireland than to Winnipeg, Manitoba.

8. Newfoundland & Labrador is *three times* as large as the total combined area of the other three Atlantic (Maritime) Provinces (Nova Scotia, New Brunswick, and Prince Edward Island).

9. The Grand Banks is an underwater plateau, about the same size as the Island of Newfoundland. Some 10,000 years ago, the Grand Banks was also an island --i.e. above water.

10. Newfoundland and Labrador are the Eastern Gateway to North America, very much farther east than any other part of continental North America.

The Newfoundland Centred World.

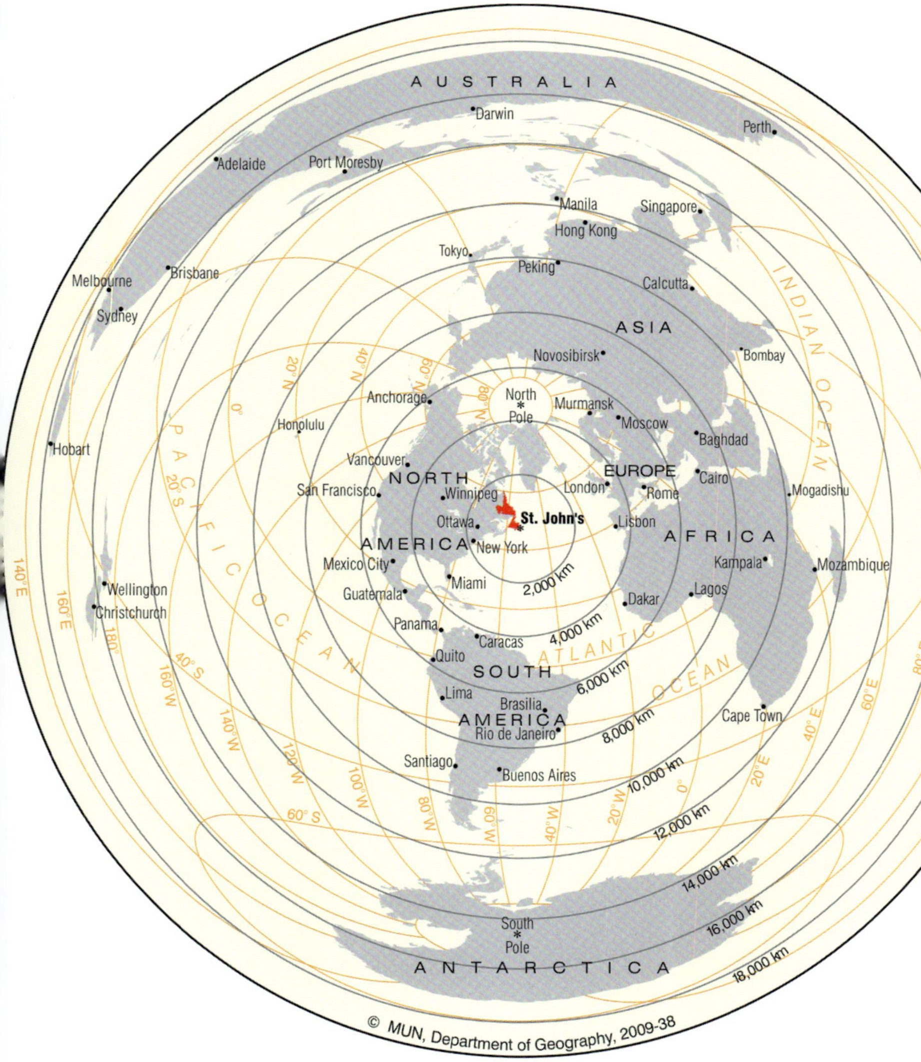

This is an AZIMUTHAL EQUIDISTANT PROJECTION centered on St. John's, Newfoundland. Only distances and directions measured along straight lines radiating from the centre are true. All straight lines passing through St. John's are great circles. Deformation of the earth surface increases outward from the centre an measurements taken other than through the centre are inaccurate.

SCALE along any straight line through the centre

1000 0 2000 4000
Kilometres

1000 0 1000 2000 3000 4000
Miles

Projects Based on We Love Thee Newfoundland.

These 20 Projects were initiated by the Johnson Family Foundation, their Staff, and Funding Partners. Expert teams were carefully formed, which could include: architects, historians, scientists, engineers, writers, researchers, structure and exhibit designers, graphic artists, landscapers, sculptors, fabricators, stoneworkers, photographers, and all the construction trades.

1. The Signal Hill Lookout Project.
2. The Grand Concourse Authority.
3. Concourse Historyboards® and Little Rests.
4. The Winston Churchill Monument.
5. The Johnson GEO CENTRE.
6. Community Historyboards® of N. & L.
7. Memorial (University) Clock Tower.
8. Rotary Young Children's Playground.
9. Merchant Marine Memorial.
10. Royal / Canadian Navy Memorial.
11. Newfoundland Coat of Arms in Granite.
12. The GEO CENTRE Solar System.
13. The Railway Coastal Museum.
14. Newfoundland & Labrador Dog Sculptures.
15. Harbourside Park / Gilbert Memorial.
16. The GEO CENTRE Titanic Story.
17. Tommy Ricketts V.C. Memorial.
18. Cruiseship Authority of N. & L.
19. Johnson GEO PARK and Stoneworks.
20. Memorial University History Rotunda.

Every single Project has been a success.

PJJ

1

2

3

4

5

6

7

8

9

10

18

CRUISESHIP AUTHORITY
OF NEWFOUNDLAND.

John Cabot Leaving Bristol, 1497. Painting by H.B. Goodridge.

Courtesy Newfoundland Historical Society.

The Landing of Sir Humphrey Gilbert. Painting by H.B. Goodridge.

Colonial Building.

(Completed in 1850.)

The Newfoundland National War Memorial.

(Unveiled July 1, 1924.)

The Newfoundland Regimental Caribou Monument, Bowring Park.

The Merchant Marine & Royal / Canadian Navy Memorials, St. John's.

The Marine Institute of Memorial University.

18

A Golden Rule for Newfoundland & Labrador.

By: Paul J. Johnson.

World War II finally put Newfoundland in the spotlight as "Europe's Doorway to North America". Britain, Canada, and the United States learned three vital lessons about Newfoundland. *First*, if there were to be a German invasion of North America, it would start with Newfoundland. *Second*, to combat the U-boat menace to Allied convoys in the vulnerable mid-Atlantic sector, a powerful naval base was needed in Newfoundland. *Third*, in attempting to air-ferry thousands of aircraft to England, Newfoundland's Gander and Goose Bay Airports were the only practical ones for departure.

Newfoundland's historical and strategic importance should have already been well-proven by many notable events in the previous 1,000 years. "Eventually the obvious becomes obvious":

- The Vikings, settling first from Norway to Iceland, then to Greenland, eventually came to Northern Newfoundland 1,000 years ago. Their settlement at L'Anse aux Meadows marked the very first contact of two branches of humankind, completing the encirclement of the earth.

- Five hundred years later, almost every one of a dozen European explorers, looking for a short ocean passage to China, "discovered" Newfoundland and Labrador all over again.

- John Cabot and others found a shallow, underwater plateau (almost the size of Newfoundland) off the east coast of the island. It became very well named "The Grand Banks". For the next 500 years, almost every European seacoast nation pursued the bountiful Grand Banks Fishery.

- In the 1800s, to provide immediate communication, transatlantic telegraph cables were laid on the ocean floor connecting Europe to Newfoundland, then on to Canada and the United States.

- In 1901, Marconi received the first transatlantic wireless signal on Signal Hill, St. John's, Newfoundland.

- In 1919, the first Newfoundland to Europe flight.

- In 1937, the first, huge, transatlantic "flying boat" planes refuelled in Botwood, Newfoundland, to and from England and the United States.

- In 1938, Britain opened the world's largest airport in Gander, Newfoundland, to refuel civilian flights crossing the Atlantic.

Financial Outcomes with Our Commission of Government.

In 1939, by radically reduced spending, and starving many Newfoundlanders, the Commission of Government had brought the public debt down from $ 100 million to $ 18 million. By 1945, with the huge wartime expenditures, and extra tax revenues in Newfoundland, our "skinflint" Commission now had a surplus of $ 32.5 million, including a $ 12 million interest-free loan to Britain.

In addition to the Commission's *five major* wartime shortcomings (Chapter 2, pages 18 and 19) there was a *sixth* extreme omission. Throughout the war, the Commission failed to carry out necessary maintenance, repair, rebuilding, or replacement of our worn-out roads, bridges, railway equipment, rail-beds, coastal boats, wharves, dry docks, and other public properties. The Commission could not claim they did not have enough money to "do the right thing". It was just another case of the Commission's neglect of matters that were too awkward or troublesome for them to organize and complete.

Some Very Fundamental Questions.

The Commission, having been disasterously negligent before and during the war, after the war committed its *seventh* misdemeanour. It could have made representations on Newfoundland's behalf about our country's badly worn-out public works, to seek to repatriate and re-equip our workers, businesses, and industry. After the war, tremendously rundown and exploited Newfoundland saw *no* reconstruction or reparation payments, such as the American Marshall Plan lavished on our previous *enemies* Germany and Japan. Because the Commission never sought appropriate treatment, "used and abused" St. John's and Newfoundland were simply "left in the lurch". The Commission got what we Newfoundlanders routinely expected - - *nothing*.

"Skullduggery" in High Places.

Newfoundland was out of debt and showing a surplus by 1943. By clever connivance, the Commission managed to stay as our government right up to the day we joined Canada. We now KNOW that toward the end of the war Britain and Canada discussed Newfoundland's Confederation with Canada. An "independent" Newfoundland and Labrador was "not acceptable". Britain's repeated promises to return Responsible Government "at the request of the people" were circumvented. A simple plebiscite could have provided our "request", following which a constitution could have been determined by an elected body. Instead, Britain and Canada decided on our "National Convention" pretending it was the proper way to determine "our request to return to Responsible Government". After the Convention voted for Responsible Government, the British Dominions Office and the Commission decided we should have a Referendum vote. When Responsible Government was again the top choice, they decided we had to have still another vote.

Those three examples of Newfoundland being manipulated by others show that supposedly reliable and honourable commitments can be easily circumvented, especially if connived in secrecy.

So, What About "Our People & Our Heritage" ?

Five years after WWII, without having recovered Newfoundland's promised Responsible Government and bargaining rights, we sent two well-intentioned delegations, not expert in constitutional law, to negotiate with Ottawa about our "Terms of Union" for Confederation. It was a seriously one-sided confrontation against VERY experienced, hard-nosed senior bureaucrats.

Since 1949, we have had six decades of rarely satisfying negotiations, trying to secure equitable and workable arrangements from the top Federal officials. Their invariable approach to Provinces is nay-saying, inefficient administration, and vindictive reprisals.

Some bureaucrats, politicians, businessmen, and union leaders fail to understand that simply trying to "gain the upper hand" creates mistrust and bitterness. Civilized, constructive negotiation requires open examination of *everyone's* advantages and disadvantages, and opportunities and limitations. If Ottawa *never* intends to be open-minded, fair, and conciliatory, we must complain publicly and confront them with our strongest demands, negotiated by the most experienced and toughest advocates we can find.

In Newfoundland, we finally seem to understand the pathetic consequences of being obliging. When dealing with scheming adversaries, we must *stop* abiding by our old "Golden Rule":

"Those That Make the Rules Take the Gold".

Unlike the extremely decent, fair-minded, friendly Canadian people (with whom the writer resided for seven very pleasant years before Confederation, and did business thereafter for another 50 years), it is the obvious intention of senior Federal officials to use their dominant position to *never* let any Province gain "a lion's share" from the Province's own resources. That negative approach, and the condescending way that Federal politicians "dole out" their grants and programs, has *stifled both* Canada and its Provinces.

Since Confederation, until recently, almost without exception, Newfoundland and Labrador has had incredibly sad and bad experiences in *our* results for the development of *our* natural resources. We simply cannot ignore or abide the following, rotten, indisputably unjust, *outright-exploitive* situations:

Our Iron Ore is exported in a raw state, out of the Province.

Our Churchill Falls Hydro power is practically given to Quebec.

Our Offshore Oil is all exported, unrefined, to the U.S.

Our Fishery is never-ending nonsense under Federal Control.

Would *any* citizen of Canada agree with such outcomes for their own Province ? How could *anyone* not be indignant over these outrageous results ? Newfoundland and Labrador must *stop* assuming that decency and fair play are forthcoming from Ottawa.

With our Province's present, resolute determination to get "a fair deal", our bargaining with both "the Feds" and resource-development companies has proven what *can*, *should*, and *must* be done (e.g., Voisey's Bay and Hebron). Our over 10,000 educators and more than 65,000 post-secondary graduates will support a more enlightened, tougher approach for *our* benefit - - and the future of *our* Province.

We should all commit to implement a *brand new* Golden Rule for Newfoundland and Labrador:

"*We* Own the Gold, and *We* Set the Rules".

"God Guard Thee Newfoundland" is all very well, but just "praying" will not work. "The Lord Helps Those Who Help Themselves".

Paul J. Johnson.

INDEX

Abbott, D.C., 285
Addison, Lord, 238, 282-3
Admiral Scheer, 85
Air Ferry Service, 98
Alderdice, Frederick C., 11, 196
Amerika, SS, 133
Amherst, Colonel William, 190
Ammon, Lord C.G., 165, 222-4, 251
Amulree Report, 203, 205
Amulree, Lord W.W.M., 12-3, 163, 211, 281
Anna T, SS, 149
Anstey, Capt. George, 41, 133
Antonia, 82
Argentia, 21, 42, 79, 83-7, 89, 109, 119-20, 131, 136, 140-2, 199, 214, 254-5
Army, British, 33, 44, 130
Atlantic Charter, 20-1, 120, 214-5, 246, 255, 315
Atlantic Ferry Command, 83, 97, 255
Attlee, Clement, 161, 216, 251, 282, 306
Bailey, Charles, 266, 274
Baldwin, J.R., 265, 273
Bank of Canada, 57, 258-9
Bank of Nova Scotia, 258
Bank, Royal (*See* Royal Bank)
Bases for Destroyers, 38, 49
Batteries, 37, 42-43, 53
Battery, The (St. John's), 42, 50, 134-5, 146
Battle Harbour, 108
Bay Bulls, 70, 186, 189, 192
Bay L'Argent, 48
Bay Roberts, 34, 44
Beachy Cove, 148
Beaverbrook, Lord, 121, 165, 212, 225
Bell Island, 34, 36-7, 41, 44, 68-9, 129, 133, 146, 148-9, 195, 247, 252
Bennett, Viscount, 165
Bermuda, 38, 130, 157-8, 215, 253
Bishop's Falls, 79, 93
Bittersweet, HMCS, 111
Black Watch, 36-7, 82
Board of Trade, 20, 204, 221-2, 251, 320
Borden, Robert, 279
Botwood, 36-8, 40, 79-84, 97, 100, 129, 213, 338
Bowditch, USS, 49
Bower, R.P., 259, 272
Boyle, Sir Cavendish, 325
Brabazon, Lord, 165-6
Bradley, F. Gordon, 264
Brant, USS, 140
Bridges, Frank, 283, 290
British Colonial Office (*See* Dominions Office)
British Empire, 2, 8, 20, 22, 32, 113, 115, 117, 155, 165, 250, 314
Broad Cove, 148
Bruton, Lt. Col. Philip, 49, 51
Buchans, 77, 80, 106, 195
Burchell, Charles J., 255, 259, 262, 279-80
Burin, 109
Bursey, William J., 41, 49-50, 132, 134
Cabot Tower, 134, 315, 321
Cabot, John, 3, 178, 313, 321, 337
Camps: Alexander, 50, 52, 62, 135, 254; Cobbs, 79; Hattie's (Hatties), 79, 252

Canadian Naval Shore Patrol, 152
Candytuft, 111
Cape Bonavista, 188
Cape Chidley, 68
Cape Spear, 40, 42, 53, 311, 321
Carbonear, 6, 44, 187
Cardoulis, John, 134
Caribou Hut, 24
Caribou, SS, 67-8, 82, 94-5, 106, 126, 143-6, 254
Carnell, Mayor Andy G., 116-7, 131, 156
Carson, William, 91
Cashin, Peter, 151
Cavanaugh, Robert J., 262
Chadwick, G.W. St. John, 222, 245, 256
Chafe, William, 78
Chambers Cove, 137, 141
Chateau Thierry, USAT, 51
Child, Sir Josiah, 185
Christmas Seal, MV, 115
Christoph von Doornum, 80, 129
Church Lads Brigade, 81, 320
Churchill Falls/River, 268, 341
Churchill, Sir Winston, 15, 20-1, 28, 120, 130, 242, 251, 253, 255, 277, 315, 328
Clarenville, 79, 84, 91
Clarenville Shipyard, 90
Claxton, Brooke, 280, 285
Clutterbuck, P.A., 238-9, 240-1, 243, 246
Clyde, SS, 80, 82
Coaker, William, 109
Coat of Arms, Newfoundland, 321, 328
Cochrane, Sir Thomas, 191
Collins, Governor John, 187
Colonial Building, 9, 11
Columbus, Christopher, 313
Confederate Association, 298
Confederates, 283-4, 296, 298-9
Constitutional Act, 293
Cook, Capt. James, 190
Corvettes, 28, 45, 69-70, 110
Coureurs de bois, 186
Cranborne, Lord, 166, 224-9, 231-2, 235-7, 242, 278
Crosbie, Chesley, 301
Crow's Nest, 24
Crown Colony, 8, 201, 251, 281
Crump, Edgar, 34
Culbert, Lt. James, 145
Cupids, 314, 322
Curling, 84
d'Iberville, Pierre Le Moine, 186-7
Daily Express, 212
Daily News, The, 54, 89, 153
Daisy, 109
Dalton, Hugh, 238
de Ruyter, Admiral, 185
Deer Lake, 44, 312
Dockyard (St. John's or Newfoundland), 11, 28, 46, 94, 98
Dominion of Newfoundland, 13, 18, 196
Dominion status, 9, 15, 201, 215, 281
Dominions Office, 9, 14, 16, 18-20, 34, 55-6, 83, 88, 159, 200, 203, 205, 212, 216, 222, 224, 226-8, 230-1, 233, 236-9, 242-5, 250-1, 256, 339
Donitz, Admiral Karl, 66-7, 69
Doyle News, Gerald S., 113, 125

Doyle, Gerald S., 112-3, 126
Duchess of Richmond, 82
Dunfield, Sir Brian, 35
Dunn, P.D.H., 229-31, 233, 261
Duplessis, Maurice, 292
Earnshaw, Philip, 39
Edmund B. Alexander, USS, 24, 41, 50-2, 85, 132-35, 254
Elliott, Major George Feilding, 155
Emerson, Edward, 36, 39, 54, 88
Empire Commerce, 81
Emrys-Evans, P.V., 163, 226
Esquimalt, HMCS, 69
Evelyn B, MV, 69
Evening Telegram, The, 33, 142, 154-65
Exploits River, 79, 178
Family Fireside, The, 112
Fanning-Evans, Claude, 34-5
Fathers of Confederation, 301, 303
Ferry Command, 83, 97, 121, 255
Financial Post, 287
First Five Hundred, 131
Fishery, 2-6, 8, 14, 22, 24, 30, 74, 92, 108, 113, 126-7, 181-5, 190-3, 195-9, 205, 217, 314, 317-18, 337, 341
Flags, 134, 321-3
Fleming, Tom, 144-5
Fogo, Senator Gordon, 298
Forestry Unit, 33, 221
Forts: Alexander, 24; Amherst, 42, 50, 53, 134, 146; Chain Rock, 42, 53; Pepperrell, 24, 51, 54, 85, 129, 131, 134, 152; Townshend, 35, 40; William, 188
Fox, C.J., 156
French Ships: *PLM* 26, 149; *PLM* 27, 69
French Shore, 9
Gander, 34, 37-8, 40-1, 43, 79, 82-4, 93, 97-8, 107, 118, 120-2, 153, 178, 198-9, 207, 213, 252, 254-5, 278, 337-8
Garner, J.J.S., 216
Garrison Church, 9
George E. Badger, USS, 140
Germany, 21, 32, 37, 52, 65-6, 69, 129-30, 149, 152, 155, 339
Giesler, Patricia, 67
Gilbert, Sir Humphrey, 3, 183, 314
Gildea, Robert, 269
Glenwood, 85
Globe and Mail, 269
Goodwill Mission, 162, 251-2
Goose Bay, 47, 83, 98, 131, 198-9, 213, 225, 255, 261
Government House, 9, 251
Governments: Commission of Government, 14-15, 17-20, 32-4, 40, 49, 53, 74-5, 83, 86, 89, 91, 99, 107, 110, 117, 131, 150, 159, 161, 164, 166, 194, 196, 199, 201-4, 206, 211-2, 214-7, 219, 221-3, 230-1, 234, 238, 243, 245-6, 251-3, 266, 281, 298, 338; Provincial, 115, 241, 293; Representative, 14, 192, 196, 221; Responsible, 8-9, 14, 74, 158, 163-4, 177, 192, 200-1, 203, 211, 217-20, 222-6, 229-33, 243, 251, 261, 266, 283, 297-8, 300-1, 303, 339-40
Grand Banks, 2, 3, 67, 178, 190, 312, 326, 337

Grand Falls, 91, 97, 195, 268
Grandmere, HMCS, 144-5
Grandy, Group Capt. Roy, 48
Great Britain, 32, 130, 156, 211-7, 219, 223-7, 229-30, 232, 235-7, 239-42, 244-7, 299
Great Depression, 11, 118, 122, 204, 211
Great War, The (*See* World War I)
Greenslade, Rear-Admiral John W., 49, 83, 131
Gregg, Milton, 295
Grenfell, Wilfred, 279
Gunston, Sir Derek, 222
Gushue, Ray, 261
Halifax, 36-7, 39, 48, 67, 69-70, 81, 85, 253, 288
Hamilton River (*See* Churchill River)
Harbour Grace, 44
Hebron, 341
Herbert, Alan Patrick, 250-1, 259
Hiatt, Capt., 54, 133
Hickey, Lt. Cdr. Lester, 70
Holt, Sir Herbert, 121
Holyrood, 150
Home Guard, 26, 33, 44
Hopedale, 222
Hopper, George D., 254, 257, 261
Horwood, Harold, 299
House of Assembly, 116, 128, 191, 201, 235, 243, 250
House of Commons (British), 196
House of Commons (Canada), 213, 226, 227, 244, 277, 282
House of Lords, 14, 165, 244
House of Representatives, 8
Howe, C.D., 265, 266, 268
Howell, Alfred T., 44
Howlett, Mayor, 116
Humber River, 179
Humber Valley, 312
Ilsley, J.L., 285, 391
Industrial Development Board, 228
International Grenfell Mission, 279
Iron ore, 34, 37, 68, 129, 146-7, 165, 252, 265-8
Jerseyside, 108
Jervis Bay, 85
Job, R.B., 251
Joensen, Capt. William, 133
Johnson Family Foundation Projects, 167-75, 328-30
Johnson GEO CENTRE, 315, 328
Jones, Edgar, 245
Keenleyside, Hugh, 261, 266
King, Mackenzie, 21, 36, 43, 162, 213, 252, 255, 262, 275, 279
King's Cove, 112, 118-9, 126, 128
Knights of Columbus, 24, 125, 254, 320
Kyle, SS, 82, 140
L'Anse Amour, 313
L'Anse aux Meadows, 313, 337
Labrador, 2, 21-2, 26, 29-30, 32, 47, 68, 93, 97, 99, 108, 113, 115, 131, 134, 178-80, 190, 194, 203, 206-7, 212-3, 220, 222, 234, 247, 250-2, 255, 263, 265-70, 277-8, 289, 292, 311-6, 318, 323, 326, 328, 337, 339, 341
Labrador Current, 179, 312
Labrador Mining and Development Company, 266
Land Settlement (Scheme), 205, 228, 234

Laurier, Wilfrid, 279, 290
Lawn (Lawn Head), 137, 139, 140-2
Leased Base Agreement, 15
Lend-Lease, 88, 130, 237
Leonard Wood, USAT, 51, 53
Lester's Field, 40
Lewisporte, 79, 84, 87, 89, 97
Livyers, 10, 185, 193
Lord Strathcona, 69, 147-8
Macdonald, Angus L., 291
Macdonald, J. Scott, 262, 280, 284
MacDonald, Malcolm, 241, 282
MacKay, Robert A. (R.A.), 280
Mackenzie, Grant, 216
Marble Mountain, 312
Marconi, 315, 338
Marine Institute, 167
Martin, Cabot, 201
Marvita, 109-1
Mascin, HMCS, 44
Matthew, 180
Mayflower, 314
McCarthy, Florry, 95
McEvoy, J.B., 201
McEwen, Group Capt. C.M., 47-8
McLean, Senator Neil, 298
McNair, J.B., 291-2
McNamara Construction, 47
Memorial Stadium, 115
Memorial University College (Memorial College), 40, 110, 197, 235
Memorial University of Newfoundland, 57, 70, 202
Merchant Marine, 65, 85, 167, 328
Merchant Navy, 26, 33, 67
Merchants: 5, 180-1, 189, 191, 194, 254, 321; Newfoundland, 291; Water Street, 257, 243; West Country 3-4, 183
Molson, Hartland, 265
Montreal, 40, 45, 82, 121, 142, 224, 266
Montreal Standard, The, 142
Moore, J. Charles, 96
Morris, Patrick, 191
Murray, Leonard W., 46
Muselier, Vice-Admiral Emile Henri, 121
Musgrave Harbour, 106
National Convention, 164, 200, 223, 227-30, 235-6, 238, 240-6, 256, 260, 264-6, 282-6, 295-6, 339
National War Memorial, 334
Naval Association, 167
Navy, Merchant, 26, 33, 67
Navy, Royal (British, RN), 3, 6, 19, 21-2, 26, 33, 183-4, 193
Navy, Royal Canadian, 28-9, 65, 110, 123, 328, 45-7
Neary, Peter, 57, 201
Newfie Bullet (The Bullet), 96
Newfie (Newfy) John, 96, 27, 28, 29, 56
Newfoundland Escort Force (NEF), 45, 47, 67
Newfoundland Fisheries Board, 189, 205
Newfoundland Quarterly, 41, 99, 23, 274, 310
Newfoundland Railway, 73-104, 107, 121
Newfoundland Ranger Force, 205, 266
Newfoundland, SS, 81

Newfoundlander, The, 114
Nfld. Patriotic Association, 115, 156
Nicholson, Col. G.W.L., 111
Noel-Baker, Philip, 298, 302
North Atlantic Ferry Command, 83, 97, 121, 155
North Sydney, 67, 94, 143
Noseworthy, J.W., 280
O'Driscoll, Joseph, 37
O'Neill, Paul, 146
Ocean Vagabond, SS, 69
Order of Canada, 127, 177
Orwell, 251
Osborne, Capt. Henry, 188
Ottawa, 35-6, 39, 42, 45, 157, 237-40, 242-3, 245-6, 255, 258, 260, 264, 266, 269-70, 280, 283-4, 287-9, 291, 301, 340-1
Outerbridge, Leonard, 253-4
Oxford, Thomas, 184
Palliser, Governor Hugh, 190
Pearl Harbor, 51, 121, 135
Pearson, Lester, 282, 285, 293, 296
Penson, John H., 39, 155, 256
Perlin, Albert B., 89, 176-8, 194, 269
Permanent Joint Board on Defence (PJBD), 20-1, 38-9, 42, 46
Petten, Senator Ray, 299
Pickersgill, J.W. (Jack), 265, 284, 286, 289, 301
Pitcher Plant, 323
Placentia, 6, 108, 118-20, 184-9
Pleasantville, 129, 131, 134
Pollux, USS, 136-9
Portugal Cove, 148, 192
Power, Charles G., 38
Power, Greg, 267
Prince of Wales, HMS, 21
Pratt, Calvert C., 260
Privy Council, 178, 292
Puddester, Sir John C., 88, 127, 229, 231, 233, 258
Quidi Vidi, 45, 49-51, 81, 131
Rainnie, Major D.V., 37, 42
Ramea, 109, 118, 126-8
Reconstruction Finance Corp., 86, 89
Red Triangle Club, 152-3
Regiments: 37, 40, 42, 43, 50, 53, 82
Reid Newfoundland Company, 78, 106
Reith, Oberleutnant Hans Edwin, 70
Rendell, Walter F., 35
Renshaw, William, 34
Richards, Morley, 212
Robertson, Norman, 240, 255, 259, 262, 278-80, 285
Roosevelt, Elliott, 255
Roosevelt, Franklin D., 15, 20-1, 38, 120, 130, 157, 252-3, 255, 283, 287, 315
Rose Castle, SS, 69, 148-9
Rotary Club, 115, 195, 328
Rouse, Corp. W.B., 146
Royal Air Force (RAF), 33, 121, 143
Royal Artillery, 33, 81, 322
Royal Bank, 57, 118-21, 126-7
Royal Canadian Air Force (RCAF), 29, 36, 38, 46, 48, 67, 83
Royal Canadian Artillery, 37
Royal Canadian Navy (*See* Navy, Royal Canadian)
Royal Flying Corps, 48
Royal Gazette, 191
Royal Navy (*See* Navy, Royal)

Royal Newfoundland Regiment (Newfoundland Army), 26, 44, 322
Russell, Herbert (Herb), 73, 75-6, 78, 82, 86-8, 91, 99, 106-7
Ryan, James V., 78
Ryan, John, 191
Saganaga, SS, 69, 147
Saint John, 81-2, 93
Sanitorium (St. John's), 125
Shakespeare, Geoffrey, 216, 226, 251
Shamrock Field, 40, 44
Shoal Harbour, 91
Short, Magistrate Nehemiah, 235, 238
Shulamite, 109-10, 133
Signal Hill, 50, 53, 134, 146, 190, 311-2, 315, 321, 328
Smallwood, Joseph (Joey) R., 114, 121, 246, 260, 264, 267, 283-4, 289, 296-9
Solomon, Simon, 191
Squadrons, 48, 257
Squantum, 314
Squires, Sir Richard, 11
St. Brendan, 313
St. Jacques, 70, 109
St. John's, 3, 6, 9, 11, 21, 23-5, 28-9, 32-4, 37-50, 53-4, 56-7, 65, 67, 69-70, 78-85, 89, 91, 96-9, 106, 109-12, 114-22, 124-7, 129, 133-5, 142, 147-53, 156, 167, 177, 179, 183-93, 195, 198-9, 201, 211-4, 216, 219-20, 222, 226-31, 233, 235, 241, 243, 245, 251, 254-5, 258-9, 262, 269, 297, 299, 301, 311, 315, 321-2, 326, 338-9
St. John's Harbour, 34, 41, 45, 70, 110-11, 131-3, 314
St. John's Housing Corporation (Commission), 117, 235
St. Laurent, Louis, 275, 284-5, 288-94, 297-8, 303-4
St. Lawrence (town), 67, 138-43, 195
St. Lewis, USS, 49
St. Phillip's, 148
St. Pierre, 121, 314
Statute of Westminster (*See* Westminster)
Stephenville, 42, 83, 89, 97, 131, 199, 214, 254
Story of Newfoundland, The, 176-194
Submarines, 28-9, 65-7, 69, 130, 148
Sunday Herald, 299, 301
Sydney, 81-82, 252
Tavnor, Capt. Ben, 144-5
Terra Nova, 91, 178
Tidal wave, 109
Times (London), 162, 276
Timmins, Jules, 266-7
Topsail, 133, 148, 192
Torbay (includes Torbay Airport), 40, 43, 46-48, 192, 198, 213
Torngat Mountains, 311
Toronto, 46, 224
Trans-Canada Air Lines, 48
Treaties: 9, 201; Paris, 190; Utrecht, 188
Trinity, 118-9, 121, 127
Trinity Bay, 6, 187
Truxton, USS, 136-8
Tucker, Gilbert, 65
U-boats: 28-9, 65-70, 93, 110, 136, 145-6, 149-50, 278, 337; *U-69*, 94-5, 144; *U-190*, 69-70, 81; *U-513*, 69, 147; *U-518*, 69, 149;

U-537, 68; Waffe Type VII, 65
UNESCO World Heritage Site, 311
United Newfoundland Party, 196
US Dock, 54
USO Recreation Centre, 54-5, 254
Veterans Affairs, 167
Veterans Guard of Canada, 41
Victoriaville, HMCS, 70
Voisey's Bay, 341
VONF Radio, 113, 253
Wages, US Army Base, 159
W Force, 39
Walsh, Albert J., 215
Walwyn, Sir Humphrey, 38, 55, 130, 156, 211, 216, 230, 234
Washington (Seat of Government), 257, 261-2, 299
Watts, G.S., 258-9
Wayfarer, The (*See* Perlin, Albert B.)
Wells, Gordon, 35
Welty, Capt. Maurice D., 50
West Newfoundland Association, 222
Westminster (Government), 218, 233, 250
Westminster, Statue of, 9, 15-6, 200-1, 215
Wheare, K.C., 245
Whelan, Capt. John (Jack), 108-11, 127, 133
Whitehall, 212, 216, 218, 221, 223, 229-32, 337, 246-7
Wild, Ira, 231, 258
Wilkes, USS, 136-8, 142
Winter, H.A., 231
Woods Labour Board, 205
Woods, Sir Wilfred W., 77, 87-88
World War I (One), 13, 33-5, 39, 78, 108, 131, 133, 156, 286, 322
World War II (Two), 19, 30, 77-8, 80, 98, 105-17, 129, 152-4, 195, 213, 250-1, 256, 271, 315, 318, 322, 337, 340
Wrens (WRNS), 46
Wright, Frank, 87-8
Wrong, Hume, 240, 280